ICEBREAKER

ICEBREAKER

The Autobiography of

RUDY GALINDO

WITH

ERIC MARCUS

POCKET BOOKS
New York   London   Toronto   Sydney   Tokyo   Singapore

POCKET BOOKS, a division of Simon & Schuster Inc.
1230 Avenue of the Americas, New York, NY 10020

ISBN: 0-671-00390-9

First Pocket Books hardcover printing April 1997

10 9 8 7 6 5 4 3 2 1

POCKET and colophon are registered trademarks of
Simon & Schuster Inc.

Printed in the U.S.A.

For my mom, whom I love and cherish.
For my dad and my brother, George,
who were the wind beneath my wings.
And to my beautiful sister, Laura.
I finally figured out that you are
the golden star that shines on me.
I love you.

Contents

Contents

Acknowledgments

A lot of very special people have been involved in making *Icebreaker* happen—some in producing the actual book, others by being participants in the story it tells. Whatever their involvement, I couldn't have done it without the tremendous support and encouragement of the following individuals.

First, I'd like to thank Michael and Nancy Rosenberg of MARCO Entertainment for all the wonderful opportunities they've given to me. I wouldn't be where I am today without them. Also, my deepest gratitude goes to Mickey Freiberg at The Artists Agency.

Thank you to Tommy Collins for giving hugs and encouragement and for giving me the incredible opportunity to be a member of his extended family. I am deeply honored.

Thank you to the many people at Pocket Books who lent their expertise, including my editor, Sue Carswell; Editorial Director Emily Bestler; Publisher Gina Centrello; Associate

Acknowledgments

Publisher Kara Welsh; as well as Donna O'Neill, Donna Ruvituso, Theresa Zoro, Steve Boldt, and Craig Hillman.

Thank you to my friends Reuben Jenkins and Wayne Leonard for always being there for me and for making such a big difference in my life—Reuben for being my best friend, and Wayne for being a father figure.

Thanks to my new brother-in-law, Andy Black, for having confidence in me and telling me that I'm the best skater he's ever seen.

To the Hulick family, who have helped me through good times and bad, thank you for your support.

Thank you to the late Rick Inglesi and James Hulick for being great coaches. I wish I'd known how to thank you while you were still here.

A special thank-you to the Yamaguchi family for giving me the love and support I needed during my teen years. Kristi Yamaguchi will always have a special place in my heart.

Thank you, John Brancato and Kevin Peeks, for teaching me how to present myself in competition, and a special thanks to John for choreographing a beautiful short program for the 1996 nationals.

Kudos to Sharlene Franke for putting the funk in my "Swan Lake." You deserve a 6.0 for your choreography.

Much appreciation to Bill Hare for editing the best music at nationals, and to Julie Rose for making the most beautiful costumes.

Thank you, Kelly and Marla Black, for giving me family support, and to the Cristobal family for always telling me that I was going to win nationals in San Jose. You were right. To Laura's skating parents, thank you for boosting my confidence when I was down.

Thanks to the Ice Centre for giving me free ice time when I was struggling to make ends meet. And thank you to Susan Hammer and the city of San Jose, for giving me my shining moment in skating and in life. I really do know the way to San Jose.

Thanks also to the McMahon family for your support, and to

Acknowledgments

the Galindo family in Los Angeles for giving us a home when we most needed one. Finally, I want to thank my coauthor, Eric Marcus, for making me feel so comfortable. Eric's friendship made it a lot easier to reach down into my soul and pull out my life story. As we talked, I felt like Eric was a part of my family. I was sad when our work was done and he left to go home, but I know that our friendship will always be there.

My collaborator, Eric Marcus, would like to thank the following people:

Thank you Rudy (and Laura) for trusting me with your story. What a life! Many thanks to my agent, Joy Harris—simply a gem. Thank you to Tom, Mike, and the late Harris Collins for their generous hospitality and for giving me a front-row seat to the world of figure skating.

Thank you to my researcher and friend, Jennifer Finlay, for leaving no stone unturned and for her deliciously wicked sense of humor. A very special thank-you to Kathy Prata and Robert Melton for their meticulous transcription work. Much appreciation to my friends, family, and colleagues for their help and support, especially Christine Brennan, Kate Chieco, Benjamin Dreyer, Stephen Frommer, Daniel Levy, Cecilia Marcus, May Marcus, Steven Milioti, Brett Morrow, Barbara Moulton, and Phil and Debra Roselin. And to my very significant other, Barney M. Karpfinger, thank you like you wouldn't believe.

ICEBREAKER

Introduction

Nobody ever wants to take a picture of me in front of the house where I grew up and, until very recently, lived with my mother. It's not that it's such a bad place. It's too nice! I think that the newspaper and television reporters are afraid that if they show a picture of my mother's comfortable, well-kept, double-wide trailer, it'll somehow diminish the drama of my story. Take my word for it, even if I grew up in a nice house in a middle-class suburb, there would still be plenty of drama in my life to write about, with a lot left over for another life or two.

Now I have the opportunity to tell you my story in my own words. In its simplest terms, this is the story of my struggle to attain a dream, although it's anything but simple. My journey from my mother's trailer in East San Jose to winning the 1996 U.S. Figure Skating National Championships at the San Jose Arena is filled with the kind of emotion and detail that gets lost in the shorthand versions of my life.

Let me also tell you what this book is not about. This is not an exposé on the skating world. Figure skating, like almost every sport and profession, has its secrets, conflicts, eccentricities, and politics. I have no interest in embarrassing anyone by revealing things that they prefer remain private. This book is not about settling scores. It's about my life and how I experienced it.

I'm hoping that my book will be an inspiration to all people who face adversity, especially teenagers, and because of who I am, gay and lesbian people, and Mexican-Americans. I'm not, however, setting myself up as some sort of role model. I can't see myself as that, although I think it's okay to look at me as an example of someone who had a dream, pursued it, and achieved it. I don't see any harm in drawing from my experience to get the push you need, or to look at what I've accomplished and say to yourself, "I want to win, too," whether that means getting a good grade on a test, getting a better job, being a good parent, or going for a gold medal.

The problem I have with the idea of being a role model is that I like to skate, skate, skate. And just because I won a medal doing what I love to do, why should that make me a role model? I don't belong on a pedestal, not for winning a medal. And when you're on a pedestal, people expect you to be perfect. Then you're always looking over your shoulder, trying not to make any mistakes. Everyone who knows me knows I'm not perfect. And if you don't know it now, you'll know it after reading my story in the pages that follow.

1

Dreams and Nightmares

I couldn't sleep. I kept tossing and turning, reliving the competition and the awards ceremony from just the day before. The more I thought about it, the more unreal it seemed. I thought to myself, "Did it really happen? Am I really national champion? Did I just dream the whole thing?" I was so worked up that I turned on the light and looked around my room for some proof that it had actually happened, that it wasn't just a figment of my imagination.

I happened to glance at the floor, and there was a copy of that day's *San Jose Mercury News*, and I immediately spotted my name. The headline read: "Rudy, Rudy, Rudy! San Jose's Galindo delivers a shocker . . ." I picked up the paper and started reading Mark Purdy's column.

Can an entire building have a lump in its throat? Saturday afternoon at San Jose Arena, it happened. The lump was a

3

size triple extra large. And the air was full of emotions that don't have a name.

"I can't describe . . . ," said Rudy Galindo when asked how it felt. "I can't describe . . ."

Forgive him his speechlessness. A kid grows up in East San Jose and ends up grabbing his hometown by the heart and doing something impossible. Are there any concise adjectives to fit that scenario? How could he have done it?

Rudy Galindo, the living, breathing quadruple jump of hard luck.

Rudy Galindo, whose skating career was thought to be finished five years ago when Kristi Yamaguchi dropped him as a pairs partner to pursue her solo Olympic medal.

Rudy Galindo, who has lost two coaches and a brother to AIDS—and his father to a stroke—in the past few years.

Rudy Galindo, who has been so broke that he sometimes has had to ride a bicycle from his mother's house trailer to practice at the Ice Centre of San Jose.

Rudy Galindo, who finished a dismal eighth last year in the national championships and was considered a nonfactor entering this weekend's event—mostly because of his balletic skating style and a hip goatee with a spiky haircut that the judges were supposed to despise.

Rudy Galindo, national champion.

You try to figure out how that must have felt when he heard those last four words. To win his gold medal, Galindo beat out two other men with five U.S. titles between them—Scott Davis and Todd Eldredge.

Figure skating, with its sequined affectations and dense politics, can produce cynicism by the rinkful. But to see Galindo skate Saturday was not only to witness a human being free of gravity and worry, but also to witness the best athlete in the house.

The drama built slowly. Galindo was the last man to skate, which turned out to be an advantage. Maybe the judges really were inclined to downgrade Galindo because of his style, as he has implied in the past. But since he was the last man to skate, after every other person had stumbled or wobbled at least once, the judges could not deny him his rightful scores—if he didn't fall.

While waiting to perform, Galindo stayed beneath the arena, pacing and sitting, wearing his sister's Walkman stereo headphones and listening to loud alternative rock and roll on KOME-FM. That way, he could not hear the ovations, not know which other skaters had slipped or where he stood.

"When I took the ice, I didn't know anything that had happened," Galindo said.

Good plan, for when the headphones came off, Galindo's feet took off. He attempted eight triple jumps—two more than any other competitor—and touched down perfectly on all eight. Over and over. Leap, spin-spin-spin, land. After each one, the applause inside the arena grew more immense, filling the space to the ceiling.

According to the U.S. Figure Skating officials, no man has previously won a national championship in his hometown. You can guess why. The pressure to perform with your friends and family sitting right there in rinkside seats can be worse than performing in front of a national television audience.

Yet Galindo was handling it fine—he even waved to a friend in the front row during his program—and the hometown palms were clapping like crazy. With 15 seconds left in Galindo's program, no one was sitting. There were 10,869 in the house, but the noise was as loud as a 49ers home game.

When his routine finally did end and the ovation soared even louder into the rafters, Galindo looked heavenward, made the sign of the cross, then glided over to await his scores, shouting his father's and brother's names as he left the ice.

The crowd had something else in mind. A chant began: "Six! Six! Six!" That's the figure-skating score for a perfect routine. It appears on the scoreboard about as often as Tonya Harding tapes her own Disney Channel special.

But the magic number flashed for Galindo. Two judges punched it. The arena lifted off to another decibel level. Galindo had won. The video screen on the scoreboard made it official a few seconds later.

Could anyone script a better finish? A kid grows up in East San Jose and becomes the first Mexican-American ever to win a national figure-skating title after every tragedy in the world visits his life, and while he has every right to gloat afterward, he does not.

"I'm still in shock," he said in his postroutine media conference, during which he refused to snap back at his critics, uttering only this: "Hopefully, they all have faith in me now."

With Saturday's victory, Galindo qualifies for the U.S. delegation to March's world championships. He also should receive thousands of dollars for appearing in ice shows. Basically, in five minutes, his bank account went from zero to solvent.

"Now, I guess I can pay for my training expenses," he said.

He wasn't joking. In football terms, Saturday was like Yerba Buena High School showing up at the Super Bowl and beating the Dallas Cowboys. Galindo's "team" was a thrifty local operation in every sense. His choreography was done by a local jazz-dance instructor, Sharlene Franke. And he was coached by his sister, Laura, who has no other world-class pupils and who spends most of her time teaching young kids at the Ice Centre, on 10th Street.

There it was in black-and-white print and color pictures. It wasn't just a dream. I really did win. The thought was breathtaking. I tried saying it out loud: "Rudy Galindo, national champion." I cracked up because it sounded so funny. But then I said it again and again, and I thought to myself, "I can get used to the sound of that."

I finished reading the article, folded up the newspaper, turned out the light, got under the covers, snuggled up with my pillow, and fell into a deep sleep for the first time in days.

On New Year's Day 1996, if you'd asked me where you could find me on January 20, the last place I would have told you to look for me would have been at the top of the podium in the middle of the ice rink at the San Jose Arena with tears streaming down my face as I accepted the gold medal for the U.S. Figure Skating National Championships. If you asked all my friends and family, every official of the U.S. Figure Skating Association, all the sports reporters and commentators who had been reporting on me since the early 1980s, they would also have told you that that's the last place I'd be.

They might have guessed I'd be crying, but I have a reputation—one that happens to be true—for being extremely emotional. Some people need years of therapy to learn how to express their feelings. I could probably use some therapy to learn how *not* to express mine all the time. But on that day at the San Jose Arena, there was no way that someone in my position, with my background, with all the losses I'd experienced, and with all the disappointments, could not cry over having achieved the dream of a lifetime. It would not have been human.

For five of the last eighteen years of my skating career, I'd unintentionally built a reputation as the skater who couldn't. I could not get through a national championship without a humiliating fall, often on the easiest jumps. I got lots of praise for my artistry, for my choreography, and for my triple-triple jump combinations. I even got standing ovations in arenas filled with thousands of spectators. But as predictable as the summer weather in San Jose, I could not skate my opening program from beginning to end without landing on my behind instead of my feet. And that was after more than a decade of building a reputation as the skater who could do no wrong, especially during the half dozen years I skated with Kristi Yamaguchi as her pairs partner.

Back at home, in the trailer where I lived with my mother, I had all kinds of medals lining my shelves and hanging on the walls of my room, evidence of my first thirteen years as a winner. Gold, silver, bronze, national, international, junior, novice, beginner. But that was history, which is what everyone thought I was until the 1996 national championships in my hometown of San Jose, where I finally got to make my place *in* history.

If the odds were against me winning the national championships in 1996, they were against me from almost the day I was born. On September 7, 1969, Jess and Margaret Galindo, a truck driver and a part-time computer-factory assembly-line worker, welcomed me into their family. I was the last of three children. George, my handsome brother (who turned out to be gay), was ten when I was born. Laura, always my father's favorite little girl, was born five years after George.

I wasn't handsome and I wasn't the favorite. But I guess I have a little of both George and Laura in me, because it turned out I was gay and feminine. These are two characteristics that aren't much help to a Mexican-American boy growing up in a working-class neighborhood. If I'd had anything to say about it, I would have been straight and masculine. But some things you don't get to choose in life.

Home was a small trailer on the wrong side of the freeway in East San Jose, a run-down neighborhood where kids are far more likely to deal drugs than figure-skate. When we were really small, Dad never let us play outside. He didn't want to lose any of us to the street or a stray bullet.

I thought our trailer was just fine. There wasn't any reason for me to think otherwise. The whole neighborhood was a trailer park, so that's how all my neighbors lived. Our house was just what you think of when you think of a trailer. It was one story, had a short flight of stairs up to the aluminum front door, and had off-white metal siding. Inside it had two bedrooms, one bath, a living room, and kitchen, all decorated with the latest used furniture. The trailer was set on a tiny piece of bare land with just enough extra room to park my dad's yellow Toyota pickup truck. Dad kept his eighteen-wheel tanker at the garage he rented, which was a couple of miles from the house. He hauled rocket fuel three times a week between San Jose and Las Vegas. So we didn't see a lot of him growing up.

The first big event in my life after being born was being sent away. I had two years with my mom, and then she had a complete emotional breakdown. Mom suffered from manic-depressive illness, which went undiagnosed until 1983, and every few years she descended into a delusional state and was hauled away in a straitjacket. I don't like to dwell on bad things in my life, so I try not to think about what happened with my mom, but over the years her mental illness really shattered our family.

Thankfully, I was too young to remember what happened when Mom had her big breakdown—or maybe I was just too traumatized to remember—but Laura tells me Dad had to call an ambulance because Mom was screaming, throwing things, carrying on about the devil, and hiding in closets. He didn't know what else to do but call for help. And when the ambulance arrived, Mom wasn't about to go quietly. She's only five feet tall, and at the time she was rail thin, but my father and the two ambulance workers had a lot of trouble securing her in the cream-colored jacket and carrying her away. She put up a fight the whole time. My sister, my brother, and I watched—crying and holding on to one another—from the corner of the living room. You could hear Mom screaming even after they closed the ambulance doors and headed down the street.

Before leaving for the psychiatric hospital, Dad came back into the trailer and told George to take charge of things at home, which he did, and without being told, Laura took charge of me. That was nothing new. From the day my parents first brought me home, Laura treated me as if I were her baby. Given my mother's generally poor mental health, Laura didn't have a lot of competition. Of course, my mom changed and fed me—she almost always managed to do the basics—but when it came to paying attention to me and giving me affection and answering my cries, it was Laura whose brown, curly hair and brown eyes I always remember seeing first.

The doctor at Agnew State Hospital told Dad that Mom would have to be hospitalized for an extended period, that it could be weeks, months, or even longer before she could come home. That must have been a terrible and overwhelming blow for my dad. Dad loved my mother and, like most men of his generation, he depended on his wife to take care of him and his kids. With Mom out of commission, there was no way he could do his job—which took him away from home most days and nights of the week—and take care of us at the same time.

After the ambulance left with Mom and Dad inside, we ran to the window and waited there until Dad came home, two or three hours later. He wasn't the kind of father who was physically affectionate with his children, so we generally kept our distance from him, but when he came through the door that night, Laura and George wrapped themselves around him, and I followed their lead.

Dad got us calmed down, telling us that Mom would be okay, then went into the kitchen and called his sister, my aunt Cindy, in East Los Angeles, to ask her if George, Laura, and I could stay with her for a while. My mother had six sisters and two brothers, most of whom lived within a couple of miles of us, so it would have been a lot more convenient to ask one of them to come look after us or for the three of us to move in with one of them, but my parents were estranged from my mother's side of the family.

My father asked Aunt Cindy if she could come get me right away, because I was much more than he could handle without my mom there, even with Laura's help. He told Aunt Cindy that he'd drive Laura and George down at the end of the week. It would be bad enough for them having to leave their friends at school, and he wanted to give them a few days to make things a little easier.

Leaving home wasn't easy for any of us, and again, thankfully, I don't remember what happened. I've had to depend on the memories of my aunt, my cousins, and my sister for this part of the story, and even without recalling it myself, it's upsetting to tell what happened.

It was my cousin Irene, Aunt Cindy's second-oldest daughter, and my Aunt Dolly, Aunt Cindy's sister, who actually drove up to get me. I'd never met them before, so when my father tried handing me to them, I did what a lot of two-year-olds would do: I started crying. Laura was there and got me to calm down, telling me it was okay, that I shouldn't be afraid. But when my aunt and cousin took me out of the house and tried to put me in their car, well, you'd think I thought someone was trying to kill me. And maybe that's what I did think. I screamed and thrashed and carried on from the minute they put me inside the car until we were on the outskirts of Los Angeles. After a half dozen hours stuck in a car with an inconsolable toddler, my aunt and cousin probably *wanted* to kill me.

I was sound asleep by the time we got to the house, so my aunt Cindy's first impression of me was of this blond little boy with rosy cheeks (the hair color and skin tone must have come from my mother's Italian ancestors, because my father's family is 100 percent Mexican), sleeping peacefully in the backseat of the car. Of course, I was sleeping because I'd cried myself into a state of total exhaustion, and my skin was red from all the tears. I hardly stirred as Aunt Cindy carried me into the house and put me to sleep in her bed.

The next morning, after a night of profoundly deep sleep, the kind that only two-year-olds seem capable of, I woke up in my new home. Aunt Cindy was gentle with me and spoke in a soft voice, so I wasn't afraid and I didn't cry, but I was too shy to say a single word to anyone.

Over the next few days I stayed close to the edges of whatever room I was in, hanging on for dear life to my special blanket. I wasn't yet certain of my new surroundings and didn't feel comfortable around all these strangers who were being so nice to me. But within minutes of Laura and George's arrival that weekend, I was back to my happy, giggly self. Still, I never let

Laura out of my sight, and she never let me out of hers. And for the first few weeks, George never let the two of us out of *his* sight. I'm sure my father told him to look after his little brother and sister, and he took that job seriously. As time passed and we all felt more secure, we gave each other more room, but for the two years we lived with Aunt Cindy, we remained a tight little family unit.

The three of us found ourselves in the middle of this huge, sprawling, and very loving extended family in a mostly Hispanic working-class neighborhood east of downtown Los Angeles. Five of my aunt Cindy's eight children were still living at home. And many of my father's ten sisters and brothers lived in the same neighborhood, along with their spouses and kids. For a two-year-old, having all of these other kids to play with and a new neighborhood to explore was a great adventure. I was the youngest of about a dozen of us who played together, and I tagged along with the group wherever they went—whether it was down the block to one of their houses or on a trip to the beach.

For my sister and brother—especially for Laura—moving so far from home, living with strangers in cramped quarters, and starting in new schools was difficult. While my faint memories from that time are almost all happy ones, I know that Laura dreamed only of going home. George was already on his way to being a teenager, and over the two years we lived in East Los Angeles, he fell in pretty comfortably with a big crowd of neighborhood kids. From the very first day, his good looks made him extremely popular with all the girls.

Given how many kids of her own she had living there, Aunt Cindy was an angel to take us in. She had a tiny, old, two-story house that was in the yard behind a bigger house, which faced the street. On the first floor there was a living room, a kitchen, a bathroom, and one bedroom. The second floor had two very small bedrooms with a closet in between, and the only way to get up there was by climbing a steep ladder.

George and Laura slept on a foldout couch in the living room, and I sometimes slept there, too, although during the first year, most of the time I slept in a little rollaway bed in my aunt's bedroom. Aunt Cindy wanted me nearby in case I woke up during the night. She quickly discovered that my special blanket was the secret to my bedtime happiness, and as long as I had it in hand, I stayed in bed until she was ready to get up in the morning.

Aunt Cindy was a great mother to me and she treated me like one of her own. She was a small lady in a family of ample women, but to me, of course, she was huge and completely enveloped me when she took me in her arms. You should see her now. She's this tiny, lovely woman with silver hair, and even though I'm only five foot six, I tower over her. But in 1971, as I tagged along with her wherever she went, I was barely able to reach the bottom of her skirt. And when George and Laura and the other kids were at school, I did my best to stay attached to that skirt every minute of the day. I guess it didn't surprise anyone when I started calling Aunt Cindy "Mama." To me, she was Mama.

Dad came to visit us about once a week, on his way to or from Las Vegas. He would usually call Aunt Cindy the day before to tell us he was coming, and the three of us kids would watch from the yard in the late afternoon for his shiny, silver tanker truck to come down the street. We didn't really have to watch, because even before we could see him, we could hear the roar of the diesel engine in the distance. It was a quiet residential street, so the sound was hard to miss.

You can't imagine how excited we were when Dad arrived. All three of us would jump up and down screaming, "Daddy's here! Daddy's here! Daddy's here!" The yard was fenced in, so we couldn't just run out by ourselves to the truck. Aunt Cindy or one of my older cousins would open the gate for us and walk us across the street, although by the time we were halfway across the road, we were sprinting for the open door of the truck's cab. We'd run right past my dad, who was invariably standing in the street waiting for us, his arms folded across his broad chest, a grin on his face and a cowboy hat on his head. Don't get me wrong, we were thrilled to see our father, but our destination was the huge sleeping area in back of the cab, which was my dad's home away from home. He built the sleeping area himself, and it had a big, comfortable bed. You should have seen us, scrambling under the blankets, tossing the pillows in all directions, squeezing our hands between the walls of the cab and the mattress, all in a mad search for silver dollars. This was a game Dad started with us after we moved to Aunt Cindy's, but we didn't really know it was a game. He let us think that the silver dollars fell out of his pockets while he was sleeping, and he told us that whoever found them got to keep them. George and Laura were so good to me, because they always left the most obviously "hidden" silver coins for me to discover.

If Dad stayed overnight, he'd let us and our cousins play in the back of the cab and he never got mad at us, no matter how much of a mess we made. But usually he stayed only a couple of hours and then headed back to San Jose. We hated to see him go, especially George, who would sit by the window for hours after Dad left, long after everyone else in the house had gone to sleep. George adored our father and really looked up to him, so it was especially hard for him to have a part-time dad during such a critical part of his adolescence. I really think that Dad's absence during those two years, and the fact that he was home so little all the other years, was the root of a lot of George's problems as he got older.

During the two years we lived with Aunt Cindy, Dad brought Mom to visit only three times, and these were not occasions for a joyous family reunion. On her first visit, which was a year after she was hospitalized, Mom didn't even seem to know who we were when she saw us standing in the yard. We knew she was coming, because Aunt Cindy had told us, but after the way Mom had behaved the day they took her away to the hospital, I think we were all a little scared. I was only three, so I wasn't fully aware of the situation, but I could sense that Laura and George were nervous, so I stayed close to Laura as my dad walked Mom into the yard.

If my mother didn't recognize us as her children, she was hardly recognizable to us as our mother. Physically, she looked basically the same. She was still small and pretty, a lot like the way Laura is now, with thick, dark brown hair, smooth olive skin, and brown eyes. But in contrast to how she had been on that awful day a year before, she was now totally withdrawn. She was like a zombie, hardly lifting her feet as she walked, not saying a word, a blank expression on her face. I got scared and hid behind Laura, who just stood there with George, watching wide-eyed as my dad said hello to Aunt Cindy, and they all walked in the house.

The whole time that Mom was there, which was only a few hours, she sat in a chair in the living room, not saying a word, and only occasionally looking around at the walls or gazing out the window. She looked at the three of us when we ventured inside, but she never tried to engage any of us, and as soon as we could escape, Laura and George and I went off with our cousins to play.

Mine was not the kind of family where parents sat their children down and had serious, informed discussions about day-to-day issues, let alone something as grave as mental illness. Not that I was old enough to hear or fully understand what was going on. But nobody made any effort to explain in a way that I could understand—or in ways that Laura and George could understand—what was wrong with our mother. So we were all left feeling confused and fearful. We couldn't understand why Mom was behaving so strangely, and we just wanted her to somehow snap out of it. We had no idea when she came to visit that she was heavily sedated and that she suffered from a serious mental illness. To us, that's just how Mom was.

On her second visit, a few months later, Dad brought Mom to stay for a week. His idea was to give Mom and us a chance to start getting to know one another again before bringing us home to live. Dad was eager to have his family back together and he was probably rushing things, because Mom was still in pretty bad shape. She wasn't catatonic the way she had been the first time, but she was still strangely quiet and wasn't always rational.

For example, while Mom was staying with us, Laura had an accident at a neighbor's house and got second-degree burns on her hand. She came running into the kitchen through the back door, crying and holding her scalded hand in front of her. Mom was at the dinette table and just sat there staring at no place in particular while Laura cried. Aunt Cindy heard all the commotion, came in from the living room, took one look at Laura's hand, and said that she needed to take Laura to the emergency room. She asked Mom to go with her because Mom was still Laura's legal guardian. Asking Mom turned out to be a mistake.

My mother reacted to Aunt Cindy's suggestion as if she thought Aunt Cindy had said she was taking Laura out to the yard to chop off her head. Maybe she was afraid that Laura was going to be committed to a mental hospital like she had been. Who knows? But she got up, grabbed Laura by her shoulders, and yelled at Aunt Cindy that they weren't going anywhere. Aunt Cindy first tried to reason with my mother, explaining that Laura's burn was serious and that she needed immediate medical attention. It was obvious to anyone that Laura needed a doctor, but my mother wasn't in her right mind and she refused to budge. Aunt Cindy tried pleading for my mother to let go of Laura, but that didn't work either, so finally she grabbed Laura by her good hand and pulled her away from Mom. Having lost the struggle, Mom sort of collapsed onto one of the dinette chairs as Aunt Cindy took Laura and me out through the back door, put us in the car, and headed to the hospital.

A few months later, Dad decided that Mom was finally well enough for us to come home, or at least he wanted to believe she was well enough. In truth, it was another ten years before Mom was properly diagnosed as manic-depressive and stabilized on lithium and other medications. Nonetheless, one weekend, almost two years to the day my aunt and cousin had come to get me, my father took us home.

For some reason—maybe I was just being a four-year-old—I was under the impression when we all got into my father's truck, we were going for a ride around the block, which was something I loved to do. The usual routine, when I was lucky enough to get a ride in the big rig, was for Dad to put me in his lap, take my little hands, place them on the steering wheel, and let me think I was actually steering the eighteen-wheeler as we cruised down the street. To me, that was heaven.

When I first climbed into the truck, I didn't notice that all our clothes were packed up in a couple of boxes and piled on the mattress in the cab's sleeping area. Also, there wasn't any big send-off. It was just my aunt Cindy and a couple of my cousins watching from the sidewalk, so there was no reason for me to think we were leaving for good. I suspect my family hadn't forgotten how hysterical I had got the last time I was taken from home, and they didn't want a repeat performance. They did a good job, because as we pulled away, I just laughed and laughed as I steered my father's truck in the direction of the freeway.

Laura and George both knew where we were going, and despite how wonderful my aunt Cindy and all our relatives had been to us, and despite the fact that going home meant living with my mother, they were still looking forward to being back in our house, to being with Dad, to seeing their friends, and to going back to their old schools. For them, there was still no place like home.

I was so mesmerized by being on the highway that I drifted off to sleep before realizing we weren't going back to Aunt Cindy's house. I slept almost the whole rest of the way and I didn't get upset at all when we pulled up at my father's garage, piled into his pickup with all of our belongings, and drove to the trailer park. I was with my three favorite people in the whole world, so I don't think it would have really mattered where we were going. The whole thing felt like an adventure.

As far as my attachment to Aunt Cindy, I can't explain it, but after I got home, I only asked for her a couple of times, and that was it. I guess that even though I called her Mama, I knew deep down she wasn't my mother. And now that I was home with my real mama, I quickly forgot about Mama Aunt Cindy. But I'm getting ahead of myself.

Mom came out of the trailer when we drove up. There weren't any hugs and kisses, but she smiled, helped us inside with our things, then put dinner on the table—all of Dad's favorite, greasy Mexican foods. We were all feeling a little wary given our past experiences with Mom, so as usual I stuck close to Laura and she stuck close to me. I don't know who was being comforted by whom at that point, but it turned out that we had nothing to worry about that night, because nothing happened. We had a quiet dinner, which was something you could never have at Aunt Cindy's house where the dinner table was always packed with ten or more people.

After dinner, while Laura and Mom cleared the table, Dad went into the living room and turned on the television. It was pretty late by then, so George got me ready for bed. He helped me get into my pajamas, took me into our little—really little—bathroom so I could brush my teeth, carried me into the bedroom that all three of us shared, tucked me in, handed me my special blanket, and said good-night.

I wasn't quite ready to go to sleep yet and just looked at everything in our room, including the glow-in-the-dark peace-sign poster on the wall, the toy trains on the dresser, Laura's dolls piled on her bed, George's clothes scattered on his bed, and some of my old toys in a box on the floor. George explained to me that this was where we'd lived before we moved in with Aunt Cindy. But as hard as I tried to remember, nothing in our room looked familiar. I didn't let that bother me, because everything *felt* familiar. That's how I knew I was home.

2

GROWING UP GALINDO

If this were the fairy-tale version of my life, this is the point in the story where I would tell you that after we moved back home, Mom baked cookies for me every afternoon; Dad and I played ball on the weekends; we sat around the dinner table and shared our stories of the day; Mom read to me at bedtime; and Mom and Dad both tucked me in and gave me a hug and a kiss before turning out the light. Of course, real life is no fairy tale, especially when your dad was away more nights than he was home and your mom occasionally acted like a character right out of a Stephen King novel.

On her good days, Mom did the grocery shopping, got the meals made, did the laundry, and took care of our family's basic necessities. There was nothing in the way of conversation, affection, or even general interest in what Laura, George, and I were up to. On her not-so-good days, Dad had to remind Mom to do the shopping and get the meals made, and on those days I'm not sure she was even aware that she *had* children. On her bad days, watch out, because it didn't take much to set her off.

One time, a few months after we came home, Mom asked Laura if she would vacuum the house. Normally, when a mother asks a child to help with the vacuuming, it's no big deal. But the way Mom asked Laura, it was as if she were throwing down the gauntlet. She was angling for a fight, and Laura tried her best to get out of the line of fire. Mom hated all the attention Dad showered on Laura, such as taking her with him when he worked on the truck at his garage and buying her presents all the time. She was jealous of Laura, plain and simple. So when Mom asked Laura to vacuum, she didn't say, "Laura, could you please vacuum the house?" It was more like, "Goddammit, get off your behind and vacuum the house!"

George saw where this was going and tried to head things off by volunteering to help out in place of Laura. But it was already too late, because before he could finish getting the words out and before Laura could get out of reach, my mother had Laura by the hair and threw her across the room.

The whole trailer shook when Laura hit the wall, and she let out a little yelp as she crumpled to the floor. Unfortunately, that wasn't the end of it. Mom took five steps over to where the vacuum cleaner was, picked it up, and with all her strength threw it at Laura, just missing her head by inches. The whole thing seemed to happen in slow motion, but it only took a few seconds for the nightmare scene to unfold, play out, and end with Mom storming out of the house.

I'd taken refuge in a corner of the living room and just watched everything from a safe distance, with my knees shaking the whole time. After Mom left, I was too scared to move. George went over to Laura, who sat on the floor sobbing, and tried to comfort her, stroking her hair, hugging her, and telling her Mom didn't mean it. And the fact was, Mom didn't mean it. She just couldn't help herself when she was overcome by these terrible rages, and afterward, she would say how terrible she felt about what she had done. Unfortunately, that didn't stop her from doing it the next time.

In general, Laura took the brunt of my mother's anger, but a few times Mom went straight for me. I was probably around nine years old the first time it happened. Mom said something mean to me and I talked back, and suddenly I was against the wall and she was pummeling me with her fists. I tried protecting my head and stomach as best I could, begging for her to stop, but she just kept hitting me with her fists until Laura managed to pull her off me. Even though I was crying hard, I could see the look of horror on Mom's face over what she'd done to me. She had her hands over her mouth and her eyes were wide, and then she ran to her bedroom and slammed the door behind her.

Laura always told Dad about Mom's outbursts, but he couldn't do a whole lot because he was away so much. I look back now and wonder if part of the reason he spent so much time out of the house was because he couldn't deal with Mom's illness. What's confusing is that at times my dad was so playful with her, giving her a pat on the behind or sneaking up on her and giving her a kiss. It must have been a terrible conflict for him between the love he felt for Mom and having to cope with her awful rages and delusions.

Dad's usual routine for the first year after we came back home was to make three round-trips each week, Monday through Friday, between San Jose and Las Vegas. On those one or two nights during the week when he was home, he'd walk through the door with just enough time to wash up for dinner. We were all happy to see him, but it wasn't like the times he'd come to visit us at Aunt Cindy's. Now that we were home, we got to see a lot more of Dad, so his arrival wasn't the special occasion it had been during our time away. We didn't go running to the door or anything like that, but we'd say hello, and Laura would always give Dad a kiss on the cheek.

At dinner, if Dad was in a good mood, he'd ask Laura and George how things were going with school, but usually not a lot was said around the table. If he was in a bad mood, he'd scold Mom for not making his food the way he liked it, and then nothing was said by any of us, and we ate in almost complete silence. After dinner, Dad sat and watched television—he especially liked westerns—and had a few beers. Sometimes we'd watch with him, but usually George was out with his friends in the neighborhood and Laura and I played just outside the trailer or in our room. By the time the ten-o'clock news was over, our whole family was in bed and sound asleep.

On the weekends, Dad left first thing in the morning with Laura for his garage to work on the truck to get it ready for another week of driving. Laura was Dad's little grease monkey, handing him his tools as he needed them. They were gone all day both Saturday and Sunday, so I'd stay at home with Mom and play on my own or go with her on errands. I could probably have gotten Dad to take me along, too, but I was one of those boys who was a lot more interested in dressing up his sister's Barbie dolls than getting under the hood of his father's truck.

In thinking about my family life that first year we were all together again, I wish I could come up with memories of doing things with my dad or even a memory of him picking me up and giving me a hug or reading to me. Dad was generous; he bought us lots of toys and clothes. But what I really wanted from my father, his time and attention, he couldn't give. I know it was partly because he worked so hard and had little free time, but it also wasn't his nature. He was an old-fashioned dad: He was the provider and the rule maker, and he took pride in what his kids accomplished. There's a lot to be said for that, but I was the kind of sensitive child who needed more, and over the next few years, I figured out how to get it. That secret, I was about to discover, was ice-skating.

It's my sister Laura to whom I owe all my thanks for introducing me to the sport that transformed my life. We had been home for about a year when Laura was invited to a birthday party for one of her school friends at the Eastridge Ice Arena, which was about three miles from our house. Laura took to the ice like a duck to water and was so excited when she got home that for the rest of the afternoon she pretend-skated all over the house, sliding across the vinyl-tiled floors. I didn't understand what she was doing, but it seemed like loads of fun to me, so I followed along behind her, shuffling my feet, and every so often Laura grabbed me and twirled me around.

When Dad came home that night, Laura asked him if she could take skating lessons. As I've said, Dad was great about giving us the things we wanted, so the following week, Laura started group lessons at the Eastridge arena.

After Laura's skating performance at home, there was no way I was staying home and playing in my room while she went off for her lesson. I would have wrapped myself around my dad's leg if I'd had to, but everybody was used to me wanting to go wherever Laura went, so I think they just assumed I'd be going along.

Before we left, I asked George if he was going with us, and he laughed and said, "I don't think so." George was a teenager with a busy social life, and I imagine the last thing he wanted to do was spend a weekend afternoon with his little brother and sister and his father at an ice-skating rink. Of course, I couldn't imagine why he didn't want to go.

Dad drove us over to the Eastridge arena in his pickup truck. I don't know what I was expecting, because I'd never been to an ice-skating rink before, but I was so excited that Dad and Laura had to strap me in with the seat belt to keep me from jumping up and down on the seat. I put up a bit of a protest, but it was only a five-minute drive so I didn't have the chance to get too worked up. I was never very good at sitting still for long. I'm still not.

The first day we went to the arena together was one of those perfect fall days in San Jose, where the air is hot and dry and all the parched plants and trees seem to be begging for the start of the rainy season. Laura said it would be cold inside the arena, so I had to wear long pants and I brought along a sweatshirt. I'll never forget the sensation of walking through the entrance of the arena, from the hot, dry air outside into the cold, moist air inside. The feeling of the cold air on my skin reminded me of when you stand in front of an open refrigerator. It made the skin on my face tingle, and it felt so good to breathe in deep. I got goose bumps on my arms, and I asked Laura to help me put on my sweatshirt.

The arena was huge, or at least it seemed that way to a six-year-old. It was a big barnlike space with a high ceiling, and it was lit like a gymnasium with those harsh high-intensity lights. We went over to a long counter where Dad rented a pair of white ice skates for Laura, and then we all sat down in the changing area, which was crowded with lots of kids and their parents. Laura put on her skates and Dad helped her lace them up. Then we walked over to the ice, which I couldn't see at first because of the low wall surrounding the oval rink. But as we got closer, I caught a glimpse through the break in the wall where people got on and off the ice, and I could see scores of kids and a few adults skating around and around the rink to a Karen Carpenter tune. They were going so fast that it looked to me as if they were flying.

I was so mesmerized by the whole scene that I didn't even notice that Laura had left us. I looked up at my dad and asked him where Laura was, and he picked me up so I could get a better view and pointed to a group of kids at the center of the ice. And that's when I saw Laura with a half-dozen other girls about her age and their instructor. Dad took me up to the stands where some of the other parents were sitting, and I watched without moving from my seat for the whole half hour Laura was on the ice.

At the beginning, Laura had one lesson every Saturday. By the third trip to Eastridge, Dad had to hold me back from running onto the ice in my sneakers. He knew I wanted to skate, but I was so small for my age that he was afraid I'd get hurt. He must have decided at some point that I was less likely to get hurt on skates than I was if I got loose and ran out on the ice in my sneakers, so he took me over to the rental counter and asked the attendant if he had a pair of skates that would fit me. The guy leaned over to size me up, then went back to where they kept all the skates and brought out a pair of white ones. Dad turned bright red and asked the man if he was trying to be funny. I didn't know at first what the problem was because the skates looked perfectly fine to me—they were the same as Laura's. "Those are for girls," my father said in a tone of voice that dripped with disgust. Boys wore *brown* skates.

Looking back, I can understand the rental guy's confusion. Given how slight I was and my shoulder-length, blond hair, and my generally feminine demeanor, you couldn't blame him for thinking I was a girl. In some ways I was more feminine in my mannerisms than Laura was. It's not as if I tried to be feminine. That's just how I was.

Up until then, no one had ever said or done anything to make me think I was somehow odd or different from other boys. But from the way my father reacted, I knew something was wrong. I'd been mistaken for a girl, which was apparently a bad and humiliating thing to a man like my dad. I didn't help matters any when I burst into tears. I didn't fully grasp what was going on, but I felt like I'd done something terribly wrong, and tears seemed like the appropriate response.

By the time Dad started lacing up my brown rental skates, I'd stopped crying and wiped the tears off my cheeks with the sleeve of my sweatshirt. Dad didn't say a word the whole time and didn't make any effort to comfort me. He was a real cowboy type of guy, and I'm sure it couldn't have made him happy that his little boy had been mistaken for a girl. I assure you that that was hardly the last time it happened, but it was the only time that Dad was a witness to it. After that first trip to the rental counter, Dad let me go to the rental counter by myself, and whenever there was a new attendant, out came the white skates. And right on cue, I'd burst into tears because I felt so ashamed and embarrassed. Through my tears I'd have to explain that I got the brown skates.

Once Dad finished lacing and tying my skates, I stood up. Suddenly I was tall! The two-inch-high steel blades gave me a whole new perspective on the world and offered a considerable challenge to getting from one place to another. Dad held my hand to keep me upright as we walked across the rubber mats to the edge of the ice. I was so eager to get on the ice that I almost dragged my dad onto the ice with me. He let go just in time, and I took off across the ice like a sailboat across a lake. Well, maybe not quite so gracefully as a sailboat, but I certainly flew.

A lot of times I've been asked what it was like the first time I stepped onto the ice, and I always answer by saying that it's impossible to describe. Probably, the better answer is that the sensations are indescribable, because no matter what words I use, my description falls short of describing the actual experience. Taking that into account, let me say that as I skated around the rink, it felt as if gravity had dropped its hold on me. It was like flying. It was exhilarating. It made me feel alive. I felt powerful. It was fun. And I was instantly hooked.

For the next year, every time Laura went to Eastridge for her lesson, I went along and skated around and around and around as many times as I could. Not a single time did I have to be encouraged to get on the ice, but lots of times Laura had to drag me off.

While I skated, I always kept an eye on what Laura's class was learning, but not until Laura started private lessons a year later did I begin paying closer attention. Laura had done really well with her group classes, and the teacher recommended that she start taking lessons from a private instructor. Laura's new instructor was Colleen Blackmore, a very attractive, brunet Australian woman who always dressed in bumblebee yellow ski pants and a matching jacket.

During Laura's five-days-a-week lessons with Colleen, I stood over by the boards—which is what you call the low wall surrounding the ice—and watched everything Colleen taught Laura to do. Then I'd try to do the same things myself. That's how I learned to do little bunny hops and how I mastered shoot-the-ducks, which is when you do a knee bend on one leg and keep the other leg straight out as you glide across the ice. I also learned the first jump they teach you in skating, the waltz jump, and the next jump, the salchow. I learned all of these jumps just by watching.

Sometimes I really struggled to follow along, because Laura is right-handed and I'm left-handed, so I had to improvise and do everything the other way. I could see Colleen laughing sometimes as I tried to do half-revolution jumps and, eventually, whole-revolution jumps, which at first landed me butt-first on the ice. Colleen wasn't the only one who thought it was funny. I'd sit there on the ice laughing at myself, too. Sometimes falling really hurt, but I was having so much fun that I couldn't help but laugh.

After Laura's lesson, Colleen often came over to me, patted me on the shoulder, and said, "Rudy, you're good!" I lived for that praise, and the next time I'd try even harder to do everything perfectly. Apparently, Colleen thought I was good enough to start lessons myself and she talked to Dad about taking me on as one of her students. Dad knew how much I loved to skate and he also knew from watching me that I was a good skater with a lot of potential.

Dad wanted to surprise me with the news, so one day at the arena, instead of letting me walk over to the rental counter, he took me into the pro shop. Laura had gone ahead of us to the dressing area and was already lacing up her skates, which Dad had bought for her when she started individual lessons. In the shop, Dad picked up a pair of beautiful, black Riedell figure skates and asked me what I thought of them. I told him I thought they were really nice—and they *were*, especially in comparison to the brown rental skates I'd been using. Then he said, "I think you should have your own skates if you're going to take private lessons." My jaw just about hit the floor. I said, "You mean it?" He smiled and nodded yes, and you can imagine how I reacted. I jumped up and down in excitement and just about fell over one of the store displays.

When Dad finally got me to sit still for a minute, he had me fitted for my very own pair of skates. Now I would be like all the other real skaters and walk into the arena with my skate bag over my shoulder and go right to the changing area and put on my black figure skates. I can't tell you what a big deal it was at the rink when you had your own skates. It was a status symbol like no other, and it made me feel special.

As soon as Dad finished helping me put on my skates, I ran out to the ice to show Laura what Dad had bought for me. I got on the ice and raced across to the center of the ice where Colleen was giving Laura her lesson. You should have seen the expression on her face when I said, "Laura, look what I've got." She didn't know about the new skates, and Dad hadn't told her that her private lessons were about to be lessons for two. Laura looked down at my scuff-free, brand-new skates and said, "Oh, no! Now you're going to follow me *all* the time!" Well, she was right!

The year I started taking lessons was memorable for two reasons that had nothing to do with skating: We moved to a new house, and I had my very first crush.

Dad had been saving money for a few years to buy a new house in a safer neighborhood nearby, but he had second thoughts once Laura and I both started taking skating lessons. From the beginning, it was pretty apparent that we were both good and that we might have skating careers ahead of us. Dad was afraid that he wouldn't be able to afford a new house, the expenses of lessons, and all the other costs that go along with having two skaters in the family, so he decided to hold off on committing himself to big mortgage payments.

We couldn't really stay where we were, because with the three of us growing up, the trailer had become extremely cramped. By the time we moved, I was seven, Laura was twelve, and George was seventeen. The room we shared, which Laura called our closet, had been too small for the three of us since we first got home from Aunt Cindy's. And for the last two years we lived in the trailer, George had slept on the couch in the living room on the nights he was home. A lot of nights he stayed over with friends.

I think Dad also thought Mom might do better if we lived in a bigger place, especially after she had another one of her episodes. It happened on a day when Dad was on his way back from a trip and George was out. Mom wasn't working at the time, so she should have been home when we got back from school, but she wasn't. We figured she'd gone out to pick up groceries because her car was gone, but after a couple of hours we started getting really worried.

At around five o'clock, Laura and I went outside and sat on the steps of the trailer to watch for her, and after a half hour we spotted her blue Honda in the distance, coming up the road. Mom was driving really fast, too fast, and when she finally braked, she lost control of the car and crashed into the trailer right across the street from us. Almost immediately, she put the car in reverse, swung it around, pulled up in front of our trailer, and screeched to a halt in a cloud of dust.

By this point Laura and I were on our feet, holding on to each other, more than a little frightened. The front and back doors of the car opened, and out stepped Mom and these three guys who looked as if they'd been living on the street. It was quite a scene.

I don't know where Laura found the courage, but she started screaming at Mom, telling her to stay away from the house. "Get out of here and take your friends with you!" Mom slammed the door of the car, started walking toward us, and yelled back, "I'm going into my house and I'm bringing my friends!" Laura yelled at her again, telling her to stay away, and then my sister grabbed me, took me in the house, and bolted the door.

From inside, we could see Mom running from window to window, trying to figure out where she could get in. Even if any of the windows had been open, they were too far off the ground for her to reach. But she pounded on the outside walls and banged on the door, screaming for us to open the door. After a few minutes of this, Laura went back outside and told Mom again to leave: "I don't care where you go, just get out of here!" I could hardly believe the force of Laura's voice, but Mom and her friends got back into the car and drove off. Laura came inside and rebolted the door, and then we waited on the sofa for Dad to get home. We were both shaking; Laura because she was angry, and me because I was scared.

A few weeks after this incident, which landed Mom in the hospital for a few days, Dad took all of us, including Mom, over to a trailer park on the other side of the freeway and showed us the three-bedroom, two-bath, double-wide trailer he'd decided to buy. It wasn't Graceland, but to me it was a palace compared to where we'd been living. There was so much space! I ran from room to room to room, imagining what it would be like when we could finally move in.

The following month, Dad got some of his friends to help pack up our belongings and move everything into the new house. I couldn't wait to go, and because I didn't have any real friends where we lived, there were no tearful good-byes. Dad had been pretty strict about not letting me go out of the house, and when I did, I had to stay right next to the trailer. There were a few kids I played with on rare occasions, but mostly I played with Laura at home or I played on my own.

The new house was great, and Mom seemed to do better; she got angry less frequently, and if it looked as if she was going to go off and have a fit, it was easier for us to stay away from her. So in that regard, moving made a big difference.

There was only one thing I didn't like about the new house: For the first time in my life, Laura and I weren't sharing a room. And with George out most nights, I was lonely sleeping in a room all by myself. It was a corner room with windows on two walls and was about eight feet by twelve feet. It had two single beds, perpendicular to each other, and separated by a corner table, with a lamp on it. And on one wall we had a dresser, and that was all.

Sometimes I'd sneak into Laura's room and climb into her bed, but she liked her newfound privacy and almost always sent me back to my room. Being on my own at night was a big adjustment, especially after George moved out the following year, when he graduated from high school.

* * *

There was no question that moving to a new place was a big deal. But a far bigger deal was my first crush. This time, I didn't go anywhere new, but the ground moved beneath my feet.

There is nothing else in life quite like puppy love, and given what an emotional child I was, when I fell for my first love, I fell like a block of ice breaking off a glacier into the ocean. But at least the block of ice has the ocean water to break its fall. For me, I just kept on going.

I'll call him Johnny Rivera. I spotted him the first day of second grade at Arbuckle Elementary School in San Jose. We were let out into the yard for recess, and within minutes I caught sight of him. My heart felt as if it skipped a beat and then it started pounding in my chest. He was breathtaking—an Italian-looking James Dean type with slicked-back jet-black hair, light skin, full lips, and liquid brown eyes.

Johnny was dressed in the uniform of the day: baggy pants, a white T-shirt, and sneakers. He was over in the part of the yard where the fifth and sixth graders hung out, so all I could do was look at him from a distance and later that night, dream about him in my sleep.

After a week of staring across the school yard and catching glimpses of Johnny at the beginning and the end of the school day, he and a couple of his friends came over to our side of the yard during recess. I don't know quite how I found the courage to go over and talk to him, but having a crush can make you do things you wouldn't dream of otherwise. So, I just walked over and said, "Hi, I'm Rudy," in the most casual kind of tone you can imagine, which was in extraordinary contrast to the explosions going off in my head. I asked him his name, and he said, "I'm Johnny, Johnny Rivera."

The fact I didn't faint is nothing short of a miracle because at that moment I was so excited I couldn't breathe. Johnny could see I was in trouble, and he put his arm around my shoulder and asked me if I was okay. Okay? With Johnny Rivera's arm around my shoulder, was I okay? I was in heaven! Every muscle in my body relaxed under the weight of his arm and I took a deep breath. If Johnny had left his arm there all day, I would have been a very happy boy, but as soon as he saw that I was all right, he gave me a friendly pat on the back and headed back to his friends.

I know there are people who believe that those of us who wind up gay or lesbian are somehow recruited or made gay by the circumstances in which we grow up. I definitely wasn't recruited by anyone, including Johnny. He was nice to me, but an innocent arm around the shoulder was as far as it ever went. Some people also like to believe that it's the fault of the parents when a child has feelings of attraction for the same gender, but all the reputable experts on this issue agree that your relationship with your parents and how they raise you has nothing to do with your innate sexual orientation.

At the time of my crush, I didn't know anything about homosexuality, but I definitely knew how I felt about Johnny Rivera. Those feelings toward Johnny were so fundamental to who I was—and am—that even if I'd tried to stop my feelings, I'm sure I couldn't have.

Even though I knew nothing about homosexuals—I didn't even know the word—I'd apparently already absorbed enough from the world around me to know that a crush on another boy was something I shouldn't talk about with anyone, including Laura. So I didn't, although for anyone watching, it must have been pretty obvious that I had a thing for Johnny Rivera.

During the rest of the school year, whenever I had the chance during recess to be near Johnny, that's where you would find me. I lived for those rare occasions when he'd put his arm around my shoulder.

After second grade I never saw Johnny again because I had to transfer to a different school. It would be a very long time before I had another crush, but I had plenty of memories with which to console myself. You don't ever forget your first crush or that intense feeling of falling in love for the first time.

The reason I had to change schools was because of skating. Between the lessons and the required practice time, it was impossible to get to school when classes started at 8:30 A.M.

That was about the time Laura and I were just getting off the ice, so I needed permission to come in by 9:00 or 9:30. It wasn't a problem where Laura went to junior high, but the principal at Arbuckle didn't believe in seven-year-olds coming to school late regularly. I can't say now that I disagree with him, but at the time skating was more important to me than anything. Somehow my father managed to get me into another school, in the foothills on the other side of the freeway, where the principal was more flexible.

By any standards but my own, our schedule was demanding. I loved skating so much that I didn't mind going to bed when most kids my age were settling in for an evening of television. We skated five days a week, so Sunday through Thursday we were in bed by 7:30 P.M. At 4:30 A.M. the alarm went off in my parents' bedroom and Mom would go into the kitchen, start breakfast, and make our sandwiches for school. Fifteen minutes later she'd come wake us up. Laura and I took our showers the night before, and we always laid out our clothes for the next day before going to bed, so we were dressed and at the breakfast table by 4:50. The hot oatmeal, topped with brown sugar, was already set out for us by the time we sat down. We ate, probably faster than we should have, raced to the bathroom to brush our teeth, grabbed our schoolbooks and our skate bags, and headed out the door by 5:00.

Mom drove us the three miles to the rink, dropped us off, and by 5:15 we were on the ice, practicing our figures. (Figure skating, by the way, gets its name from the figure eights and other patterns that you cut into the ice with your skate and retrace over and over. This used to be the most important part of skating competitions, but it was dropped by the U.S. Figure Skating Association after 1990.)

Most of the kids, about eighteen of us in all, got to the Eastridge arena around the same time. When the kids headed for the ice, the mothers who stayed to watch headed for the stands. I felt bad that my mother didn't stay. I thought she didn't care about me the way the other mothers cared about their kids. Looking back, I can't blame her for going home to start her chores. For a lot of the mothers, being at the rink was a social time, but given my mother's mental illness, interacting with the other mothers would have been well beyond her capabilities. She was too nervous and shy even to look at them. And besides, watching a bunch of kids practice their figures is—at best—boring. Still, most of the mothers stayed, and that was the standard by which I unfairly measured my mom.

Each of us practiced our figures for forty-five minutes on his or her own strip of ice. At 6:00 we had a half-hour group lesson with Colleen Blackmore, which was followed by another twenty minutes of figures practice. Then we got off the ice, took off our skates, and warmed up for the freestyle session, which was when most of us had private lessons.

The warm-up was about ten minutes of stretching on the floor and air turns, where you practice your jumps as if you're on the ice. Then we put on our freestyle skates. (You use different skates for figures and freestyle, so each of us had two different pairs of skates. For figures, the bottom of the blade—the rocker—is flatter than the freestyle blade. And the toe pick, which is the row of teeth cut into the front of the blade, is smaller and higher up. For freestyle, the blade is designed for greater speed and jumps. The bottom of the blade is slightly concave, and the toe picks are larger and closer to the ice so you can use them to propel yourself off the ice into a jump.)

Once we were back on the ice, we skated freestyle, which is the kind of skating most people think of when they think of figure skating—turns, spins, crossovers, jumps—for about an hour and a half. During that time, I had a twenty-minute private lesson with Colleen. Every day we focused on a specific jump or spin. If I was learning something entirely new, we might spend several days on one jump or spin. And every day we worked on my program, which at the beginning was about a minute long. Laura's program was a minute and a half long and more difficult than mine. We finished around 8:30, which was when Mom came back to pick us up and drive us over to school.

Like every coach, Colleen had her own way of doing things.

She was strict and could be harsh when you did something wrong. Because I was such a sensitive kid, I was reduced to tears regularly. Colleen made it clear that she didn't like it when we cried. She wanted us to be tough and professional, so when any of us cried, she asked us to leave the ice and go cry in the bathroom in private. What I wanted when I cried was just to be comforted, but when we were on the ice, the hugs and the pats on the back were reserved for when you did a good job.

Colleen's way of doing things forced me to become a perfectionist. I didn't want to be criticized for doing something wrong, and I hated being sent into exile when I cried. And, of course, I wanted the compliments and the hugs when I did things the way I was supposed to.

After my first few months on the ice, Colleen was so impressed with my skating that she asked my dad if she could enroll me in a competition in Squaw Valley. After sitting in the stands cheering at all of Laura's competitions, I was really excited about the idea of being in a competition of my own. I loved the whole atmosphere at the competitions: the crisp, cold air of the arena, the way the sound echoed through the arena when the announcer said the name of each skater before he or she got on the ice, the music, the costumes, the choreography, the cheering spectators, the way the winners would get so excited and jump up and down, and best of all, the awards ceremony. I found the whole extravaganza mesmerizing, and I was thrilled by the prospect of being a part of it instead of watching from the stands.

I was also excited by the idea of going on a long trip with Mom, Dad, and Laura. I wished George could go with us, but after he graduated from high school he went to work full-time at the local Taco Bell, working behind the counter filling orders. He had odd hours, so even if he'd been interested in our skating—which he wasn't—there was no way he could have gone.

The whole trip to Squaw Valley was like a vacation, beginning with the long drive. I loved the place where we stayed and thought it was exotic. It had individual rustic cabins, each with a fireplace, so at night we'd sit in front of the fire and it felt as if we were way out in the wilderness.

The four-day skating event was sponsored by the U.S. Figure Skating Association—the same organization that puts on the annual amateur national championships. At the time, Laura and I represented the Mission Valley Ice Skating Club. You had to join a local club to compete in a USFSA event.

I was competing at the beginners level, which is usually called preliminary, but the whole competition had an Indian theme, so my group of ten boys from the Bay Area was called Papoose Men. The preliminary group is mostly for kids ages seven to nine, although there were sometimes exceptions, as there was at this event for one chubby fifteen-year-old kid we nicknamed Papoose Moose. We thought that was funny.

At my level, we did only a freestyle program, whereas Laura had to do both figures and freestyle. I skated my program to "The Flight of the Bumblebee" and did four different jumps: an axel, a double salchow, a double loop, and a double toe loop.* I fell on the double loop that night, but in practice I was already doing a triple loop, which in those days was incredible for an eight-year-old.

After the competition was over, the results were posted in the lobby of the arena. Papoose Moose won, and I came in third. Dad and Laura went with me to see the results, and Laura jumped up and down with me. She didn't win any medals, but she was happy for me that I had won one during my very first competition. I'll never forget my dad standing there with a big smile on his face. You could tell that he was bursting with pride that his little boy had placed third. So I wasn't the most masculine kid in the world, but I was an award winner, and that made him extremely happy.

I loved the awards ceremony, which was held right after the competition. I discovered that it was a lot more fun when you're standing on the podium looking out at the audience

---

*You'll find a list of descriptions of jumps and spins in an appendix at the back of this book.

than when you're in the audience looking down at the podium. From where I was standing I could look at the audience and see out the huge windows to the snowcapped mountains beyond. It was awesomely beautiful.

Once we were on the podium, we were each given our awards. I was the first of the three skaters to be handed his award, and I held it over my head just as I'd seen the other kids do at all of Laura's competitions that I'd gone to. On cue, the audience applauded. And for a change, I held back the tears. As I said, Colleen didn't like her students crying in public.

After the awards ceremony, the first person I showed the award to was my dad. It was an unusual medal, because in keeping with the event's theme, it was made out of Indian beads. Dad held the medal in one hand, and he ran his fingers over it as if it were a precious object. When he was finished looking at it, he handed it back to me and gave me a pat on the back. It was the start of a ritual that we repeated again and again throughout my career.

3

THE MAKING OF
A LITTLE CHAMPION

Up until third grade, I really liked everything about school, from art and music to math and reading. And I liked doing well. For example, in second grade, the teacher rewarded the students who did well each day by writing their names inside a big smiley face that she drew in one corner of the blackboard. I made every effort to please my teacher, always doing my homework on time, volunteering to answer questions, always behaving as I should, and for this I got my just reward. Day after day, my name stayed on the board.

There was only one day when I didn't make it onto that coveted list, and it's a day I'll never forget. My teacher was at the piano playing "Love Makes the World Go Round," and the whole class was singing along. I was feeling mischievous, so I made a funny face at one of my classmates across the room. She didn't think it was so funny, and after the sing-along she went to the teacher and told her about the terrible crime that I'd committed. The teacher told me, in front of the whole class, that what I had done was wrong, and then she erased my name from the smiley face on the board. In a matter of seconds I went through a range of emotions. First I felt embarrassed for being singled out. Then I felt guilty for what I'd done. Then I felt angry at my classmate for turning me in.

My initial instinct was to get out of my seat, walk across the classroom, and knock that little girl to the floor. But I didn't, because I knew that would mean I'd be off the list forever. So I kept my feelings inside, and by the end of the next day, my name was back where I thought it belonged. Whether it was on the ice or in the classroom, I was one competitive kid.

In third grade, however, my attitude toward school took a dramatic turn for the worse, mostly because of how my third-grade teacher treated me. She didn't agree with the principal's decision to let me come in late. I wish she had expressed her opinion to the principal or my dad, but her way of dealing with her resentment was to take it out on me. Often when I came into class, she'd say in the most sarcastic way, in front of the whole class, "How was your skating?" As an eight-year-old, the way I interpreted her attitude toward me was to think that she was jealous of my skating, so I tried not to let it get to me, and I got through the day as best I could. It was hard not to get angry at my teacher, but I never said anything to her, the principal, or my parents. I thought it would only make things worse.

After school, I'm afraid I sometimes took out my frustration and anger on some of the neighborhood kids. As I'd hoped, once we moved to the new trailer park, Dad relaxed his rule about my having to play at home. I never asked him why, but I assume it was because I was older and because he felt that our new neighborhood was safer than the old one. So I started making friends with some of the kids who lived nearby. I never had any problems with these kids, and we'd play tag together and build forts out of leftover construction material. I had a best friend named Tim, and building forts was our favorite thing to do. We would go under the large porch that was attached to our mobile home and make rooms out of Styro-foam boards, the kind used for insulation. The two of us always built the fort, while our other friends looked on. When we were done, sometimes we'd invite everyone in to join us.

But there were other kids in the area who weren't a part of my clique. Most of them were Asian or black, and these were the kids I went after. I'll leave the psychoanalysis of my behavior to the professionals, but to this day I can't quite understand why I chose to taunt these kids with ethnic slurs to draw them into a fight. Of course, it never occurred to me that I was a member of an ethnic minority as well. I thought of myself as all-American, like my friends, most of whom were Anglos.

I was still quite little in stature, so you might think it was a bad idea for me to pick fights, but as long as the fights were one-on-one, there was no question who would win, because I would go crazy. I'd call these kids names, and when they came at me, I let loose with everything I had. I'd go for their heads, punching, scratching, and pulling their hair until they were on the ground crying.

Given that I was beating up two or three kids a month, it's no surprise that their parents came to speak to my mother about my behavior. My mother would listen, then she'd apologize, and that was the end of it. Neither she nor my dad ever told me that what I was doing was wrong, and they never punished me. Even at the time, I thought that was a little strange, but if they didn't want to punish me, I wasn't going to twist their arms.

In actuality, I didn't need my parents to tell me that what I was doing was wrong. I knew it. For the first five or ten minutes after I beat up a kid, I felt great. I felt powerful and I got a lot of satisfaction from physically assaulting some unsuspecting kid who had no idea what I was waiting to let loose. But then after a while I'd calm down and the adrenaline would stop pumping, and I'd get this uneasy feeling. I'd think to myself, "How can you do that to another person? What was the point of that?" At the time, I didn't have a word for what I was feeling, but I know now it was regret. Fortunately, that sense of regret in combination with my increasing commitments to skating helped me rein in my rage after a year or so of being the neighborhood's littlest bully.

For the most part, what I did after school was as benign as building forts. Sometimes I tagged along with Laura and her friends and watched them as they jumped rope or played hopscotch. But Laura didn't always appreciate having her little brother as her shadow. I remember one time when Laura got angry at me for following her out of the house and told me to go back in and play with one of her dolls. Well, I decided to play with the doll I liked best. My dad had given Laura this three-foot-tall doll with beautiful curly hair. It was the kind of doll you're not supposed to take out of the box. But I thought she could use a shampoo and haircut. So I tore open the box, took out the doll, removed her dress—I didn't want to get it wet—put some shampoo in her hair, and started cutting it. When Laura came back, she took one look, said, "Oh, my God!" and screamed at me for ruining her doll. Well, I don't think I really ruined her doll, but I have to admit that I did give her a permanent bad-hair day.

After school, I also sometimes watched television—I was hooked early on in my life to the soap operas, especially *All My Children* and *General Hospital*. Of course, my favorite thing to watch on television was figure skating. But there wasn't nearly as much figure skating on television when I was growing up as there is now, so it was a relatively rare treat when Laura and I could park ourselves in front of the TV and lose ourselves in the excitement and drama of a national figure-skating competition.

You would think that after watching as much figure skating on television as I did that I had figure-skating role models. But from an early age, I always wanted to be myself, so rather than wanting to be like Scott Hamilton, the Olympic gold medalist, I'd imagine that I was skating against him. It sounds pretty goofy now, but at the time I really let my imagination take over.

In our trailer we had sliding glass doors with curtains, which

Mom drew at night. I'd pull the curtains open so I could see my reflection in the glass. Then I'd skate a routine that I choreographed on my own, to music that I played on my Show & Tell record player. Of course, I was my own judge, so I'd give myself a 5.8 (out of a possible 6.0). Then I'd roll the dice for Scott Hamilton's score. For example, if I rolled a five and a six, his score was 5.6. If I rolled a six and a one, the score had to be 1.6, since in skating you can't score over 6.0.

After I rolled the dice, I'd write down the scores on a piece of paper, fold it up, and give it to my mother and ask her to post it in the hallway on the wall. After she posted the scores, I'd go look at the final results and act really surprised that I'd won. Then I would jump up and down and clap and scream, just as I saw the skaters and their coaches do at competitions. In my fantasy competition, with the way I played the game, there was no way I couldn't win.

Besides beating an imaginary Scott Hamilton, one of my favorite things to do after school, which I only got to do a few times that first year after my brother moved out, was to go with George for rides in his new car. George liked lots of attention, and that desire guided him to a silver Trans Am with a big bird painted on the hood, the kind of car that says, "Look at me." It also had "pay attention to me" mufflers to match the hood's artwork, so it literally called attention to itself.

George would pick me up at the trailer and buckle me into the front passenger seat, and we'd cruise down the streets in our area, honking at people George recognized and feeling incredibly cool. It made me think I was special to be riding with my big brother in the hottest car in our neighborhood.

The rides stopped abruptly that Christmas, because after Christmas George was not exactly welcome around the house. George chose Christmas morning as the time to announce to the family that he was gay.

Now, Christmas around the Galindo house was always a big deal, especially for my father, who did everything he could to make the holiday festive. He spent days decorating the entire outside of the house with white lights. Our Christmas tree was a sight to behold—we had enough lights, decorations, and tinsel to cover the tree at Rockefeller Center. You should have seen all the presents, lots of expensive toys, clothes, and model trains. Everything I asked for was always there under the tree. My father wasn't a rich man, but there always seemed to be enough money to provide for us throughout the year and still spoil us at Christmas.

So it was Christmas morning when George chose to make his declaration, and we were all in the living room waiting for him to get there so we could open the presents. There was no way I was going to sit calmly and wait, so I went from gift to gift, checking the names to see which ones were for me. At about 10 A.M. we heard George pull up in his Trans Am, and then he stumbled into the house before flopping down on the sofa, sprawling across its entire length. Looking back now, I realize he was on something, but at the time I was so focused on what was inside all the boxes that I hardly noticed. Given what George planned to tell the family that day, I can understand why he felt he needed to dull some of his nerves with drugs.

George didn't have an easy time getting our attention. Several times he said, "I've got to tell you guys something," but Dad was busy getting coffee in the kitchen, Mom was busy pouring it for him, and Laura and I were busy around the tree.

After a few more attempts at getting our attention, and after raising his voice to the point where we couldn't avoid noticing him, George said, "I'M GAY AND I LOVE MEN!" Well, that certainly got Laura's and Dad's attention right away. Mom, as I've noted more than once, didn't have the greatest hold on reality, and she just stood in the doorway to the kitchen with her usual blank look. I was too young to really connect with what George was saying, but once Dad started screaming at him, it began to sink in. What George had said about himself was the same thing I felt toward Johnny Rivera, and what we had in common was something that made my dad furious.

My dad's first response was to get this confused and angry

look on his face. Then he managed to spit out one word: "What?" George sat up on the couch and repeated with an edge of hostility in his voice, "I'm gay and I love men!" At that point Dad blew a gasket. "Goddammit, men don't go with men. God didn't make you that way. You go with women and you have babies." After that, George didn't say a word; he just sat there staring as Dad paced the room yelling over and over again about how men didn't go with men. After Dad exhausted that particular line of thought, he started in about how George had spoiled our holiday: "How dare you come here on this special day and ruin our whole Christmas." With that, George got to his feet and said, "Fine, I'll leave so you can have your Christmas," and he walked out the door, got in his car, and sped off. I have no idea where he went that day.

As George drove off, Laura ran into her room crying. Mom didn't move from where she'd been standing. Dad threw himself into his big easy chair. And all I wanted to do was open presents. I'd heard more than I could handle for that day and I just filed away the whole incident somewhere in my memory to be dealt with when I got a little older. I didn't do this consciously; no eight-year-old does. But my automatic emotional defense systems kicked in, and I went on as if nothing had happened.

After that day, George stayed away from the house. I can't blame him, given how Dad had reacted, and Dad made no effort to reach out to him. Looking back, I think George pretty much knew the kind of reaction he'd get from Dad, and I don't think he chose Christmas Day by accident. I think he decided to "ruin" that day because he was angry at Dad for lavishing so much attention and resources on me and Laura. Since Laura had started skating—and then once I started skating—the whole focus was on the two of us. George was pretty much left to fend for himself, as he had been for virtually all his life. When he was still living at home, no one ever seemed to notice or comment when he was out late or stayed out overnight. What George really needed at that moment in his life were a couple of strong and accepting parents who could help him get over the difficult hump of adolescence. But unfortunately for George, he'd have to struggle through life on his own.

Life for me at that point was anything but a struggle; it was an exciting challenge where the focus was almost entirely on the love of my life, skating.

After my first competition in Squaw Valley, Colleen enrolled me in another half dozen competitions throughout the following year. The first was at the Eastridge arena, where Laura and I skated every day. That was the first time I experienced the rush of competing before a home audience—although to say that there was an audience is probably an overstatement, because there couldn't have been more than a hundred people there to watch the competition, and everyone there was a member of the local skating club or was somehow related to one of the competitors. Still, a hundred people can make a lot of noise, and it really pumped me up to have the support and extraloud applause of my skating friends and their parents. Their enthusiasm encouraged me to do my best.

Of course, Laura and Dad were there to cheer me on as well, and even my mother came along. For a second time, I skated to "The Flight of the Bumblebee," and this time I beat everybody hands down. Being on the podium in Squaw Valley had been great, but at Eastridge I discovered that being on *top* of the podium is even better. I loved first place, and I could tell from how loudly my father cheered when I got my award that he loved it, too.

After winning at Eastridge, I won most of the competitions that followed during that year. Many of them were in central California, but we went to Santa Barbara a couple of times, too. My dad almost always took us, and not because he had to, because Colleen could have taken us and we could have gone with other families from our skating club. Dad went because he loved to go. He was one of the few fathers who came regularly, and he enjoyed being around everyone, especially all the mothers, who adored him. My dad was charming, good-looking, and something of a flirt, so it was easy to understand why they all liked him so much.

My father's interest in skating, despite his presence and financial support, didn't extend much beyond going to competitions and cheering for me and Laura. He wasn't the kind of skating parent who told us what to do or how to skate, and he only came to practice once a week or so to see how we were doing. He never commented on our programs, our choice of music, or our costumes. That was probably a good thing, because a lot of the parents get far too involved and turn into skating versions of stereotypical stage mothers.

Mom came to the local competitions, but she almost never went to the ones out of town. The travel made her too nervous and she never enjoyed being around so many people. I'd like to say that I got used to the fact she wasn't at the boards or in the stands cheering for me and Laura. I'd also like to say that I was compassionate and understood that she couldn't be a mother like all the other skating mothers. Unfortunately, I was young and needy, and that my mother couldn't come close to meeting my needs made me mad more than anything.

At this point in my skating career, I trained year-round and entered a half dozen competitions during the season, which lasted from May to September. The preliminary-level skaters were limited to local competitions, but that changed as you moved up through the ranks. After preliminary, the categories are prejuvenile, juvenile, intermediate, novice, junior, and senior. Generally, you had to take figure and freestyle tests to move up from one category to the next.

Once you reach the intermediate level, if you make it through the qualifying events, you go on to regional competitions, but that's as far as you can go. Qualifying novice skaters go from regionals to sectionals and then nationals. The country is divided up into three sections, and in each section there are three regions. In my section, which covered the whole West Coast, the regions are Southwest, Central, and Northwest. If this is beginning to sound as confusing as the annual Westminster dog show, with all the different levels and all the different clubs, well, there are some frightening similarities, especially when you begin to see how subjective the judging can be.

Most of the early competitions that I participated in during the first couple of years I skated are just a blur to me now, but one that stands out was about a year after Squaw Valley. I had moved up to prejuvenile boys and went to the Oktoberfest in Marysville, California. I won the figures portion of the competition and the freestyle as well. I did a really polished double loop, and when I got off the ice after finishing my program, I was surrounded by a group of little girls. A couple of them, who, as I think back now, must have had crushes on me, handed me teddy bears and told me how wonderful I was. I thought to myself, "Wow, I must be pretty good." Looking at photographs of myself from that time, when I was about nine, I can see that I often had a cocky look on my face. With so much success I was beginning to take myself a little too seriously.

I wish my parents had been there to rein me in when I began to think of myself as God's gift to the skating world. But they weren't really aware of the monster growing in their midst. Mom wasn't up to it, and I think Dad was having so much fun soaking up all the compliments from the other parents that he didn't notice what a spoiled brat I was becoming.

Part of the problem was that Dad generally didn't get to see me at my most demanding and temperamental, and Mom apparently didn't share with him what I was up to when he was out of town. It was hard for Mom to say no to me, so most of the time I simply got my way. On those rare occasions when she decided to risk saying no to me, I was quick to turn on her. For example, some days I didn't want to go to school after skating practice. Most of the time Mom just drove me home and let me sit in front of the television all day. But a few times she insisted I had to go to school, and I threw a tantrum and screamed and cursed, using the most awful profanities you can imagine.

I apparently knew my father well enough not to try the same

spoiled-brat routine on him. If he made a decision, like when he said I had to be in the house at a certain time, it was law, and I didn't dare contradict him. I'm not sure what I was afraid of because he never hit me. But I think it may have been that bellowing voice of his. His just raising it made me tremble like a bowl of Jell-O.

My off-ice behavior aside, I was doing so well during my second competitive season that Colleen had me skip from prejuvenile to intermediate because she felt I was ready for intermediate sectionals, the next level of competition. Colleen handled all of the arrangements for my qualifying tests, which left me free to focus on what I liked doing best. It's great to have someone else taking care of all the arrangements, but over time, as I was to discover, there's the danger of becoming helpless as all your practical needs are met before you even know what they are.

As I moved up through the ranks to intermediate men, I placed in the top three at every event, which only added to my swelling sense of self-importance. It's somewhat ironic that we were called men when we were so young. At ten, I was among the youngest intermediate men. I'm not sure I even had the maturity to be called a boy, let alone a man. In hindsight, when I'm feeling unkind toward myself, big baby seems like a better description.

I liked the idea of jumping from level to level, or at least I did until I went to my first competition as an intermediate skater, which was held in Stockton, California. In Stockton I discovered that all the other skaters were two and three years older than I was. Add to that the fact that I was small for my age, and you can imagine how intimidating it was to be in the locker room with all these boys who towered over me.

At the Stockton competition, I placed third after the figures, which wasn't too terrible. But in the past, if I placed third in figures, I usually pulled up to first or second place after doing my freestyle program. Not this time, and I had no one to blame but myself.

There was a big park across from the ice arena in Stockton where we went to hang out and wait before the freestyle competition. Dad and Colleen and lots of the other parents and kids spread out blankets on the grass. A lot of the kids took naps, but as usual I couldn't sit still. I wanted to go to the little amusement park and the petting zoo and run around. As I said, I usually got my way, which wasn't always a good thing. By the time I got on the ice later that day, I had zero energy and I fell more times than I care to remember.

As I dragged myself off the ice, I knew there was no way I could have won; I still thought that I'd at least secured third place. But when the scores were posted in the lobby of the arena, I saw that I'd dropped to fourth. Not only had I not won, I wouldn't even be on the podium to get second or third. No award. No applause. No praise from my father. I was devastated and ran from the arena crying.

Colleen caught up with me outside, and after I stopped crying, she sat me down and explained to me that I wasn't always going to get an award, and that part of being a competitive skater was being a good sportsman. This was a painful lesson. Colleen walked me back inside and made me shake hands with the three skaters who had won awards. She stood there and watched me as I said congratulations and shook their hands. She was right to force me to do it, but at that moment I hated doing it and I hated her.

I didn't realize it, but Colleen was acting like a mother toward me, trying to teach me proper values. In my fantasies, having a loving mother didn't mean having to do things I didn't want to do. But as my relationship with Colleen grew closer, and she became more parental, I began to see that a mother-child relationship was complicated. And given that Colleen was also my coach, you can probably forgive me for being a little confused about exactly what my relationship was to her and how she fit in with my real parents.

This confusion began after my first year working with Colleen, when I started staying over at her house on occasion. Colleen lived in San Jose, up in the foothills, with her three teenage children. She'd fix dinner for me and was very affectionate. I especially loved the way she tucked me in at night and gave me a kiss on the cheek. It reminded me of when I was living with my aunt Cindy.

When I slept at my own house, Colleen often called to make certain I was in bed on time. She wanted to make sure I got my rest, and often she just liked checking in. When we traveled to out-of-town competitions, Colleen kept even closer track of me by having me room with her. In 1982, for example, when I went to Indianapolis to compete in my first national championship as a novice skater, my mom and Laura shared one room and Colleen and I shared another. It was so expensive for all of us to go to Indianapolis that my father stayed home.

Colleen took good care of me in Indianapolis. The night before my first practice, she prepared a special pasta meal for me and put me to bed early so I'd have plenty of rest for the next day. She asked my mother and sister not to disturb us, because she didn't want anything to interfere with my practice session the following morning. Colleen was looking after me like a mother hen, and I just soaked up all the coddling and the attention. The next day, after practice, she had me take a nap, then woke me about an hour before we had to leave for the coliseum.

Suddenly, right before we were to leave the room, there was a knock at the door. Before Colleen could make a move, I ran to the door and opened it, and there was my dad in his cowboy hat. I was so excited that I jumped into his arms, hugged him, and yelped, "Oh, my God, you made it!" Colleen had no idea Dad was coming and she got very mad. She pulled Dad outside the hotel room, closed the door behind them, and started yelling at him. Through the door, I heard her tell him that he had no right to cause such a distraction just before the freestyle program. The whole thing quickly escalated into a screaming match, with my dad yelling that he paid the bills and that Colleen had no right to tell him what he could do, and that he wanted to see me. Colleen wouldn't budge and told my father he could see me after the competition.

By the time Colleen came back into the room I was crying. First of all, the yelling frightened me. Second, the whole situation was confusing. I loved my dad and wanted to be with him, but I knew that Colleen was looking out for my best interests, so I felt torn between Colleen and my father. It was awful.

Before Dad left, he poked his head in and said he'd see me after the competition. Colleen tried to comfort me, saying that everything was okay. After I calmed down, she helped me finish getting dressed, and we left to catch the bus to the coliseum. I needed to focus on my skating now, so I put the argument that I'd just witnessed out of my head. I was already in the habit of taking things that I found too painful to deal with and pushing them aside. I knew that if I was going to win the competition, I had to push this out of my mind, too.

When we got to the coliseum, the first thing I had to do was stretch, which Colleen always helped me with. I held on to her hands as I did knee bends and then leg kicks. Then she cradled me, with her arms around my back, so I could do back bends. It seemed to me that helping me helped Colleen stay calm, although I could still tell she was nervous, because she was so quiet. I thought Colleen was more nervous than I was.

When it was my turn to skate, Colleen reminded me to smile a lot and to acknowledge the judges with a little "Hey." Colleen really emphasized skating for the judges and performing for them, which is exactly what I did that night. They must have been happy with what they saw, because I won. I was the new novice national champion! The audience cheered. Colleen hugged me and said how proud she was of my performance. Mom, Dad, and Laura told me the same thing, and, of course, I was proud of myself.

Nationals in Indianapolis proved to be a landmark for Laura as well, but it was a very different kind of landmark from mine, and it was one that was dictated by money.

Over the past couple of years, it had become clear that money was a problem. Laura wrote all the checks for our dad, because he could hardly read or write. She'd go over the bills with him and he'd complain about how expensive everything was. I'd listen and get scared that he was going to say we shouldn't skate anymore. One time when he was yelling about all the bills, I got so upset that I ran out of my room and said, "Fine, I'm going to quit." And he said, "No, that's not what I'm saying." He explained that he loved the fact that we skated, and he didn't want us to stop, but it was an enormous burden, and sometimes he just needed to let off steam about it.

My father actually made pretty good money, but with two of us taking skating lessons and traveling to out-of-town competitions, it was getting difficult for him to stay afloat. The U.S. Figure Skating Association provided some grant money once you were skating at the level I'd reached, and they paid the cost of international travel for the skaters, but the vast majority of the several-hundred-dollars-a-week financial burden fell on my dad's shoulders.

Laura knew that there wasn't enough money for both of us to continue skating much longer. And at sixteen, with six years of lessons under her belt, she also recognized that I was the skater with the better chance of making it to the top. So without saying anything, Laura pretended to show less interest in skating, and after Indianapolis she began cutting back on her lessons and eventually quit. What helped her make her decision was overhearing a telephone conversation in which my father tried—successfully, as it turned out—to borrow money so that he could fly to Indianapolis to see me compete. It broke her heart to hear him ask for money. Laura also went to work part-time at Taco Bell to help pay for my lessons and other skating costs. At the time, I wasn't aware of any of this. I'm still in awe of Laura's sacrifice, and terribly grateful to her for all she's done for me.

By the time I won my gold medal at nationals, I'd graduated from elementary school and was in my first year at J. W. Fair Junior High. As you might imagine, because of my skating I was something of a local celebrity. There were articles about me in the newspaper, and the principal put my picture up in the cafeteria and the school office.

My celebrity turned out to be great insurance against getting hassled for coming in late or getting teased because I was this little feminine boy who did figure skating. I was famous—at least to the kids at my school—and that's all that mattered to anyone.

J. W. Fair was a pretty rough school back then. There weren't gangs as there are today, but there were different cliques of *cholos* (Mexican boys—the girls were *cholas*). Most of the *cholos* wore baggy pants, white Ben Davis T-shirts, and Nike or Adidas sneakers. Some of them wore headbands. And a lot of them walked with a swagger, with their arms sort of hanging behind them. These were the tough kids, although a lot of it was just posturing.

Right after I won nationals, all the different groups of *cholos* wanted me to be a part of their clique. They wanted me to hang out with them after school, to go to their houses and smoke pot. My strategy was to be friendly with everyone in all the different groups, but I made a point of letting them know that I was too busy with skating to be a part of a gang, and they all respected that. In truth, I already had my "gang" at the ice-skating rink.

It's funny, so many people warned me about how much trouble I was going to have in junior high because of the tough kids, but the very kids I should have been afraid of wound up protecting me. For example, if someone wanted to pick a fight with me or looked at me funny, the *cholos* would say, "Don't be looking at Rudy that way, or you'll have to deal with us." Instead of calling me Rudy, most of the *cholos* used a couple of nicknames they came up with for me—either French Fry or Shrimp, because I was so short.

The *cholos* considered me one of their own because of my Mexican heritage. That always struck me as kind of funny because I felt about as Mexican—or Italian—as most second-generation Americans feel about their ancestry, but because of my last name, I was automatically a part of the Mexican community. However they saw me, I saw myself as a California boy. I didn't really identify with the *cholos*, and I didn't dress in any way that suggested I was a part of their world. I chose to dress like the skating kids, which was the community I felt most strongly connected to. So I wore what the other skating kids wore and that meant dressing preppy.

There were other things that made me feel isolated from the kids at school. I had an exciting life that wasn't limited to J. W. Fair or San Jose. I was a nationally recognized skater. I was written about in the local newspapers and the skating magazines. I got to travel. And I was allowed to go to school part-time. In seventh and eighth grade I had only four classes a day: social studies, math, reading, and English. I got to skip phys ed because skating made up for it, and I didn't have time for the art elective.

For the most part, I didn't feel bad about going to school part-time or missing days so I could go to competitions. But occasionally I felt left out, like when I would come back after a trip and all my classmates would be talking about what they had learned in class the day before. I tried justifying to myself that I was getting to do lots of things that my classmates never got to do, but I wasn't always convincing.

After winning nationals, even my mom started treating me differently. This was during a period when she was doing better and was less withdrawn than usual. Her illness wasn't really predictable, and this was one of those times when she was more normal-acting than others. She'd show up at school at lunchtime and wait for me outside in her car. She always brought me my favorite things from Taco Bell: two tostadas—just beans, lettuce, and sauce, no cheese, tomatoes, or onions; one taco; and a root beer.

This lunch routine just started one day when Mom dropped me off at school after skating and asked me if I wanted her to bring me lunch. I always got dropped off at 10:20; and lunch was around noon. I said I thought it would be great, and that's how it started. So whenever she dropped me off, I'd ask if she was going to be there at lunch. I was never sure whether she'd come back, so I'd look out the window at school, and when I saw her little car waiting outside, I'd get so excited. I thought it was the coolest thing for my mom to do that, and so did the other kids. No other parents brought food from Taco Bell for their kids. It made me feel special, and I was finally getting special treatment from my mom.

4

RUDY + KRISTI = ?

Throughout my career, it's been the artistic and balletic style of my skating that has set me apart from the other American male skaters, and I have Colleen to thank for setting me on that path.

Unlike many other coaches, Colleen believed that her skaters should have training in ballet, so off I went to ballet class twice a week after school, for an hour and a half. I didn't think at all about the implications of a boy taking ballet until I walked into my first class and I saw that I was the only one. It wasn't a problem for me. When you're a young male figure skater, you get used to being surrounded by girls. I always liked being around girls, but it would have been nice if there had been at least one boy, so I wouldn't have been the sole target for the teasing during class.

Given what I looked like in tights, the girls had every reason to tease me. I had the skinniest chicken legs you can imagine, and when I looked in the mirror, I couldn't help but laugh along with the girls at how I looked. I wore a pair of gym shorts over my black tights, which only served to accentuate my twiglike legs.

I can't say that I loved ballet, because I didn't, but I did learn a lot. I learned the proper way to stretch, which is how I became so limber. And I learned all the different ballet positions. When you watch me skate, you can see that I still use what I learned back then, especially in the way I hold my body and in my hand positions.

At the same time I studied ballet, Colleen introduced me to the skating of one of the greatest skaters of all time. John Curry was the 1976 Olympic gold medalist from Great Britain, and he was known for his creative balletic style. Colleen showed me a video of John in competition, and she also showed me pictures of him in all of the skating positions he did. She never told me that I had to skate like John Curry, but I found his style of skating very appealing, so I incorporated a lot of what I saw into my own skating style.

The first chance I had to use all the new things I learned was in a local exhibition in 1980. Colleen worked with me to prepare a program using music from the opera *I Pagliacci*. Instead of just skating to the music, I told the story of the tragic clown, Canio, through my skating. Colleen had told me the whole story one day at practice about how Canio kills the woman he loves in a jealous rage. I was only an eleven-year-old twerp, but I really got into the emotion of it all. So Colleen had a clown costume made up for me and she did my face makeup with a big teardrop. I did so well that I was invited by Carlo Fassi, who coached the legendary Peggy Fleming, Dorothy Hamill, John Curry, and Robin Cousins, to perform in a show he was doing in Santa Rosa with all these Olympic stars. You would think that I would have been intimidated by such an all-star cast, but I was perfectly happy to be in their company.

After three years of working with me, Colleen felt that she needed to bring in a more experienced coach, someone who could take me to the next level of my career. She introduced me to Jim Hulick, who was the top-name coach in the San Francisco Bay area. He hadn't coached any champion skaters, but he'd been a national junior pairs champion himself in 1971 and had built a reputation as a jump expert. I was pretty solid on most of my double jumps, but I needed a lot of work on my triples.

I wasn't aware of Jim's reputation, but after taking a couple of private lessons with him at the arena where he worked in Dublin, which is about a half hour north of San Jose, I knew that I wanted to work with him full-time. Jim was in his thirties, but looked younger. He was good-looking with blond hair and blue eyes. Jim always wore prescription sunglasses, even on the ice, and his laces were always untied with the tongues of his skates hanging down to the ground. I liked the look.

Jim's style of coaching suited me quite well. In contrast to Colleen, who was strict and occasionally harsh, Jim was laid-back, gentle, and encouraging. Jim knew when to praise me and when to give me a gentle push. I was the kind of athlete who did best when he was trying to please his coach, and Jim understood that about me right away and used it to his advantage and for my benefit. For example, instead of being critical when I missed a jump or fell, he'd first joke about it, then he'd tell me what I did right and explain what I did wrong, then show me how I could do it better the next time. With this positive-reinforcement approach, I was as predictable—and content—as a lapdog.

The transition from Colleen to Jim was gradual, and over a period of months I took more and more classes with Jim and fewer classes with Colleen. After being so close to Colleen, you might guess that I would have had trouble separating from her or that I would have missed her. But in a way, this was similar to how I experienced the separation from Aunt Cindy; once I stopped seeing Colleen, I never looked back.

I had only one complaint about working with Jim and it had nothing to do with his teaching abilities and everything to do with location. Because Jim worked at the Dublin rink, my mother couldn't drive me. That was too long a drive for her, plus it meant getting on the highway, and that was more than her nerves could handle. So Laura had to drive me, which she was more than capable of doing, but she did it without a license for the first few months because she wasn't yet old enough to drive. I always felt completely safe with Laura, and I had every reason to. Dad had taught her how to drive his eighteen-wheeler when she was thirteen, and from that age on, whenever Mom was out of commission and Dad was on the road, Laura drove us the three miles to the Eastridge rink. Laura was a cautious driver, so thankfully we never had an accident.

I had a lot of work to do with Jim, because after winning my novice title at nationals, I automatically moved up to junior men. If I was going to have any chance against the older and more experienced skaters, I needed to learn new jumps and I had to learn *fast* how to do them consistently.

My first competition as a junior was regionals in the fall of 1982. Apparently I hadn't worked hard enough, because I came in third. Third wasn't bad, especially since it was good enough to get me to sectionals, but given that my competition at sectionals was going to be a lot stiffer, I'd have a hard time placing high enough to win a medal. Sure enough, I came in fifth at sectionals, which meant I failed to qualify for nationals, the first and only time in my career that happened.

I have to admit that my ability to deal with disappointment even now isn't very good, and back then . . . well, I guess I could be charitable and say I was worse, but a more descriptive word would be *horrible*. Placing fifth felt like the end of the world, and I dragged myself around the house for days afterward feeling sorry for myself. Fortunately, shortly after sectionals, I had something to take my mind off the most disappointing season thus far of my competitive career. That something was an eleven-year-old skater named Kristi Yamaguchi.

The first time I saw Kristi in 1982 was at a rink in Pleasanton,

California. I don't remember exactly why I'd gone to that particular rink, but I was just skating around for fun during a public session, taking it easy following my poor showing at sectionals. During public sessions there were always kids taking lessons at the center of the ice, and Kristi was one of them. She was taking a spin lesson and I could see that she was really good. So I asked one of the coaches at the side of the rink who she was and found out that she was this hot intermediate-level skater.

In addition to being a great skater, Kristi was incredibly cute. She was a tiny, pretty Asian girl. It's not as though I had a crush on her—that would never have occurred to me—but between her size and the way she reacted when I applauded her jumps, I thought she was irresistible. She'd half-pretend not to notice me clapping, but no matter how hard she struggled to ignore me, she'd eventually give in to her emotions and her face would light up with a big smile. Then she'd turn red and get shy.

Out on the ice, there was no way I could resist teasing Kristi, but the only way I knew how to tease her was to skate by her and gently poke her in the side. She had this squeaky little voice, and I loved how she'd laugh and say, "Don't," which, of course, encouraged me to tease her even more. Given today's political and social climate, if I tried that sort of stunt nowadays I would probably be thrown out of the ice rink for sexual harassment.

My interest in Kristi had nothing to do with romantic thoughts. What I had in mind was skating pairs with her. Laura, as always, had been my inspiration. In her last year of skating, she skated pairs, and it looked like a lot of fun to me. Singles skating is extremely isolating, and I thought it might be fun to work with someone, especially someone who was as full of energy and charm as Kristi.

After seeing Kristi on the ice several more times, I mentioned to Jim that I was interested in trying pairs skating. Jim was usually good about protecting my feelings, but I guess the image of this little pipsqueak trying to do all the lifts and throws that are required of the male pairs skaters was too much for him, so he burst out laughing. I was crushed and started to skate away, but he quickly composed himself and came after me.

Jim apologized for laughing and said that if I could find someone who was shorter than I was, then he'd see about arranging a tryout. I know Jim assumed that I'd never find a qualified skater who was smaller, because I was so small myself. At thirteen, I was four feet six inches tall, and I weighed only sixty-nine pounds. Of course, I already knew the perfect partner, and I told Jim about Kristi, who was four feet two inches tall and weighed fifty pounds. Jim had seen her skate and thought she was a good skater. He had this look on his face that said, "Maybe." After thinking for a minute, he said, "I'll talk to her mother and see what she says."

A week later, Jim told me he'd got the okay from Kristi's mother, Carole Yamaguchi, so all he needed was an okay from Laura, who by that point was the person responsible for making my major skating decisions. Since my dad wasn't really interested in skating beyond going to the competitions, he was more than glad to let Laura handle the day-to-day responsibilities and decisions. Laura knew how much I wanted a tryout with Kristi, and she gave an enthusiastic okay.

Jim set up an appointment with Kristi's mom for a tryout session the following week. I was nervous, excited, and scared all at the same time. I really wanted this to work, but you never know how it's going to be until you get out there on the ice together. As luck would have it, the day of the tryout I was sick, and I spent the whole morning throwing up. It wasn't from nerves. It was from eating too much raw chocolate-chip cookie dough the night before at a skater friend's house.

As woozy as I was, I didn't want to miss my session with Kristi, so I had my friend's mother drive me to the rink anyway. Despite my desire to get out on the ice with Kristi, I could barely stand up, let alone skate. Carole was very sweet with me. She said, "Maybe you should go home and have your mother make you something to settle your stomach." While she had the wrong mother in mind, I appreciated her concern. She also told me not to worry about missing the session, that we'd reschedule for the next day. As Laura and I said good-bye to Kristi's mom, she said, "I hope you feel better." Now it was my turn to blush and get shy. I wasn't used to that kind of attention.

The next day, February 16, 1983, is a day I'll never forget. I got to the arena an hour before our tryout, and every minute seemed like forever. I skated around, trying to calm down, but there was no way to stop the adrenaline from pumping through my veins. It felt as if my heart would just pop out of my chest.

Finally, Kristi arrived and I skated over to where she was standing with her mom at the edge of the rink. Carole gave me a big hello, and Kristi said hello quietly while staring at the ice. She was as nervous as I was. Jim spotted both of us and skated over, and as usual he was wearing sunglasses and his skates were untied. He said, "Okay, gang, let's go!" Carole gave Kristi a hug and a kiss, wished us both good luck, and we skated out to the center of the ice.

The first thing Jim asked us to do was synchronized crossovers; it's the most basic skating move you do as a pair. He showed us how to hold hands, but Kristi was giggling so much that it took a while to get it right. By then, a couple of dozen people had gathered up in the stands to watch us.

I knew how to do crossovers from watching Laura do pairs, so I knew to watch Kristi's feet and cross over at exactly the same time she did. We did it perfectly the first time, and as we skated around and around the center of the rink, our small cheering section, which included Carole and Laura, urged us on. We were the Mighty Mites!

Jim worked with us for about a half hour putting us through a range of basic moves. I couldn't get over the difference between singles and pairs. This was so much more fun. Instead of learning things by myself, we learned new things together. I had someone to talk to and I had a playmate who liked to play on the ice as much as I did. I couldn't imagine anything better.

The tryout went really well, and after the lesson, Jim talked to Carole and Laura about Kristi and me taking a lesson once a week, just for fun. Everyone saw how great we were together, so the answer was yes.

Before long, one lesson a week turned into two, and that was in addition to my regular singles lessons. I liked pairs better, but I was already successful as a singles skater, and there was no reason to give that up for pairs. Skaters rarely do both singles and pairs, but that didn't matter to me. I didn't see any reason why I couldn't do both.

My morning skating schedule stayed the same as it had always been, except now I also practiced our pairs program, but on my own. I'd do all the footwork and pretend that I was lifting Kristi as I skated across the ice. After my morning lessons and practice, I'd go to school, and in the afternoon on Tuesdays and Wednesdays, Kristi and I would meet at the rink during a public session for a half-hour pairs lesson with Jim, then after that we'd practice by ourselves for another hour and a half.

Learning pairs was a lot of work, but it was so much fun mastering new tricks together. Once we'd fully mastered crossovers, Jim taught us a pair camel spin. Next was side-by-side jumps, which was a real challenge at first because Kristi and I spin in opposite directions. I'm left-handed and Kristi is right-handed, so while I spin to the left, Kristi spins to the right. That meant before doing a jump we had to cross in front of each other, and then she'd jump to the right and I would jump to the left, like mirror images.

From jumps, we went to lifts. I was such a little twig that I think no one could believe I'd ever be able to lift Kristi over my head. But I was deceptively strong, and after two weeks of practicing an overhead lift on the ground, we got out on the ice to give it a try. We skated crossovers, got up a little bit of speed, and then positioned our hands; I took a deep breath and lifted Kristi into the air. All I could say was "Oh, my God!" I was so caught up in the moment that I forgot all about the turn I was supposed to do while Kristi was in the air. I heard Kristi say,

"Turn, turn," and so I turned one revolution and then set her down. We were so excited over what we'd accomplished that we instantly grabbed each other and hugged. Then we did the same lift again and again and again until it was perfect. I had this incredibly joyful sense of accomplishment, and what made it even better was that we were now two friends working together.

I was never someone who got close to other kids easily, but with Kristi, from almost the very first time we skated together, I felt like Kristi and I were best friends. We worked hard, but we also laughed a lot and had fun clowning around. And as the months passed, we began spending time together off the ice, as well, going to the mall with Carole and every now and then to the movies. It's nothing unusual for kids that age to have a friend they do lots of things with, but for me it was something totally new.

When Kristi and I started taking pairs lessons, it was just for fun. I don't think either of us thought in terms of being competitive pairs skaters, especially since we both had increasingly successful singles skating careers. It's rare for singles skaters to also compete in pairs, mostly because each discipline is so time-consuming in its own right. Add to that the logistical nightmare at competitions where scheduled practice times and competitions overlap, and it's easy to see why it's so rarely done at all and certainly *never* done in the top ranks.

Only a few months after Kristi and I began working with Jim, he decided we were good enough to be entered in a competition. For our first time out, he chose a small event at the Pickwick Arena in Los Angeles. Kristi's mom drove us down, and we stayed with Kristi's grandmother, who didn't exactly welcome me with open arms. The first time she met me she said to Kristi, with me standing right there, "Why couldn't you pick a nice Japanese boy to skate with?" Kristi rolled her eyes and walked with me into another room. She told me not to pay any attention to what her grandmother said, and that she was actually a nice woman, just a little old-fashioned. I wasn't convinced and stayed as far away from her as I could.

For our first skating program, Jim choreographed a two-part, two-and-a-half-minute routine to two pieces of music. For the fast part we skated to "In the Mood," and for the slow part we skated to the theme from the movie *Gone with the Wind*. The program included some really fun moves, including what can best be described as a whirly cartwheel, and we also did a throw axel, which is a move where I threw Kristi into the air as we skated across the ice and before landing she would execute a single axel.

We were amazed by the audience response, but we didn't have much perspective on ourselves. For one thing, we were both small, and at thirteen and eleven, we were young in comparison to our sixteen- and eighteen-year-old competitors. Second, the audience could see that we were having a great time. As we got off the ice, people ran up to us and told us how wonderful we were and that we had to keep skating together. Kristi and I looked at each other and started giggling. Of course we were going to continue skating together. We were having too much fun not to.

That first summer Kristi and I skated together, the summer of 1983, there was one huge worry for me on the horizon. In June I graduated from eighth grade, and that fall, I was supposed to go to Independence High School in San Jose. But there was one catch. Because of my skating schedule, which was getting even more demanding because of my work with Kristi, I needed to arrange my schedule so I could start my school day at 10:30 instead of 8:30. The question was, would they let me?

Dad made an appointment for us to meet with the school's principal, and he brought along a letter that Jim wrote explaining my skating schedule. I remember being incredibly nervous as we walked into the school the day of our meeting. On our way into the office, my dad patted me on the back and told me not to worry, that he was sure it wouldn't be a problem.

Well, it *was* a problem, and it didn't help when Dad explained that it hadn't been a problem for me to come in late for elementary or junior high school. The principal said he understood our dilemma and realized that I had a promising skating career—"But high school is different," he said. "It's far more demanding. For Rudy to get a proper education, he has to take all his classes." He finished by suggesting that I find a way to rearrange my skating schedule.

I walked out of the principal's office feeling despondent. What would I do? I had to go to high school. What if we couldn't find a school in our area that would let me come in late? I tried to think of a way to rearrange my schedule so I could still get enough time on the ice, but it seemed impossible. In the afternoon, the ice arenas were open to the public, so the only time I could be on the ice without weaving in and out of crowds was in the morning. I was already getting up at 4:30 in the morning to be on the ice by 5:30, so starting my day any earlier was impossible. One option was to cut back on my practice time, but in my mind that was out of the question. So the only thing that could give was school.

Despite what the principal said about getting a proper education, my father was completely supportive of my going to school part-time. He knew how important skating was to me, and he didn't put a lot of emphasis on education. Dad never went to high school, so going even part-time was a lot more than he'd done himself.

Before Dad had a chance to find another high school for me, he happened to overhear a skating parent at the rink talking about getting a tutor for her daughter so she could do home study instead of regular high school. That was the answer. Dad asked for the name of the tutor, and he made an appointment for us to go see her.

We met with the tutor, who worked out of her home. She was a reasonably nice middle-aged woman and, as I was soon to discover, not a terribly demanding teacher. She talked to my dad for a little while, and they arranged for me to come in twice a week for a couple of hours. The rest of the time I'd work on my own, which would leave me free to focus on my skating. I was thrilled, because now I wouldn't have to worry about missing classes or having teachers get angry at me for not keeping up.

When the school year began, instead of going to Independence High, I went to my tutor's house twice a week at around eleven, right after skating. The first thing I did was hand in my assignments, which ranged from homework in math and English to book reports and research papers about athletes. While the tutor sat at her dining room table and looked over my work, I'd go in the kitchen and look in her refrigerator for something to eat. The whole setup was pretty informal, and I was perfectly happy to take advantage of it.

On occasion, my tutor gave me tests on whatever I'd been studying. And before I left her house, she'd give me my assignments for the next time. By one or two o'clock I was on my way home, where I spent about an hour a day on my homework.

Early on, I got a sense that my tutor didn't pay a lot of attention to my work, so just to see if she really read my papers, I made up a book report. I wrote the first few paragraphs the way I normally would, then I wrote sentences that were all mixed up. I handed in the report, trying the whole time not to laugh, and the next week the book report came back with the usual approving check marks. I should have gone home and told my father, because the tutor was not only wasting my time, but totally wasting his hard-earned money. While I was going through the motions of getting an education, I really wasn't getting one. Nevertheless, I was completely focused on my skating, and school was just getting in the way. To me, the less I had to do, the better.

For the next three years, I went to my tutor's house twice a week, and then I quit. I didn't see any point in going beyond eleventh grade just so I could get a high school diploma. Instead, I took a test to get my general equivalency diploma

(GED), which I figured would be more than enough for me to get through life.

I'm often asked if I missed anything by not going to regular high school. I did miss something, but not what most people think. Over and over, I've heard people say that the thing you miss is the social life. I don't agree. In skating, there's plenty of social life if you want it. I also got to travel to distant places that none of my school classmates ever had the opportunity to go. But what I didn't get was the kind of well-rounded education that everyone needs to go through life without feeling like an idiot. While I've traveled the world, I still couldn't tell you the first thing about the history or political significance of the places I've been to. Of course, part of that is my own fault, for not making more of an effort to learn on my own, but an equal part of the blame goes to my less than adequate education.

I'm surprised that the U.S. Figure Skating Association doesn't have some kind of educational requirements for young skaters who participate in USFSA competitions. I think there's got to be a way for the USFSA to come up with a monitoring system to make sure that skaters who compete in their sanctioned events get a proper education in school or through a tutoring program that's not simply an excuse to skip high school. And if skater's don't meet the minimum requirements set by the USFSA and fail to maintain grades at a certain level, they shouldn't be allowed to skate.

On the other hand, maybe it shouldn't be the job of the USFSA to make sure skaters get an education. Ideally, the parents and skaters should be making responsible choices. But I know that that's not happening; just look at my example.

5

ARE YOU MY MOTHER?

The fall of 1983 should have been a relatively happy time for me. I didn't have to go to regular school anymore, so I didn't have to worry about coming in late or missing classes. Kristi and I were doing well in our competitions. But something wasn't right. And I know this because it took almost nothing to set me off. I found myself snapping at Jim when I couldn't get a particular move on the first try. I had no patience for my mother, no matter what she did. And whenever Laura tried to ask me if anything was bothering me, I told her to leave me alone. If I wasn't on the ice, the only place I wanted to be was in my room at home—alone, staring at the ceiling or sleeping.

My bad mood peaked at the October sectional championship, which was held at an arena near Los Angeles. Kristi drove down with her mom, and they stayed with Kristi's grandmother again. Fortunately, Dad and Laura decided to come, too, so we drove down together and stayed with my aunt Cindy.

Thankfully, I was spared another scary encounter with Kristi's grandmother, and I was glad to have the chance to see my aunt and all my cousins. My extended family welcomed me with open arms and fawned all over me, but I still felt like putting my fist through a wall.

Kristi and I were competing in both singles and pairs, but pairs came first. We faced ten teams from around the state, and after watching all of them in practice, I felt confident that we'd win. On the ice during the competition, we were awesome. Even better for me, once we were on the ice, performing in front of an audience, I could set aside all my frustration and anger for at least a few minutes and enjoy myself. We did a side-by-side double lutz, which was unheard of in novice pairs back then, and we also did a double flip. The crowd was on its feet even before we finished.

After all the pairs had skated, Kristi, Carole, and I went out to look at the scores, which were posted in the lobby. Dad and Laura were still up in the stands. Despite my expectations, we came in second. That was all the trigger I needed, and I had a complete meltdown in front of all of the other skaters, coaches, and parents. Carole Yamaguchi had about as much patience for that kind of behavior as Colleen Blackmore did, and like Colleen had done, Carole took me aside. In a very firm tone of voice she said, "Don't you *ever* do that in public again!" And then she explained to me that I was going to have to learn to deal with disappointment, that we weren't going to win every competition, especially since we were still relatively unproved. That seemed reasonable, but it wasn't the disappointment I was having trouble with. It was something entirely different, but I didn't know what it was.

This is the point in the story where you would hope that the child psychologist comes in, because I was clearly a kid with some serious problems. I wasn't just a temperamental teenager who needed a talking to. I was a troubled kid who was struggling with a deep well of barely controllable rage. Unfortunately, I didn't come from the kind of background where

70

people sent their kids for counseling, so this was something I was going to have to wrestle with on my own.

In the singles competition, I had another tantrum. I always did well in figures, but I missed a turn and landed in ninth place. I felt like a complete failure, especially after working with Jim so hard all year. This time, I waited until we were in the car on the way back to Aunt Cindy's house before I flipped out. I imagine that Dad and Laura must have wondered if I'd inherited my mother's mental illness, because I went about as crazy as she sometimes did.

When my mother had fits, she sometimes threw things at my dad. That day in the car, I screamed at the top of my lungs and kicked the inside of the car: the doors, the back of the seat, anywhere my feet would reach. Dad yelled at me to stop, and Laura struggled to get me to quiet down, which I finally did, though with great resistance.

As soon as my dad parked the car in front of Aunt Cindy's house, I jumped out and ran away. I didn't know where I was going, but I ran as fast as I could, block after block, through the streets of East Los Angeles, dressed in my figure sweater and polyester pants. Eventually, I ran out of steam and hid in an alley next to a grocery store. I sat on the ground, leaning against an overflowing Dumpster, which is where my sister and father found me hours later, still crying for God knows what reason.

It was unfortunate that I didn't get professional help at that age, but I was very fortunate that Carole Yamaguchi decided to take me under her wing. Carole's love and attention really helped neutralize a lot of my anger. She made me feel loved, and she made me feel like I was part of her family. On the practical side, Carole took care of everything from filling out the registration forms for our competitions and buying us matching practice outfits to making sure we got plenty of sleep and the right things to eat.

After our competition near Los Angeles, Carole started

inviting me over for dinner with the Yamaguchi family. I loved going over to their house. In stark contrast to our trailer, the Yamaguchis lived in a big beautiful suburban six-bedroom house in Fremont. It had three bathrooms, two living rooms, a dining room, a huge kitchen, and a big backyard. Everything was modern and spread out.

At dinnertime every night, the whole family sat down together. There was Kristi's dad, who was a successful dentist; he was very quiet, and while he was completely supportive of Kristi's skating, he rarely came to competitions. There were Kristi's younger brother and older sister, neither of whom skated. And there was Carole, and of course Kristi and me.

In my family, if we were lucky, we all sat down to a meal together—with the exception of George—a couple of times a week. And you can bet we didn't eat the kind of healthy food that Carole prepared. For almost every meal, my mom made the Mexican foods that my dad liked. But Carole made something different every night, always using a cookbook. We had lots of Japanese food, white rice, different kinds of vegetables, teriyaki chicken—so many things I'd never eaten before. Carole even got me to eat broccoli, which I hated—it was the only thing I ever had in common with President Bush. But Carole forced me to eat it because she said it was good for me. "You can't leave the table unless you eat what's on your plate." Finally, I got hooked on broccoli. I still crave it.

It was impossible for me not to compare Carole to my own mother, although in retrospect I wish I'd kept my thoughts to myself. Mom didn't do any of the things that Carole did for me. She didn't care if I got enough sleep or ate the right foods. I could have been out on the ice in rags and she wouldn't have known the difference. Beyond all the practical things and all the good food, Carole was loving toward me in a motherly way, much as Colleen and Aunt Cindy had been. Carole gave me hugs and kisses whenever she said hello or good-bye, and as I had in the past, I just soaked it up.

Thinking about the contrast made me feel resentful toward my mother, and occasionally it would boil over and I'd tell

Mom that she didn't care about me in the least. That, of course, would make her mad, and then I'd feel even more resentful toward her and all the more adoring of Carole.

Because I wasn't in regular school anymore, I got to spend a lot of time with Carole during the day. Often, Carole and I would drop Kristi off at school after practice and then go back to the house. I'd do some homework, and then I'd watch the soaps while Carole cleaned the house and started on dinner. Sometimes we'd watch the soaps together or go run errands or just talk about skating. I don't think I could have dreamed of a more perfect mother.

As the months passed, I spent more and more time with Kristi and Carole and less time with my own family. By now, Laura was in her late teens and she had a life of her own. With Carole looking after me, Laura felt she could let go of that responsibility and focus more on her own life, which included skating with an ice show, coaching, and having a boyfriend.

My father also seemed perfectly comfortable with my growing attachment to Carole and Kristi. I was a little surprised, but he never said a word about my being home less often, and he and Mom never called me when I was at the Yamaguchis— even when I stayed with them overnight. I was always the one to call home to let them know where I was and where I'd be spending the night. That made me feel as if they didn't care about me, but I consoled myself with the knowledge that Carole loved me and that I had Kristi as my best friend.

At the Yamaguchi house, Carole set aside a bedroom just for me. It was a lot larger than my room at home, with a nice big bed, plush pillows, and crisp sheets. Everything was so nice and new in comparison to what I was used to. I liked the whole thing so much, I secretly hoped that Carole would invite me to move in full-time.

By 1984, the second year that Kristi and I were skating together, we were on the ice five days a week and had developed a pretty set routine. Carole was the first to get up, at around 3:45 A.M. After getting dressed, she went into the kitchen to make lunches for Kristi and her siblings to take to school. Then she'd set out our cereal, Cheerios for me and Cap'n Crunch for Kristi. When she was done in the kitchen, Carole opened the door to my room and turned on the light to signal that it was time to get up. I'm not one to bounce right out of bed, but I liked skating so much I never needed to be reminded a second time that I had to get up. I just needed a minute to get my bearings and I was on my way to the bathroom to wash up.

Carole's next stop was Kristi's room. Waking up Kristi took more than turning on the lights. She was always so sleepy that most often Carole had to help her get dressed. Within a few minutes, Kristi would wander into the kitchen, rubbing her eyes as she walked over to the kitchen table. She'd pour two drops of milk in her cereal bowl, and then hand me the container of milk; I'd fill my bowl almost to the rim. Kristi thought that was disgusting and always made a face at me.

We took our cereal with us out to the car and ate it while Carole drove over the San Mateo bridge on the way to the rink. As soon as she was done eating, Kristi went to sleep in the backseat, and Carole and I would talk for the rest of the half-hour drive. There was always so much to talk about, like what was going to happen at an upcoming competition, gossip about other skaters and parents, everything you can imagine.

We got to the rink at 5:00, put on our skates, and did forty-five minutes of figures. Then from 5:45 to 6:30, we did singles freestyle. At 6:45, we had another forty-five minutes of figures before doing pairs freestyle from 7:30 to 8:15. Then there was an ice cut—they smoothed out the ice with a huge machine—and it was figures all over again at 8:30, and freestyle again at 9:15. After that, we'd drop Kristi off at school, and Carole and I would head home. I was off on Saturday and Sunday, but Kristi only got Sunday off. To me, this was the ideal life. I loved skating and I loved being a part of the Yamaguchi family.

Still, I don't want to leave the impression that my time with the Yamaguchis was perfect, because like any family situation, it wasn't. With two kids who were stars (one of whom was me), and two who weren't, there were bound to be tensions, and sometimes I even argued with Carole. I was a teenager, and as happy as I was to be a part of Carole's family, I wasn't always easy to get along with.

The one thing that really began to bother me, other than feeling like my own family didn't care about me, was something I'd managed to put out of my mind for years. After my first crush on Johnny Rivera, I'd never had feelings for another boy. I suspect the episode where George came home to tell us he was gay had something to do with suppressing any thoughts like that I might have had. And probably something else my dad said to me on a number of occasions made me instinctively repress any possible crush or feelings of attraction for men. Sometimes, out of the blue, my father would say to me, "Rudy, you better not be gay, because if you are, I'll haul you up by your balls to the highest tree." That was a very scary thought, and I hoped he was only kidding.

No matter what my father said or how badly he reacted to George's announcement, by the time I hit my midteens, it became increasingly difficult for me not to notice men I found attractive. I remember one time being at the movies with Kristi and some of her girlfriends when I had a particularly difficult time keeping my thoughts to myself. We went to see Tom Cruise and Val Kilmer in *Top Gun*. When Tom Cruise first appeared on the screen, all the girls started screaming, and my first instinct was to scream right along with them. But I bit my lip. I was afraid of what Kristi would think of me. I was also afraid that if she knew I was gay, she wouldn't want me to touch her, which would have meant the end of our pairs skating. I could imagine giving up singles skating, but not pairs.

Even though I didn't say anything about being gay, some people, like Kristi's brother and his friends, had no problem figuring it out. As I've said before, I'm feminine. Not all men who are feminine are gay, but lots of us are. The stereotype didn't come from nowhere. So around the time I was struggling with my feelings, I had to contend with Kristi's brother and his friends hassling me. They would pass me in the hallway at the house and I'd hear one of them say, in a voice loud enough for me to hear, "Kristi skates with a faggot," or just "Faggot!" Then they'd all laugh and run into Kristi's brother's room. It hurt my feelings that they would call me names, but it's not as if they were telling me anything I didn't know. So I'd yell back at them, "Yes, I am, and so what!" That usually kept them quiet for a little while.

Because Carole and I talked about everything, and because she made it clear to me that she loved me, I thought I could confide in her that I was gay. I just assumed that she'd accept it without a problem. By this time I was sixteen, and I'd known Carole for nearly three years. So one morning at practice, I told Carole there was something I wanted to talk about. She suggested we talk after we left Kristi off at school.

After leaving Kristi, Carole and I drove to a nearby parking lot. She asked me what I wanted to talk about, and flat out I said, "I'm gay." She said, "No, you're not!" It turned into a big back-and-forth. I'd say, "You don't understand, I really am!" and Carole would say, "No, you're not. You can't be gay. You like girls."

Of course I liked girls, I told her, but only as friends. She kept trying to convince me that I wasn't gay, I kept saying that I was, and before long I was in tears; I just wanted to get out of the car and go home.

What I didn't know at the time was that Carole's reaction was pretty typical of most parents'. She was upset by what I told her and didn't want to believe it was true. She was in total denial. I imagine that some of what was going through Carole's mind had to do with skating. Given the all-American image of the U.S. Figure Skating Association, my being gay could only be a major liability in a pairs career that seemed to have limitless possibilities.

After that day, Carole and I never discussed the subject again. Considering the way she reacted, there was no way I was going to bring it up. For one thing, Carole's love and support were important to me, and the last thing I wanted to do was drive her away. Just as important, I wanted to continue skating with Kristi, and I didn't want to do anything that could jeopardize our partnership. If I made too many waves, I was afraid Carole would break up our pair and send me on my way.

Because we never talked about it again, I think Carole convinced herself that she was right, that I wasn't gay. But I knew that being gay was forever, and that whether she liked it or not, there was nothing I could do about changing my sexual orientation. After our conversation and following a few days of awkwardness, things seemed to return to normal, but for me it would never be like it was before. For the rest of the time Kristi and I skated together, I always felt like things were on edge and that if I did anything wrong, Carole would send me packing. Our relationship, which for me had always been based on love, was now based on fear. That feeling of security I'd so enjoyed was gone forever.

6

RUDY + KRISTI =
A CHAMPION PAIR AND
A PAIR OF CHAMPIONS

When sports journalists wrote about me and Kristi during our first few years together, they talked about our being an overnight sensation, because we moved so quickly from obscurity to center stage. To me it didn't seem so fast—we had to work awfully hard to get there, day after day, month after month, practicing the lifts, jumps, spins, and footwork that make up the short and long programs. Most people can't imagine—and I can hardly believe—the amount of time, and the endless repetition, that went into creating and perfecting something that, at its best, was supposed to look effortless.

It was anything but effortless, and when you're as young as we were, a single year represented a big chunk of time. But in comparison to other pairs, the half dozen years it took to go from our first silver medal at the 1984 sectionals to our first senior pairs national championship gold medal in 1989 was lightning fast. For us, it was a relatively bump-free ride up through the ranks—until 1987. That's when we discovered the downside of moving up so quickly.

Because of all our successes, by 1987 we made it to senior-level competition at the national championships. The problem was, we were only sixteen and eighteen, so in comparison to the other skaters, who were all several years older, we were both still kids. And physically, we were the smallest pair on the ice. In practical terms, that meant that at the '87 U.S. Figure Skating Championships in Tacoma, Washington, we were just about run over by the more experienced skaters during the practice sessions. We were terrified of getting hit, so most of the time we just stayed along the boards, and we never got to skate our full program.

I don't know if it was that we didn't really get to practice or just the pressure of skating in the major leagues, but we got into trouble during our short program. We started out great, and the audience got into it from the start, clapping along with our cha-cha music. That, however, made it hard for me to hear Kristi trying to tell me that her lace was undone. We were flying across the ice, doing jumps and lifts, the audience was clapping away, and Kristi was trying to talk to me. In the middle of our really fancy footwork, I finally heard her say that her lace was undone, so I finished the move by pushing her through my legs, then I stopped her so she could look at her skate. She looked down and said, "Oh, no, it's *not* untied!"

By now, we were falling behind our music, and Kristi started dragging me, trying to get me to catch up. I stopped her and said that we should go to the judges and tell them what happened. We were already going to be marked down for stopping in the middle of our program, and I hoped that by explaining what had happened they'd let us start over. I was wrong. They made us start from where we'd stopped. It was embarrassing and it was going to cost us, but I didn't think it was the end of the world. For a change, this time I was the calm one.

Our marks were terrible, but they could have been worse.

Out of sixteen pairs, we were in eighth place. Kristi was so upset that she ran off and we couldn't find her. We looked everywhere and even got the security guards to help us. Then it occurred to me to recheck the women's dressing-room bathroom, which Carole had already searched. I walked into the bathroom, which was empty—all the skaters had already gone home—and I looked under the door of each stall. I found Kristi in the second one, standing on top of the toilet seat, her hands over her face, sobbing silently. I pushed open the stall door and took her by the hand as she got down from the toilet. Then I gave her a big hug and told her that everything was all right, that we still had the long program to do, that we'd go out there and show them we meant business.

Show them we did. Kristi and I skated an almost flawless program to music from the *The Tap Dance Kid*. We got a standing ovation and the judges gave us scores high enough to push us up to fifth place overall. Considering that this was our first time out as seniors, and the youngest seniors at that, we both felt great about being the fifth-ranking pair in the entire country.

Kristi and I ended the year at the junior world championships in Brisbane, Australia. Even though we were seniors, because of our age and our standing we still got to compete in junior worlds. It was so much fun being in a place that was warm in December, walking around in shorts and T-shirts, nothing like what it was where the junior worlds were usually held, places like Canada and Europe.

Because I'd won junior worlds the year before, I was ineligible to compete in singles, but Kristi was competing in singles, and we were competing in pairs together. We talked about how great it would be if we could take home the pairs championship and Kristi won in singles, so that we'd have all three medals between us. And that's exactly what we did, and we returned home thinking that as long as we continued working hard, nothing could stop us from becoming senior national champions.

* * *

Even as Kristi and I continued skating our way to the top, several things conspired to bring us down, from adolescence and the pressures of dual careers to injuries and the illness of our coach. As a result, over the next year, cracks in our partnership began to show.

People in the ice-skating world and the reporters who wrote about Kristi and me had already been speculating for a couple of years on how long Kristi and I would be able to manage three different careers: hers, mine, and ours. It wasn't such a problem when we were starting out, but as we moved up through the ranks and found ourselves trying to juggle demanding and conflicting schedules at competitions and trying to find enough time to do all the necessary training, it became a daunting challenge.

I was the one who blinked first. Going into the '88 nationals. I'd been feeling particularly insecure about our partnership, I'm not sure why. I thought it was important to show Carole that I was serious about pairs, and I decided that the best way to do that was to demonstrate that I didn't care nearly as much about my singles skating as I did about pairs. I did that by putting little effort into my singles programs at nationals and consequently I placed tenth overall. A few months later I announced I was giving up singles to focus entirely on pairs. My announced retirement had the desired effect: Carole let me know how pleased she was that I'd quit singles.

What I didn't realize was that by quitting singles, I was now entirely dependent on what Kristi did and had left myself no room in which to maneuver. If Kristi decided to go her own way and focus on singles, I would be left to pick up the pieces of my aborted singles career. Of course, I didn't think about that until it was way too late.

At the same time our professional relationship was changing, my personal relationship with Kristi was changing as well, and not for the better. I still spent many nights over at the Yamaguchis, but Kristi and I were no longer childhood playmates. At sixteen and eighteen, we were both well into adolescence, and the last thing Kristi seemed to want to do was hang around with her pairs partner. She had her own friends, and when they made plans to do things, they no longer included me. Unlike Kristi, I didn't make friends easily, and to me, she was still my best friend. My response to being excluded was to beg her to take me along to the mall or wherever. Of course, that led Kristi to exclude me even more. It must have been suffocating for her to have me around all the time, trying to tag along much in the same way I had with my sister years before.

One aspect of adolescence that Kristi and I shared that I couldn't tell her about was our growing interest in boys. So I didn't dare say a word to Kristi when I momentarily overcame my fear of what Carole would do if she ever found out about my being with a guy and allowed myself to get involved with someone.

It was the summer of 1988, and a strikingly handsome guy— about a year younger than me—was hanging out at the pool at our trailer park. The girls swarmed around him like frenzied fans at a skating competition, and he seemed to take lots of pleasure in the attention. I was sure he was dating one or more of them.

Brad (not his real name) was about six feet tall, sandy haired, tanned, and built. He had a perfect swimmer's body, and while I generally found Italian-looking guys more attractive, Brad was certainly nice to look at. And unbelievably, he liked looking at me! At first I didn't notice his interest in me, but in the pool, he'd come by and splash me and occasionally grab me and sort of wrestle with me. I can't say I minded, but it was a little confusing because I was certain he was straight.

About a month after I first saw Brad, he came by the pool one afternoon while I was paddling around and called me over to the side. He said, "I'll see you at your place tonight at ten." Before I could even consciously register what he'd said, I said, "Okay." Then he walked away and left me in shock. I didn't know what to think. Did he say he was coming over for the reasons I thought? Or was he just coming over because he wanted to be friends? When I thought back on all the looks he'd given me and the horseplay, only one conclusion could be drawn from his self-invitation. And I was terrified, not because of the possibility that I was going to get physical with a guy for the first time—that was something I wanted—but of what my parents would think if they found us in my room together (Laura had moved out a couple of years before and was living in an apartment nearby with a roommate).

I don't think I was so worried about my mom, because even though we'd never talked about me being gay, I'd always spoken openly around her, and whenever I saw a guy on television I thought was cute, I'd say so. And Mom either agreed or disagreed with my assessment. But I never said anything like that when Dad was home. I knew how he felt about George's being gay, and I figured it would be safer for me, and less painful for him, if I spared him the knowledge that he had two gay sons. So Dad was the one I worried about, especially because I knew he'd be home. Since his retirement the year before, he was always home.

An hour before Brad came to my house, I was pacing back and forth in my room, climbing the walls in a state of excited panic. I wanted Brad to come over, I wanted to be with him, but what if we were caught? And if we were caught, would Carole somehow find out?

I wound up not having to worry about my parents, because they went to bed just after nine-thirty. So then I could focus my anxiety entirely on anticipating what was going to happen. I had no experience, so what was I supposed to do? Was I supposed to let him make the first move, or was *I* supposed to make the first move? As I was caught up in my reverie, there was a knock at the door. I glanced at the clock. It was exactly ten o'clock.

Brad was at the screen door, and I put my finger to my lips to indicate that he should be quiet. I opened the door and for a moment took in the sight of him in a faded pair of jeans and a white T-shirt. He was breathtakingly beautiful, and in that moment I felt so *not* beautiful that I couldn't understand what interest he had in me. But there he was, standing in my living room, and I led him by the hand into my little bedroom.

I'd wasted my anxiety over who was going to make the first move, because it started with a mutual hug and went from there. I can't tell you that it was everything I'd imagined, because I hadn't imagined what it would be like, but it was fun and it felt perfectly natural. It wasn't anything romantic, because clearly our interest in each other didn't go much beyond the physical. It wasn't until I let Brad out of the house well after midnight that I realized we'd never even kissed. As I said, it wasn't a romantic encounter, just a physical one.

Before leaving, Brad asked if he could come by the next day, and I said he could, but by morning I'd worked myself into a complete state of terror over the possibility of Carole's finding out. Rationally, I knew there was no way she could find out, but I didn't want to take any chances, so when Brad stopped by that afternoon, I told him I couldn't see him anymore.

Fear of Carole and what she would do about the future of my pairs skating with Kristi came to dominate my life. And that summer, even though she didn't find out about Brad, I thought I'd given her another reason to get rid of me when I hurt my back.

That I was so small in comparison to the other pairs men was something the sportswriters and skating people pointed to as a potential barrier to Kristi and me ever reaching the top of our profession. But I always countered those remarks by simply proving that I could do all the lifts and throws that the other men were doing. The fact was, though, I was small and, for that reason, more prone to injuries. And sure enough, that summer, at an exhibition in nearby San Mateo, I severely strained my back.

For several months leading up to the exhibition, I'd been having a lot of lower-back pain, which I guess was from the pressure of catching Kristi as she was coming down from her triple twists: I'd throw Kristi in the air, she'd do three revolutions, and then I'd catch her around the waist and set her down on the ice.

At the exhibition, we skated to music from *Romeo and Juliet*, which was an attempt on the part of our coach, Jim Hulick, to give us a more mature look. The first element in our program was a triple twist, and as I caught Kristi, I tripped on her and we fell and slammed into the wall. It must have looked really bad, because I could hear the gasps from the audience, which was instantly on its feet. This sort of thing never happened to us, even in practice.

Kristi got up, grabbed my hand, and said, "Let's go." I told her my back was hurting and that we should see Jim to make sure I was okay. We skated off the ice, and Jim checked me out and said I seemed well enough to continue. When they announced that we were going to start over, the crowd applauded.

My back was still hurting, but I was afraid to say anything because I thought Carole would say that I wasn't strong enough to skate pairs anymore and that Kristi needed a bigger partner. So we got out on the ice and skated into our first move; I threw Kristi into the air and she spun around three times; but then, when I caught her, I collapsed on top of her and we skidded into the wall once again. Kristi got right up, told me to keep going, but I was in so much pain that I could hardly get up. In the end, we couldn't complete the performance.

When we got off the ice, Carole came over and asked me what was going on. I told her I'd hurt my back. She asked if I'd just hurt it from the fall, and I told her that it had been bothering me for a while. She asked, "Is Kristi getting too big for you?" and added, "Maybe you two need to quit." It was exactly as I'd feared, but then our coach stepped in and assured Carole that it was probably a minor injury and that I was strong enough to handle Kristi even during the most difficult moves.

The next day, my dad took me to the doctor, who prescribed anti-inflammatory medication and showed me how to do a number of different exercises to strengthen my lower back. I became religious about these back exercises, because I was determined that Kristi and I would continue skating together, especially since it looked as if we had a shot at a medal at the upcoming national championships.

By the fall of 1988, it seemed only two things were keeping Kristi and me together anymore: the momentum of our success, and our coach, Jim Hulick. Jim was the glue that had kept our partnership together, but after being operated on for colon cancer shortly after our San Mateo exhibition, that glue began to weaken. Jim told us that his prognosis was good, so we didn't worry, but what he didn't tell us was that his cancer was AIDS-related. In 1988, the prognosis for almost everyone diagnosed with AIDS was, at best, poor.

Jim managed to continue with us on a generally normal training schedule throughout the fall, despite his lack of energy and his weight loss. On those days when he had to go down to Los Angeles for chemotherapy or was too sick from the side effects to come to the rink, Kristi and I worked together on our own. We'd been working together for so long that a few days without Jim had no serious impact on our skating.

Kristi and Carole were very understanding about Jim's being sick. I'm embarrassed to say that I was less than tolerant. I didn't want Jim to be sick, and I was impatient when he wasn't his usual ebullient self. At times I was petulant with Jim, and that was unforgivable, especially since Jim had now dropped all of his other skaters to focus all his energy on me and Kristi. Jim showed extraordinary courage and commitment, and I, in return, demonstrated extraordinary immaturity.

If I had any excuse for my behavior, it was that I was already feeling so insecure over my relationship with Kristi and Carole that Jim's illness only made me feel even more insecure. And as if Jim's sickness wasn't enough, a few weeks before the national championships, my father had a stroke, which was serious enough to land him in intensive care.

Dad's health hadn't been good since his retirement. He'd had diabetes and high blood pressure since the mid-1970s, and he never followed his doctor's instructions to watch his diet and stop drinking. Dad was incredibly stubborn, and the doctor warned him that if he wasn't careful, he'd wind up having to take insulin injections instead of pills. But he loved his Mexican food and his six-pack of beer, so before long he was on insulin.

I was with my dad that afternoon when he had his first stroke. We were sitting on our porch, not doing much of anything, and all of a sudden he put his hand to the side of his head and slumped over. I asked him what was wrong and he said that he didn't feel well. I knew something was very wrong, and Mom and I wanted to call an ambulance, but Dad wouldn't let us. He said he wasn't going anywhere until Laura was there. So I called Laura at her apartment and she raced over. By that time, Dad was having difficulty talking and his whole left side was drooping. The three of us got him into Laura's car and drove him to the hospital.

For the first few days, they kept Dad in intensive care. I was totally freaked out and terribly afraid that he was going to die. Fortunately, my routine at the rink helped keep me from falling apart. With nationals approaching, I had to practice every day, but every afternoon I went to the hospital to visit Dad and to drive Mom home. Laura picked up Mom every morning and brought her to the hospital, and she stayed with Dad all day. I spoke with George by phone and told him what had happened, but he thought it best not to see Dad for fear of giving him another stroke.

If you think the stroke scared my father into sticking to his diet, the answer was: no way. He hated the hospital food, and as soon as they moved him out of intensive care he begged us to bring him food from Taco Bell. Sometimes we gave in because it made him so happy, but we did it reluctantly because we knew we were only making things worse for him in the long run.

By the time I left in February for Baltimore to compete with

Kristi at the '89 nationals, Dad was home and well on his way to recovery, but still I found it hard to leave home and not worry about him. I was used to my dad being the strong guy, who was always there even if we didn't have a lot to say to each other. When I said good-bye to him to leave for Baltimore, he seemed like an old man to me. But he was still my dad, and before I left, he wished me the best of luck and said, "Let the golden star above shine on you."

In Baltimore, Kristi and I were expected to place third, at best, but we surprised everyone, including ourselves, by placing second after the short program. We did a technically challenging program, nailing the most difficult side-by-side jump of the night, a double axel, and that did the trick. Jim was so thrilled at our performance that he just about had to be restrained from running onto the ice to hug us.

We did our Romeo and Juliet routine for the long program, and we wore these beautiful midnight-blue outfits with a sparkling gold stripe. We were the only pair that night who planned to do a side-by-side triple flip. In fact, we were the only pair in the world who could do that move in competition.

During the warm-up, we kept trying to practice our triple flip and some of our other moves, but one of the rival pairs, the ones who were expected to win the competition, kept intentionally getting in our way. So we kept going around and around until we found a brief window of opportunity in which to execute our moves. I was so mad at that couple that I wanted to execute them as well, but I figured we'd get back at them by skating a great program.

From the minute we stepped onto the ice to do our long program, every move was flawless. A couple of times, I glanced over to the side of the rink to where Jim was standing, and I could see he had his hands clasped in front of him, and he nodded his head every time we landed a jump. Jim wasn't the only one responding to our jumps, because with every landing, the audience gasped and broke into cheers and applause.

In our final move, I went down on one knee and draped

Kristi over my leg. The audience was on its feet applauding and cheering, and I started crying. My emotions are always just at the surface, and in that moment I was thinking of my dad at home, so I couldn't hold back the tears.

I wasn't the only one crying. Kristi and I skated over to Jim, and he grabbed both us for a big hug and he was crying, too. I was surprised that he was so emotional, but he must have known by this point how gravely ill he was, and that this was likely to be his last national championship with us.

We walked over to the "kiss and cry" booth and waited for our marks, which were very good. (It's called the "kiss and cry" because, it's where the skaters and their coaches kiss and cry.) We moved up to first place. But Natalie and Wayne Seybold, a brother-and-sister pair who were six years older than me and Kristi and had four more years experience as seniors, had yet to skate. They were in first place after the short, so we had every expectation that they'd finish first in the long and that we'd fall to second place. But that was fine with us, because as long as we placed in the top three, we'd be going to Paris the following month for our first senior world competition.

Kristi, Jim, and I walked over to where the television cameras were set up next to the rink to watch the Seybolds. From the beginning of their program it looked like they were very nervous, and after a few awkward moves, when Wayne threw Natalie into the air, she spun around three times, landed on her right leg, and fell. The audience gasped, and Kristi and I grabbed each other. From there it was all downhill for the Seybolds. Natalie fell on another throw, catching her blade in the lace of one of her skates. She and Wayne asked the judges if they could start their program over from the beginning. I felt sorry for them, because all of us skaters work so hard all year, and it just takes one bad performance and it's over. But, of course, their misfortune was good for us, so I have to admit I didn't feel *that* bad.

The judges denied the Seybolds' request, and they had to pick up where they'd left off. They finished the remainder of their program, and the audience responded warmly. As they stepped off the ice, I kept thinking that there was still no way they were going to make Kristi and me national champions. So we stood there waiting and watching nervously for the marks to come up. None of us said a word, but we were all thinking the same thoughts, that there was no way it could happen, but there was no way, after that performance, that the Seybolds could win. The technical marks went up and it looked like they were high enough to tie us. But then the style marks went up and they were really low. We had won, and once again it was our classic scene of hugs, screaming, and jumping up and down. Kristi and I had made it to the top, and it was a moment of absolute joy for all of us. But I could hardly focus on all the excitement around me because I just wanted to get home so I could show my dad the medal.

Before the end of the championship, Kristi had another medal besides our gold to take home with her. In the singles competition that followed the pairs, she won the silver.

A month after nationals, Kristi and I were on our way to Paris for the world championships. It was an unforgettable trip, but not because of anything we did on the ice. We did fine and placed fifth overall, which is incredible for your first time out as a senior pair at the world championships. But what made the trip truly unforgettable was my first kiss.

After Kristi and I were done with our part of the competition, Kristi still had three more days until she finished the singles portion of the world championships. So while she was busy practicing and competing, I was out on the town going to clubs with some of the other skaters, both male and female. Carole made it clear that she didn't like me staying out late, but I was being a rebellious teenager, and for a change, I didn't listen to her. I'm glad I didn't.

One of the places we went to was called the Boys Club. I don't know if it was specifically gay, but one of the other skaters had heard it was a great dance place. It also turned out that the guys there were gorgeous. One very husky, tall man—

I'll call him Christophe—came over to talk to me, but he didn't speak much English and I couldn't speak any French. Despite the language difficulties, Christophe managed to convey that he liked me and wanted me to go with him to his place. I said yes, and we left the club and Christophe hailed a taxi.

I must have been out of my mind, because here I was in Paris, in a cab with a man who seemed to be twice my size, going to his apartment in God-knows-what part of Paris. But I was a nineteen-year-old with raging hormones, and Christophe was an attractive and romantic twenty-five-year-old who was very interested in me.

When we got to his apartment, Christophe showed me his boxing trophies, but despite his obvious prowess in the boxing ring, he was the sweetest and gentlest guy you could imagine. He enveloped me in his arms and kissed me. I'd waited a long time for that first kiss, and I just about fainted. But I didn't dare faint, because I didn't want to miss a second of it.

As Christophe kissed me, I started thinking about what Carole would think, and that suddenly spoiled the whole thing. I pulled away from Christophe and looked at my watch. It was four in the morning. I knew Carole would kill me if she heard I was out this late. So I indicated to Christophe as best I could that I had to go back to my hotel. He sweetly asked me to stay. That much I could understand, but I said that I had to leave, and he walked me down to the street to hail a cab. He opened the door of the taxi, put his arms around me again, and in public, on a Paris street, with the cabdriver right there, kissed me passionately. I still can't believe I left him there on the sidewalk because I was afraid of what Carole would do. But skating with Kristi was my life, and this was far too big a risk. I never saw Christophe again, but I'll never forget him.

7

SAYING GOOD-BYE

After the high of becoming national champions and then finishing fifth in Paris—not to mention my encounter with Christophe—it was virtually all downhill. Or at least it was for me. On her own, Kristi was doing well, steadily improving her standings from event to event and earning invitations to top international competitions.

On the one hand, I was glad for Kristi that she was doing well, but her increasing success without me, and all the attention she was getting from the media and the skating establishment, just fed into my fear about our future together. Perhaps it was an act of desperation, but during this time I changed the spelling of my first name to match Kristi's. I became "Rudi" Galindo. Given that Kristi was trying to put more distance between us, I'm sure my new name made her nuts.

* * *

In the midst of Kristi's success and my increasing anxiety about the future, Jim's health continued to decline. The doctors had discovered a new cancerous tumor in his chest, but Jim continued to shield us from the truth. Still, he was missing more and more practices, and you could see just by looking at him and by how skinny he was getting that he wasn't getting any better.

Despite how sick Jim was, I didn't know he was dying, and I'm not so sure he'd even acknowledged it to himself. He'd even promised to be with us when we got to the Olympics in 1992, and I wanted to believe him. So with Jim's reassurances, I tried to put that worry aside and I concentrated on something that seemed a more imminent crisis than Jim's health. Kristi's longtime singles coach, Christy Kjarsgaard, announced that she'd be getting married in the spring of 1989 and moving to Edmonton, Alberta, with her new husband. Despite Kristi's reassurances to me and the press that we'd always be together, she decided to move to Edmonton following her graduation from high school in June to continue training with Christy. For me that would mean either commuting between Edmonton and home or giving up pairs skating with Kristi. Carole gave me that option, saying that it was my choice. At the time, it didn't occur to me that I could go back to skating singles, and I couldn't imagine finding another pairs partner so late in my career. I soon began my long commute between Edmonton and San Jose.

Even though I was usually in Edmonton only a week at a time, I hated being there. I stayed in a furnished apartment several blocks from the Royal Glenora sports center, where Kristi was training. While Jim was still well enough, he flew up several times to work with Kristi and me, but most of the time I was there all by myself. I felt incredibly misplaced. I'd never lived on my own before; I'd always been with my family or with Kristi's family. Now I was far from home and very alone. On the other hand, Kristi had her coach and she had all of her friends at Royal Glenora, who made it clear that they had no interest in spending time with her "faggot" friend. They never used that word to my face, but I heard it behind my back many times.

When I was in Edmonton, Kristi's coach usually picked me up at my apartment building for practice, but a couple of times she forgot, and I had to walk down the hill several blocks to Royal Glenora in snow up to my knees. Maybe I'm exaggerating a little bit, but that's my memory of it, and being left standing in the snow only reinforced my feeling that I was an afterthought.

On the ice, Kristi and I seemed out of sync. That wasn't surprising, given that we hardly had the opportunity to work with Jim anymore and that skating pairs was clearly no longer Kristi's priority. Because of Jim's failing health, I thought that he would step aside and turn us over to another coach, but he was a very determined man and wasn't going to give up yet.

Despite our admittedly unorthodox training situation and our increasingly icy relationship, Kristi and I still did well at the two international competitions we attended late in the year. We finished second at Skate America in October, which was really encouraging to me and made me think that maybe things weren't over after all. And then Thanksgiving weekend we went to Kobe, Japan, for the NHK Trophy competition.

Kristi and I flew to Japan directly from Canada, and we met Jim at the hotel. We hadn't seen him in several weeks, and we were shocked by how much he'd deteriorated. He was seated in a wheelchair and he was so frightfully thin that he seemed lost in his clothes. Jim's father had traveled with him because Jim was too ill to travel alone. It was heartbreaking to see Jim in that condition. He was clearly in the last days of his life, but despite how ill he was, he wanted to be there. I imagine that Kristi and I must have meant a lot to Jim for him to get on a plane as sick as he was to be there for us.

During our program, I fell on a triple flip, and we ended up placing fourth. With Jim so sick, I don't think that either of us really cared what place we were in. I just remember feeling like my life was out of control. I'd let everyone take care of everything for me in the past, and now with Jim sick and Dad sick and Carole focused on Kristi and Laura back at home focusing on her own life, I was lost. I didn't know what to do, so I just let the current carry me along.

From NHK, Kristi and I went on a short tour of Japan, and Jim flew home with his father to Los Angeles. Jim had trouble breathing on the plane, and he went directly from the airport to the hospital. After a few days, he went home to his parents' house for a few days, took a turn for the worse, and returned to the hospital. It was on a Sunday that Kristi spoke to Jim one last time. She told me later that he couldn't say much, but that she said, "Thank you for everything." Not realizing how close to death Jim was, I never had a chance to talk to him again before he died on December 10, 1989. He was thirty-seven years old.

Four days later, Laura and I drove down from San Jose for the funeral, which was held at the Forest Lawn Cemetery in Covina, California. Carole and Kristi came down on their own and we met them there. All I remember from the funeral was that there were lots of people and that the setting, with all its hills and trees, was beautiful. Mostly I was just numb, hardly able to absorb the fact that Jim was dead. He'd been a steady and reassuring presence in my life for so many years that I couldn't begin to think about what his loss would mean to me. My way of dealing with the pain of his death was to set it aside and go on. It was all I knew how to do.

Five days after Jim died, Kristi's grandfather, who'd been one of her biggest supporters, died of lung cancer. After all this I don't know how we pulled things together to get ready for the upcoming national championships in Salt Lake City, which were only a month away, but somehow we muddled through.

Before Jim died, he'd asked his friend John Nicks, a top coach in Costa Mesa, California, to work with us, and we spent a week with him in December, going over the programs we'd learned with Jim. Kristi and I were already pretty solid with our new routines, so John was there mostly to give us a few pointers and provide whatever anchor he could now that Jim was gone. It was an awful role to be thrown into, but John worked hard to fulfill his promise to Jim to look out for us through the world championships.

Kristi, John, and I all met in Salt Lake City for nationals in February of 1990. Although Kristi and I were the returning national pairs champions, the real focus was on Kristi, not on us. Since her silver-medal performance the year before, Kristi had gone from being a newcomer to being a major contender for the national singles title and, looking down the road, a potential gold medalist at the 1992 Olympics. At least that's what the skating insiders were saying at nationals.

The rumors were flying at nationals that Kristi and I were on the verge of breaking up, but Kristi said that she didn't want to be forced to make a choice, that she wanted to continue skating pairs and singles, and that if she were forced, choosing "would be difficult."

What seemed equally difficult was for Kristi to juggle her schedule at nationals so that she could compete in both singles and pairs. As unwilling as I was to see how stressful the whole thing was for her, I couldn't help but acknowledge that Kristi's schedule was daunting. For example, the day of our short program, Kristi had to be at the compulsory figures competition at 11 A.M. in Bountiful, Utah, about a half-hour drive from Salt Lake. Then while the other women competitors had time off, Kristi and I practiced during a session that had been reserved for junior skaters. We'd missed the morning pairs practice because of Kristi's compulsory figures, and John Nicks had to pull two of his students off the ice to make room for us. After we finished our practice, I got off the ice and Kristi continued working with her coach on her singles programs. Then she went back to the hotel, took a nap, got up, had dinner, and met me at the Salt Palace arena for our short program. To anyone looking in from the outside, it was clear there was no way that Kristi could continue with this kind of schedule and reach the top in both singles and pairs skating. But I wasn't looking in from the outside. I was standing right next to Kristi, and from where I stood, even trying to be sympathetic, she had no choice but to continue skating with me.

Given how crazy everything had been in our lives, it was no small miracle that Kristi and I skated well enough in Salt Lake City to win the gold medal and hold on to our national title. But despite what some people had predicted, Kristi didn't take home the gold in singles. She placed second, which was attributed by many, including Kristi and Carole, to her exhausting schedule.

During the three weeks between our win in Salt Lake City and the world championships in Halifax, Nova Scotia, we once again faced the challenge of finding time to practice. With Kristi in Edmonton, our new temporary coach, John Nicks, in Costa Mesa, and me in San Jose, it was a logistical nightmare.

I tried to put the best face on it, and I went down to Costa Mesa for a couple of days to work with John on my own, while Kristi stayed up in Edmonton to work with her coach on her singles skating. So I worked with John on a few different things that he thought we needed to change in the long program, and then I flew up to Edmonton and taught Kristi what I'd learned. It was very frustrating, and we had a hard time trying to work it out by ourselves.

Kristi and I faced significant competition in the field of seventeen pairs expected to compete in Halifax, but that was the least of our worries. We had plenty of other things working against us: my morale, Kristi's focus on singles, and our lack of consistent training and coaching. And then things got worse. Just before I got on the plane to Halifax, my father had another stroke and wound up in intensive care all over again. The damage this time was worse, and I was on the phone with

Laura twice a day for updates. It was pretty clear that Dad was going to make it, but he was going to need lots of rehabilitation.

Somehow I managed to block everything out for our short program, and I started out strong, but Kristi lost her footing during the footwork portion and we never recovered our momentum. Still, we placed fifth, and if we did well enough in the long program, we might move up to third and win a medal.

We were a mess in the long program. In fact, we were such a mess that we were better the first time we practiced the program than we were that night. From our first jump, it was just one mistake after another. I singled out of a side-by-side triple, then Kristi singled on another side-by-side triple, and then she stepped out of a double axel. So much was going on that we couldn't hold it together anymore. The only consolation was that we did well enough to hold on to fifth place, which guaranteed that the United States could send three pairs to the following year's competition. If we'd finished lower, then only two could have gone. But after the incredible career Kristi and I had had, this was a very small consolation for an embarrassingly poor performance.

Kristi managed to do a little better in singles, but not by much. She fell twice in her long program and wound up in fourth place overall, just missing the bronze medal, which she'd been counting on.

I didn't want to think about it, but in an article that appeared a few days after the world championships, Ann Killion, a sports columnist for the *San Jose Mercury News,* asked the question that had to be asked: "By competing in two events, is Yamaguchi failing to reach her potential in either?" Killion quoted Carole Yamaguchi as saying that Kristi would have to consider dropping one event: "I think she's going to have to think seriously about that."

I could hope as much as I liked that Kristi was going to drop singles, but no one who knew anything about skating would have thought that.

After the worlds, Kristi and I headed out on a month-long

exhibition tour. And through twenty-five cities I skated with Kristi on autopilot as I waited for the other skate to drop.

Shortly after I returned home from the skating tour, Laura got a call from Carole asking us to meet with her, Kristi, and an official from the U.S. Figure Skating Association at an office at the Dublin arena on April 26. No one had to tell me what that meeting was going to be about, because I already knew. After so many clear signals, how could I not?

In preparation for the meeting, I went out and bought Kristi a teddy bear. She'd given me two teddy bears for Christmas one year, and I wanted her to have one from me. As angry as I was with her and Carole, I still cared about Kristi. I also prepared a cassette tape on which I recorded the song "Memory" from the Broadway show *Cats*.

The whole day of the meeting is still a blur to me. I don't even remember the drive there, but Laura and I went into the office and sat down. Kristi and Carole were already there, along with a judge from the USFSA. After being so close with Kristi and Carole, it seemed like a ridiculously formal setting, but then Kristi was on her way to the big time now, and I guess the USFSA wanted to make sure our divorce was nice, polite, and official. They apparently had a lot riding on Kristi's rising career, and I imagine no one wanted this thing to blow up in the press and damage Kristi's—or the association's—image. I was determined to play along and not show anyone how upset I was. Although I was more accustomed to letting everyone know exactly how I was feeling, this was one of those rare times when I decided to keep my thoughts to myself.

The meeting took only a few minutes. The official explained that Kristi was giving up pairs skating to focus on her singles career. With that, Kristi started crying. I didn't cry, because I didn't want them to see how upset I was, but there was plenty to cry about. Our six and a half years together was over. All that we'd accomplished as a pair was behind us. Everything I'd worked toward with Kristi was gone. There would be no more national championships, no more world competitions, and no

Olympics. Even worse, now I'd have to go home to tell my father. Since recovering from his first stroke, he had told me on several occasions, "Rudy, I'm not doing so great, but I'm hanging on for the Olympics." I worried that he'd give up the fight to live once he knew there was no Olympics to look forward to.

When the official was done talking, I handed Kristi the teddy bear and the tape I'd made for her. We hugged, but neither of us said anything. I couldn't even look at Carole; I just turned away and walked out of the office. Laura followed and we headed for the car. During the half-hour drive back to San Jose, I kept trying to imagine how I was going to tell Dad what had happened. But I couldn't imagine. I didn't want to imagine. I knew that no matter how I broke the news, he was going to take it hard.

Laura and I walked into the house, and I sat down across from my father, who was sitting at the kitchen table listening to the television. His sight had gotten so bad that all he could do was listen. I told Dad what the meeting was about and that Kristi and I were through as a team, that I was on my own now. I'd never seen my dad cry before, but when I finished telling him the news, a single tear slipped down his cheek. He didn't say anything, and for a few seconds we both just sat there. Then I got up from the table, went to my room, closed the door, lay down on my bed, and sobbed.

8

Starting Over

I had two choices after Kristi and I separated. I could let my depression overwhelm me, just curl up in my room and disappear, or I could get out on the ice, go back to singles skating, and prove to everyone that I didn't need Kristi to be a champion. Fortunately, I had plenty of anger to drive me, so within four days I had a new coach and was back on the ice doing jumps I hadn't done since I'd dropped singles skating two years before.

I don't want to give the impression that I was able to put the breakup with Kristi behind me in a matter of days. I was upset and hurt over being left high and dry. For a long time I could see things only from my perspective and could not even consider that maybe the split was the best professional move for Kristi. But in the days and weeks following the final meeting, despite how wounded I felt, I really tried to get on with my life, and in that regard, I couldn't have had a better cheerleader than my new coach, Rick Inglesi.

Rick was from back East and was this really enthusiastic, funny, high-energy guy in his midthirties. And he was also very good-looking. I wasn't attracted to him, but he was Italian and looked like the kind of person you'd see on *Melrose Place*. He also drove a Harley motorcycle, which really impressed me. I've always found the tough-guy image very attractive.

I'd known Rick for a number of years from seeing him at competitions and at the rink in Belmont, where he taught part-time. He was always nice to me, and I thought he was amazing. He was the kind of guy who was up at three in the morning, did his workout at home, cleaned his house, went grocery shopping, and was on the ice at five-thirty in a remarkably good mood. I knew Rick was the kind of upbeat person I needed at that point in my career, someone who would help me stay positive, look ahead, and not dwell on the past.

It was no secret that Rick was gay, which was important to me. You spend a lot of time with your coach, and I wanted to be completely comfortable with the people around me. If I thought a guy was cute, I wanted to be able to say something to Rick without having to worry that he'd think badly of me and send me packing.

Unlike most ice-skating coaches, Rick had started out in roller-skating. He'd won a national title, then switched over to ice-skating. He did singles, then pairs, and he'd won a junior national pairs title skating with a Japanese-American partner. I thought that was an interesting coincidence. Eventually he quit competitive skating and then skated for Holiday on Ice all over the world. When he retired from that, he started coaching.

I was too shy to phone Rick myself to ask him to be my coach, so I asked Laura to call for me. Rick's initial response was very positive, and he and Laura arranged a time for our first meeting. So the next day I went to the rink to meet with Rick and skated around while he finished up with a student. When he was done, he called me over and gave me a big hug, which was just what I needed, because by that point I was pretty nervous. It had been a long time since I'd skated on my own. The hug put me completely at ease.

Right off, I told Rick that it had been a long time since I'd done all my triple jumps, so he'd have to bear with me. Before I quit singles in 1988, I was doing five of the six triple jumps, everything but the triple lutz. But in pairs, I was only doing a triple toe and triple flip. He said, fine, he was there simply to see how I skated. Now I was nervous. I didn't want to make any mistakes, so I did four of my five jumps. I landed all of them, but I skipped the triple axel, because I didn't feel confident that I could do it without falling.

After doing the fourth jump, I skated over to Rick and he put his arm around my shoulder. He said I was great, that it looked as if I'd been doing my jumps the whole time. Rick's goal was to build up my self-confidence, which was pretty shot after the breakup, and he started pumping me up right from our first lesson.

The only drawback to working with Rick was that he gave lessons at two different arenas—at Iceland in Berkeley on Tuesdays and Thursdays and at Belmont on Mondays, Wednesdays, and Fridays. So twice a week I had a long commute to Berkeley. My car was on the verge of dying, so I got up at three in the morning, drove to the nearby Fremont BART station, and took the train all the way to Berkeley. I got lucky, though, because after a few months, Rick decided to work full-time at Belmont.

Our goal for the year was to see if I could place in the top ten at the 1991 nationals, to show people that I could skate well on my own. And then for the following year, the goal was for me to place in the top seven or eight with the hope of getting assigned to one of the international competitions. The U.S. Figure Skating Association meets every spring to decide which of the top eight skaters from nationals gets to represent the United States at the various annual international competitions.

In the back of my mind, I'd already laid out the whole scenario for my comeback. After the second year, I pictured a sort of step-by-step rise to first place by the 1996 national championships, and then a spot on the Olympic team in 1998.

But I kept those thoughts to myself, because a lot could happen from one year to the next.

Most of my work with Rick was on my triples, especially my triple axel. I also had to lose some weight because I'd bulked up for pairs so I'd have the strength to lift Kristi. Now the extra pounds were making it difficult for me to do all the jumps. I kind of hated to take it off, because I thought the added weight made me more attractive. Rick wasn't so concerned with my weight and told me to just do some push-ups. With all the work we were doing on the ice, I dropped about ten pounds without really trying.

Pretty early on we started preparing my programs for the 1991 season, which started with sectionals at the end of 1990. We just assumed I'd do well enough at sectionals to go to nationals. Rick chose the music for me, did the choreography, and chose my costumes as well. He liked handling everything on his own, and I trusted him. I generally liked his taste in costumes, which ran from dramatic to just over the edge. It was during my years with Rick I got my reputation for wearing flashy, sequin-covered costumes.

Rick's choreography was angular, very different. He wanted to do modern things, so he incorporated jazz and funk moves. For my short-program music, he chose "Cancan" and he had me wear black pants with a red-and-black-striped T-shirt. I also wore a black scarf wrapped around my neck.

For the long program Rick chose music from the Broadway show *Cats*. (Thankfully he steered clear of "Memory.") My costume was this beautiful tight unitard with beading that suggested cat stripes, and I also wore lightweight velvet leg warmers. The one really unusual part of the costume was that the sleeves came down to a point and covered much of my hands. What made it unusual was that only the girls wore costumes with points. But I have big hands, which Rick and I thought could be made less noticeable if they were partly covered up.

I don't know what Rick and I were thinking when we went with the points, because I imagine they only drew more attention to my (unintentionally) effeminate hand positions. Nobody said anything to us about the costume, but my hands were something the judges would have plenty to say about—at least in private—over the coming years.

At Pacific Coast sectionals, I came in third and surprised a lot of people, who had written me off. I would have been happier if I'd come in first, but I tried my best to focus on our goal, which was simply to get to the 1991 national championships at the Target Center in Minneapolis. The most important thing I could do was just be there and show that I hadn't given up. It would also be a way for us to assess how good I was in comparison to the other top U.S. skaters. Was I even good enough to bother making the effort to come back as a singles skater? That was what we were about to find out.

My short program was just okay, and I came in twelfth out of twenty. My long program only helped me move up to eleventh place, but I was proud of the fact I landed six of my seven triples. I struggled hard to make myself feel good about what I'd accomplished, but after winning the national pairs championship twice in a row, eleventh place as a singles skater was hard to swallow.

The best and most encouraging part of my being at nationals was the audience's response. At first it felt a little strange to be the sole focus of attention, to be all alone in the spotlight, but before I was halfway through my short program I was really enjoying that I didn't have to share center stage with a partner.

The hardest part of being at nationals was watching Kristi compete. I guess I didn't have to watch, but I couldn't just stay in my hotel room. So Rick and I went up into the stands and watched, like all the other spectators. I tried to stop myself from hoping that Kristi would do badly, but it was hard to resist imagining her going home *without* a medal. Of course, given that she was favored to win the gold, that was pretty unlikely. The fact that for the first time she didn't have the demands of skating both singles and pairs only made it more likely that she'd get to the top.

Sure enough, Kristi's short program was perfect. She placed first. (Rivals Tonya Harding and Nancy Kerrigan came in second and third.) Despite myself, I stood and cheered along with everyone else at the end of Kristi's program. Part of me was instinctively excited for Kristi. Although I was mad at her, deep down I still loved her.

For her long program Kristi wowed the audience—including me and Rick—with a program skated to music from the opera *Samson et Delila,* but she fell on one of her triples and dropped to second place. Tonya Harding landed a triple axel, the first woman in the country to land one in competition, and she took the gold. One of the judges even gave her a perfect 6.0. Nancy Kerrigan got the bronze.

As we packed to go home, I couldn't help thinking that Kristi was heading for the world championships, while I was going back to San Jose. It didn't seem fair. All I had to look forward to was a full year of hard work before I'd get a chance at nationals again. And there was nothing for me at home. Laura was living with her boyfriend about a half hour away. I had no close friends. And George, whom I hadn't seen much of for years, had disappeared completely after it was discovered he'd embezzled $25,000 from Taco Bell. The police had been to the house to question us, but we had no idea where he'd gone.

I hated being at home. I was feeling angry, lonely, and frustrated, and there didn't seem to be much I could do about it other than lose my temper. Right on cue, that's exactly what I did. I can't remember what set me off or what the argument was about, but my father and I really got into it, yelling at each other so loud that I'm sure they heard us several trailers away. The argument climaxed with my declaring that I was moving out.

I went to my room, called Laura, and told her that I had to get out of the house, that I couldn't stand being there anymore. She calmed me down and told me I could come stay at her place for a little while, in the spare bedroom. She said she'd come by to get me in a few hours, which would give me enough time to pack.

Even at the time, I knew that the fight with my father wasn't the only reason I wanted to get out of the house. Besides feeling that at age twenty-one I was too old to be living at home with my parents, Dad's health was going downhill from the diabetes, and I couldn't bear to watch my big, strong father turn into an invalid. I also couldn't imagine being there when he died. At the time, I didn't think about how selfish it was for me to leave my mother with the full responsibility of caring for my father. I was just focused on getting away, and this fight was a perfect excuse.

By the time Laura got to the house I was packed and ready to go. She helped me take my things out to the car, and then we came back in so I could say good-bye to my dad. He said, "I guess this is it," which was the first thing he'd said to me since our fight. And then he started to cry. While I felt terrible, I just couldn't stay.

Laura tried to make Dad feel better, telling him that I wouldn't be far away. And I tried to reassure him, too, telling him that I was only moving out for a while, that I'd be back. But in my heart of hearts I hoped I'd never have to go back. It was time for me to be out on my own, even if "on my own" really meant depending, once again, on the kindness of my sister.

I was relieved to be out of the trailer, and being with Laura again was comforting. Living there with her boyfriend, whom I didn't know very well, was a little awkward for me, but for the most part we all got along pretty well.

Despite our quarrel, I stayed in touch with my father. We spoke on the phone every several days, and I tried to get home once a week. While I loved him, there wasn't really a lot for us to talk about, and our phone conversation was the same every time. He'd say, "Hi, Rudy. How's it going? How's your skating? Keep your training up. Come by once in a while." That was about it, and for both of us it seemed to be enough.

Shortly after I moved in with Laura, it was time for the world championships, but unfortunately I wasn't going. I probably shouldn't even have watched, because I knew I'd feel bad watching the pairs competition and I'd feel even worse watching Kristi. But I couldn't *not* watch, so at least I did the smart thing and watched it with Laura.

The defending world women's singles champion, Midori Ito of Japan, was favored to win her second gold medal—at least that was the scenario before she fell over the boards and into a television camera pit while attempting a combination jump. I instinctively cringed when she fell, and I felt so bad for her because it's incredibly embarrassing when you fall in competition. And this was even worse than a regular fall. But she got right up and finished her program. I admired her courage, but it wasn't enough for her to come close to beating out Kristi, who received the first perfect 6.0 of her career. Tonya Harding placed second, and Nancy Kerrigan got the bronze.

After her silver at nationals and her gold at the world championships, Kristi had become what the press called "America's new skating sweetheart." I wasn't willing to admit it to myself, but given how well she was doing, Kristi had made the right decision to focus on singles. Was I jealous? Sure I was! How could I not be?

Shortly after worlds, I was back on the ice, training for the upcoming 1992 season. I'd planned to take more time off before starting in again, but Rick kept calling me, telling me how much I was missed at the arena: "It's not the same without you. The kids love you so much." Soon enough, I was back on the ice. It wasn't all Rick's doing, because I was actually looking forward to starting work on my new programs and clowning around with Rick's younger skaters. If I was going to climb back to the top, I had a lot of work to do. And besides, as always, being on the ice was the only thing in my life that lifted my spirits.

The other bright spot for me that year was a new friendship I'd been nurturing with a guy named Reuben. I'd spotted him a year before while I was at the Eastridge rink getting my new skates fitted. I looked out on the ice, and there was this chubby black guy in his late twenties practicing crossovers. He was trying to be casual, acting as if he knew what he was doing, but every once in a while he'd trip on himself and then struggle to stay on his feet. And his jumps? I'd never seen anything so funny, and I stood there trying not to laugh out loud.

We happened to walk out of the arena at the same time, and he noticed that I was carrying a new pair of skates. We fell into a conversation and he started telling me the best way to break them in. He said, "The best way is to wear them in the bathtub." I cracked up, and he wanted to know what was so funny. I told him that I was a competitive skater and that I'd broken in lots of new skates, but never in the bathtub. I introduced myself, and that's when I found out that Reuben was one of Laura's students. He, of course, recognized my last name, and he also knew about me from my years with Kristi.

After the first time we met, I'd show up at Eastridge once a week or so, just to have some fun on the ice, and that's when I usually saw Reuben. We'd skate around and then hang out together off the ice. I liked his personality. He was funny, outgoing, and kind of crazy. He was also gay, and I liked the idea of having a gay friend.

By the time I moved in with Laura, Reuben and I had begun to develop the kind of friendship where we could have one-word conversations; we always knew what the other was thinking, and we both had slightly wicked senses of humor. Laughing with Reuben was a nice antidote to my all too often dark moods.

After we knew each other for a while, Reuben invited me and Laura over to his house for a barbecue. He lived in Concord, across the Bay from San Francisco, in this beautiful condo with his partner, Wayne; they were the first gay couple I'd ever met.

Wayne was very nice to us, and I liked him, although he was reserved in comparison to Reuben. He was about ten years older than Reuben and equally chubby. Wayne described himself as coming from white trailer trash, but he'd clearly come a long way from where he started. From the look of the condo, you could tell that Wayne and Reuben were very successful. It turned out that they both worked for the same high-tech medical-supply company. They had such normal, quiet lives that I had to admire them. I thought I'd be lucky if I could ever meet someone and have the kind of stable, married life that they did.

I was glad to have Reuben's support throughout the year leading up to the 1992 nationals. He'd occasionally come to my practice sessions and stand there at the side of the ice along with all the skating mothers. I'm sure some people thought that Reuben was my lover, but I didn't care. What I cared about was that Reuben was my friend and that he felt strongly enough about me to get up at five-thirty in the morning and come to the cold arena and stand by the boards just so I had someone there to cheer me on when I needed it.

One of the reasons I needed Reuben to cheer me on that year had nothing to do with skating. I came home one evening and Laura told me that George had been arrested. Within no time, before I even had a chance to see him, he was on his way to a prison in Vacaville, which is nearly two hours north of San Jose, to serve out a year-and-a-half sentence. I called Reuben to ask him what I should do about George; I felt so helpless and wanted to do something. Reuben suggested that I write to my brother, which is what I did, and that's how George and I got to know each other, really for the first time since I was a child.

In my letters I told George about my skating and how Mom was doing, and he'd write back with stories about life in prison. When I wrote him, I'd put some money in the envelope, and I'd have Mom write a little note signed, "I love you."

In one of his letters, George told me that he was HIV-positive. I knew that George had been involved with many different men over the years, and I also knew that he wasn't the most responsible person in the world, so I wasn't surprised. Still, it made me sad to know that my brother would in all likelihood die sooner rather than later, and it made me even more determined to get closer to him during whatever time he had left.

George asked me not to tell our parents that he had HIV, and I honored his wish. There was no point in telling them now, because it would just have given Dad one more thing to hold against George, and Mom would have been overwhelmed with worry. There would be plenty of time to deal with that once George started having symptoms.

For some reason I didn't hold it against George that he was in prison. He was my brother, and I thought it was time for me to open my heart to him. He had his troubles, and I needed to be there for him, just as he was there for me when we lived with my aunt Cindy. Besides, I was just about all he had. Dad never wrote him; he still couldn't accept that George was gay. And Laura was so mad at him for embezzling that she wouldn't have anything to do with him. So that left only me.

Back on the ice, Rick and I were working hard on perfecting my triple jumps and mapping out my new programs. My plan with Rick for the year leading up to the 1992 nationals was basically the same as it had been the year before, except this time my goal was to make the top eight, so I'd at least be eligible to be considered for some of the international competitions. I'd traveled so much in the past that it felt unnatural not to be going overseas. If I could do well enough this time out, I'd be on a plane and on my way to somewhere exciting.

My first hurdle came in December, when I competed at the Pacific Coast sectionals. It didn't help that I was skating with a stomach flu, but I still managed to skate a great short program, without a single mistake. For the long program, I landed my first triple axel but fell on the second. As I got back on my feet, I felt like I was going to throw up, but I told myself to hold it down for another couple of minutes. I got back on my feet, kept on going, took my bows, and made a run for the bathroom. Miraculously, I did well enough to hold on to first place.

Rick and I flew to Orlando for the national championships with our fingers crossed. I skated great in the practice sessions, and although I wasn't doing the really difficult jump combinations—they weren't consistent enough for me to use them in competition—I was getting all kinds of compliments from other skaters and their coaches about how beautiful my skating was. But rather than making me feel confident about my skating, the compliments left me feeling crushed under the weight of everyone's expectations. I started worrying about what people would think if I didn't skate just as well in the competition as I had in the practice sessions.

The night before the competition began, I couldn't sleep. All I could think about was what everyone had said about my skating, and then I'd imagine myself falling on the ice in front of all those people during my programs. What I should have been visualizing were flawless, easy programs, but I was too caught up in my fear of failure to imagine what everyone else seemed to think I was capable of doing.

Luckily, my nightmare didn't come true. I skated both programs without falling, but I was so cautious that I skated without any real energy. It was almost as if I were just going through the motions, and the judges marked me accordingly. With the help of Rick's great choreography I managed to get eighth place and polite applause from the audience, a far cry from the gold medals and standing ovations of my last couple of years with Kristi.

Rick was quick to reassure me that I'd done a good job, and he was excited for me because I was now in the running for internationals. I didn't want to seem like a spoilsport, so I did my best to share Rick's excitement, though it was a real struggle not to be overwhelmed by frustration. After so much success early in my life—winning medals and being national pairs champion—eighth place didn't feel like a comfortable place. And besides, this was the championship that determined who would be going to the Olympics. This was supposed to be a high point in my career with Kristi, our final step before going to the 1992 Olympics. Instead I was a no-name singles skater going nowhere particularly fast.

As you can imagine, watching the pairs competition at nationals was torture. Instead of being on the ice with Kristi as the defending national pairs champions with a chance of winning a trip to the Olympics in Albertville, I was up in the stands with Rick watching waitress Calla Urbanski and truck driver Rocky Marval take home the gold. They would be going to the Olympics along with silver medalists Jenni Meno and Scott Wendland and bronze medalists Natasha Kuchiki and Todd Sand. And, of course, Kristi would be going to the Olympics, too. She won the national championship in senior ladies; she got standing ovations for both her programs.

I went home to lick my wounded ego and to watch the Winter Olympics on television. I must have been really desperate for attention, because I agreed to let a local news station videotape me watching the women's singles competition. They wanted to see my reaction to how Kristi did at the Olympics, and I did my best to give them the performance they wanted. Surprisingly, I didn't have to work very hard, because I was genuinely nervous watching her skate and I found myself cheering her on.

After Kristi beat out Midori Ito of Japan for the gold medal, the reporter asked me how I was feeling. What could I say? I said that I was happy for her. What I didn't say was that I was miserable for myself and, once again, boiling over with rage.

As I usually did, I took out my anger on someone close to me. This time, Laura was on the receiving end. I don't remember what the argument was about—and neither does Laura—but it got really heated, and just as Laura was about to hit me, her boyfriend walked in. From the way things looked he thought I was trying to hit Laura, and he pretty much threw me out of the house. I couldn't believe it, but Laura didn't stop him.

I had two choices. I could go home to my parents again, or I could call Reuben and ask him if I could come live with him and Wayne. (It never occurred to me to find a place of my own because I didn't have any way of paying for it.) Calling up my father was out of the question, so I called Reuben. By this time he and Wayne had sold their condo and were temporarily living in a two-bedroom apartment in Belmont while they looked for a new house.

Reuben said he thought it would be okay, but he needed to talk it over first with Wayne. I was sure Wayne would have some reservations, especially since the two of them were living in a small apartment and he, unlike Reuben, didn't really know me. But after discussing it with Reuben, he agreed to give it a try. The next day Reuben called to tell me I could move in, so I packed my things and Laura drove me over. We were on speaking terms by then, but she made no attempt to convince her boyfriend that he should let me stay. I couldn't be mad at Laura, because it was my own fault.

I thought it would be a lot of fun living with Reuben and Wayne, and a lot of times it was, but we all had to make adjustments. They had to get used to having an overgrown adolescent in the house, and I had to get used to living with a couple of people who often acted more like parents than friends. The biggest problem at first was the lack of space, but that changed a few months later when we moved to their new house in Belmont.

For me it was an ideal arrangement because I got to live with Reuben, whom I liked very much, plus I didn't have to pay rent and they paid for all the food. I was only making a little money from coaching a few hours a week, and the token grant money I got from the U.S. Figure Skating Association all went to skating. I wasn't exactly in a position to support myself. So to make up for not paying rent, I'd always make sure the dishes were done when they got home and that the house was clean. It was the least I could do to pay them back for their generosity.

Most days were pretty much the same. I'd get up before they

did and I'd take one of their cars to the arena. By the time I got home at ten or eleven in the morning, they were already at work. The rest of the day I did all sorts of things. I'd do my stretching, clean for a while, and play with the dogs: Sara, a rambunctious beagle, and Buddy, a rather subdued mixed shepherd. If necessary, I'd go shopping. By the midafternoon, I didn't have much to do, so I watched a lot of TV. I didn't have any friends other than Reuben and Wayne, and my family was down in San Jose, so I felt pretty isolated and alone. By the time Reuben and Wayne came home, I was so excited that I'd go running to meet them, just like Sara and Buddy.

Usually, Reuben and Wayne brought fast food home for dinner. Other times, if Reuben got home early enough, he'd cook. And sometimes I'd surprise them with my burritos, which they loved. After dinner they watched TV, then went to bed. I still had so much energy that I wanted to stay up and talk, but there was no one to talk to other than the dogs, and while I tried talking to them, they weren't good listeners.

As I anticipated, I had an easier time getting along with Reuben than with Wayne. Reuben was my friend, and Wayne took more of the father role with me, which I both liked and didn't like. I liked when he came to see me practice at the arena or came to competitions. He took pride in my accomplishments, like a father would. On the other hand, I sometimes felt as if he were treating me like a child, telling me to clean up my room, telling me when I could go out, telling me I had to be home at a certain time. I didn't like that at all, so we wound up having arguments about it. But Wayne would remind me that if I was going to live in their house, I had to live by their rules, which were quite a bit more strict than the rules at Laura's or my parents' house.

I also wasn't used to anyone telling me to take responsibility for everyday things, like keeping a checkbook and filling out my own USFSA grant applications. In the past, someone else had always taken care of those things for me—my dad, Carole, or Laura. So Reuben and Wayne sat down with me and showed me how to keep track of the money I was getting from my students and how to balance my checkbook. They also made me fill out my own grant applications. I wanted them to do it, but they emphasized that I needed to take responsibility for my own life, that it was time for me to grow up. They were right. I was twenty-two years old and I still felt that I needed to be taken care of.

When I really needed them, Reuben and Wayne were good listeners, and a lot of evenings I'd pour out my frustrations about skating. I didn't know if I should continue competing or just quit and try to get into an ice show and make some money. I'd been skating since I was eight years old, and I didn't know if I'd ever win a medal again. They were both very supportive. They'd tell me what a wonderful skater I was, that whatever I did, they were behind me 100 percent, and that they would love me whether or not I won medals or even skated. Then they'd tell me to go to bed and that I'd feel better in the morning, which I usually did.

Reuben and Wayne never told me what to do as far as my skating went. It was always up to me. But they knew that no matter how much I complained I still wanted to compete and make a name for myself. I needed to prove myself. I couldn't just give up, not yet.

One time, when I was feeling really angry about not doing better in competitions, I announced that I was going to Mexico to skate, where I knew I could make the Olympic team. I expected that Reuben and Wayne would try talking me out of it, but Wayne went into my room and started packing for me. He said, "You want to go, go!" Then he asked me when my bus was leaving. I didn't know what to do, so I finished packing my suitcase and went to bed. I don't think they were surprised to find me at home when they got back from work the next day.

One of the things that I really loved about Reuben and Wayne was that they always had faith in me. Even after the 1992 Olympic Festival in Los Angeles, where I totally bombed, they believed I could make it. *I* didn't even believe it at that point. It was awful. I skated like an amateur, and it was entirely my own fault. I hadn't been taking my training seriously; I thought I could depend on my natural talent and jumping ability. All the other skaters were doing serious weight training and working out on the treadmill, while I laid out in the sun working on a rich, dark tan. I could blame my coach for not pushing me, but Rick wasn't that kind of coach. I wanted someone who was easygoing, who didn't push, and that's exactly what I got.

Skating wasn't my only problem at the Olympic Festival. My costume was a disaster. It was designed to complement my long program, which I skated to an electronically synthesized version of Stravinsky's "Firebird." I thought the costume was really cool, and in the dressing room all the kids were oohing and aahing when I put it on. It's difficult to describe, but it was supposed to look like flames against a black background, with flesh-colored fabric covering the upper part of my body. The flames, which were made out of sequins, went from the top of one side of my body all the way down my leg. It's probably the only one of all the costumes I've ever worn that truly deserved to be called flamboyant—and boy, was it. The judges hated it, and after my program, they told Rick I should get rid of it.

Between my terrible skating and my flashy costume, I figured I'd never get sent to an international that year. The USFSA hadn't met yet to decide who was going where, and I was sure they'd find a reason not to send me. I knew that the last thing they wanted to do was send an effeminate, flamboyantly dressed, underachieving skater to represent the United States in an international competition. Reuben and Wayne kept telling me I'd get chosen to go; they were right, but there was a catch.

The USFSA sort of offered me Prague Skate, one of the second-tier international competitions, but first I had to qualify in a competition against the seventh-place skater from nationals. It was a skate-off, and the two of us went to Las Vegas to compete against two world-class skaters, one Canadian, one Romanian. I couldn't afford to rely on my raw talent this time, and I worked really hard to prepare for the competition. It paid off. I beat out the other skaters, placed first, and won my spot at Prague Skate.

Getting Prague Skate was just the boost I needed. I hadn't been out of the country for a skating competition since Kristi and I had gone to Nova Scotia for our final world championship in 1990. The trip to Prague was set for October, just before sectionals, so I had a couple of months to get myself ready. I'd been working with Rick on my triple lutz—the only one of the six triple jumps I hadn't used in competition—and I got it consistent enough to use it. I also started working out with weights in the gym that Reuben and Wayne put together for me at their house.

In the middle of my training for Prague Skate, I took a day off to drive up to Vacaville. George's year-and-a-half sentence was up, and it was time to bring him home. I was very excited, because after corresponding with my brother, I felt close to him in a way I'd never been close before.

I'd daydreamed a lot during the time George was in prison about what it would be like when he came home. We were brothers and we were both gay, so I figured we could hang out together and have fun and go to all the clubs. At least that's what I had hoped would happen.

It was a two-hour drive to the prison, and I asked one of the skating mothers I'd gotten friendly with to come with me. Chris Miller is about ten years older than I am. She's straight, but completely comfortable around me, and sometimes we went out to a local gay club together. I was nervous about going to get George on my own, so I was glad to have the company.

When we got to the prison, we couldn't find the special unit for people with HIV, but after some driving around, we finally figured out where we were supposed to go. We were a little early, so we waited by a tall fence topped with barbed wire. It was a long way from the world of figure skating to the Vacaville prison. It was hard to believe that this was where my big brother had spent the past eighteen months.

After a few minutes, we saw a long line of men approaching the gate, and there was George. He was tanned from being outside so much, and he was really skinny from not eating—in almost every letter he'd talked about how much he hated prison food. As soon as he got past the gate, he gave me a big hug, and I introduced him to Chris.

George was hungry, so we went to Jack in the Box for Jack tacos, which were his favorite. Even if Taco Bell had been his favorite, I don't think we would have gone there—for obvious reasons. Over lunch, George told us stories about prison and how this giant of a guy had claimed him for a boyfriend. George didn't like the guy, but George also wasn't much bigger than I am, so there wasn't a lot he could say once he was chosen. It sounded like a nightmare to me, but George had managed. He always did.

On the way to our parents' house, George suggested we stop at one of the clubs he used to go to, so off we went to this gay dance bar in San Jose. I think part of the reason he didn't want to go right home was because he was nervous about seeing Dad. He knew that Mom would accept him as she always had, but Dad was another story. While Dad had agreed to let George live at home, it was mostly out of a sense of obligation. I'm sure if George had had any other place to go, he would have gone there. But he didn't have close friends, and he didn't have any money.

It was early evening by the time we got to the club, and lots of people were already there, and most of them seemed to know George. We had a few drinks, and George spent most of the evening running around talking to friends and trying to pick up guys. At some point, without telling us, he left with someone. I figured that this was George's first day of freedom, so I tried not to get mad at him for leaving Chris and me there.

I think the hardest part for George after prison was being at home with our parents. Given how Dad felt, I'm still surprised he let George move home. But on some level, because my father's health was deteriorating and he needed help getting around, Dad was probably grateful that George was there to help Mom take care of him. I know Mom was looking forward to having George home, but George didn't make it easy for her. He had little patience for her and got mad at her a lot. But despite how George treated her, Mom tried to keep him happy, or at least well fed. So it didn't take long for George to get back all his weight.

George was handsome and always well groomed. He never let me forget that he was better-looking than I was and that he didn't have any trouble picking up guys. I didn't care that he got guys to go home with him; I didn't see it as a competition. My one concern when we went out together was that the guys George picked up should know that he had HIV. I was always telling him that he'd better tell whomever he was trying to sleep with that he was HIV-positive. I didn't feel it was fair for him not to. In the months that followed, there were times when I told them myself. George would be putting the make on some guy and then excuse himself to go to the bathroom or something, and then I'd go over and ask the guy if he knew that George had HIV. I'd say it because I knew George wouldn't, and often, by the time George got back, the guy was gone. We got into some terrible fights over this. All George seemed to care about was having a good time, and he could care less about anyone else's health. That attitude infuriated me, but I tried hard not to let my anger overwhelm my love for George. It was a real struggle.

I guess I could have stayed home and not gone out with George, but I liked being with him. Sometimes it was fun, and I also thought I should keep an eye on him. So about twice a week we'd go out together. He'd pick me up at Reuben and Wayne's and we'd go out to the bars. He and I were so different, like night and day. I'd sit there at the bar and George would be dancing on the pool table, going up to guys and propositioning them. People would come up to me and say they couldn't believe the two of us were related. We looked alike, but he was so wild.

And the more he drank, the worse it got. George's favorite thing to drink was screwdrivers, and after two or three he'd get really vicious. All he'd care about then was having a good time and finding someone to go home with. A lot of times he'd disappear and leave me with no way to get home. I'd have to call Chris or Reuben and Wayne to come get me. Other times, I'd want to leave so I could go home and get enough sleep to skate the next day, only he wouldn't go. A couple of times, when I tried reaching into his pocket to get his car keys so I could leave, he just about tried beating me up. He'd give me a really hard shove and then stop himself. But you could see the drunken hate in his eyes.

This was not how I'd imagined things would be when George came home. I thought we'd have fun. I thought he'd be my buddy. I could never have imagined him being so crazy at the clubs, being so angry at me. And on top of everything else, he'd always be trying to pick up guys I was talking to. If I was interested in someone, George would have to have him—it was like some insane contest. I tried not to let it get to me because I knew it was mostly the alcohol talking, but sometimes I got angry and was hurt by the awful things he said to me. Most of the time, when he was acting cruel, I turned my attention to the bartender and just talked about skating. I'd try to ignore that George was carrying on like a cheerleader in the next room. I'm not kidding. He'd tear up newspapers and make big pom-poms and do really crazy things. A few times I tried to bring up how he was behaving, but he'd accuse me of being jealous because he was getting all these guys. He'd say, "I can get any guy I want, and you can't get anyone." The truth was, I didn't want anyone, at least not for a one-night stand.

Despite some late evenings out with George and a couple of hangovers, I still managed to get into really good shape by the time I got to Europe for Prague Skate.

In the days leading up to the competition, I was getting all kinds of compliments at the practices about how trim I looked and how well I was skating. I loved the compliments, but as usual I had trouble dealing with the expectations and the pressure that went along with them. And sure enough, I skated my worst short ever. I stepped out of the triple axel, double toe.

121

I did a double flip instead of a triple, and I landed on two feet instead of one. I was in such shock that I just stood there for a moment and shot a look over to Rick—it was an "Oh, my God!" look—but Rick was still smiling. I marveled at his ability to always be so sunny and good-natured.

Then I went to do a spin and I almost fell. It was humiliating, and when my technical marks came up, they were so low that I thought I was seeing things. I got 3.9s and 4.0s. The only thing that saved me from last place—there were thirty skaters—was the style mark. I got 5.7s across the board, good enough for fifth place.

I was so mad about skating badly in the short that I turned around and skated a flawless long program. I got all my triples—*everything!* I stepped off the ice and into a crowd of well-wishers who told me I was the best and that I was going to go all the way to the world championships. It was a first-place performance that pulled me all the way up to second place overall and a silver medal. Finally, after more than two years, I was back in the running.

I went home from Europe totally psyched for sectionals and couldn't wait to get through them so I could get to nationals and prove myself. At sectionals, which were held in Las Vegas, I did a clean short program and a good enough long program to take first place. That was exactly where I wanted to be as I headed for nationals.

By the time I left for the '93 nationals in Phoenix, I had my two new programs even more solid than they were at sectionals. Rick choreographed the short and long programs with lots of really elegant balletic moves, and I skated both of them to classical music. The costumes were neat and simple—no sequins. We'd learned our lesson and we decided it was best not to antagonize the judges. It wouldn't hurt to have them on my side for a change.

I had great practices all week in Phoenix, and I felt awesome, just totally relaxed. I hadn't felt that good going into a competition since my first national championship with Kristi. All I needed was to get third place—then I'd be back on the

podium for a medal and on my way to the world championships.

When it was my turn to skate and the announcer called my
name, I felt this rush of adrenaline. I took a couple of deep
breaths, stepped onto the ice, and got into position. The music
started and I headed into my first triple. As I picked up speed,
just before my takeoff, this voice in my head said, "You haven't
missed all week long, it'll be perfect, here goes," and then bam,
I was down on the ice. I didn't just fall, I slammed into the ice,
really hard. For a split second, I sat there, too stunned to move.
When the shock dissipated, my first instinct was to get off the
ice and beg the judges to let me start over. But the music kept
going, so I was on my feet, trying to catch up.

I placed seventh. If this had been 1991, I would have been
ecstatic over doing that well. But it wasn't 1991, and I was
beside myself over having fallen again in competition, and I
was ready to chop off the head of anyone who came near me.
Rick was the first one to get to me backstage, and as usual, he
was upbeat, trying to pump me up, telling me not to worry,
that I still had the long program the next day. I don't know
what I said or what kind of attitude I threw him, but it was bad
enough that suddenly he was furious, calling me a spoiled little
f-----g brat. I was shocked. Rick never said things like that. He
turned around and walked away, and I got out of there as fast
as I could. I didn't wait around to see Reuben and Wayne or my
sister, Laura, who had been watching the competition from the
stands.

I ran back to the hotel, feeling like I wanted to scream, like I
wanted to jump out of my skin. I couldn't understand what was
going on. Why was I having so much bad luck? Was my comeback simply not meant to be?

Laura eventually showed up at my room and held me while I
cried. She was great. She always knew how to talk to me, and
in a really gentle voice she said, "Just block it out. Tomorrow's
another day. You'll do great. We all have confidence in you."
After a while, I calmed down and Laura left me to sulk on my
own.

Sure enough, the next day I used all of my anger over blowing the short program, and I did an incredible long program. But because my competition was very strong that year, even with a perfect program I could only get fourth, and I felt lucky to do even that well. That pulled me up to fifth overall, one place ahead of Todd Eldredge, the two-time national champion. After bombing in the short, I was really happy to come in fifth. For Todd, after two national championships, sixth place must have been devastating.

By the time I got home from nationals, my life really seemed to be on track. I'd done well enough at nationals to make me eligible for a top-tier international competition such as NHK or Skate America. With continued hard work I had every reason to expect I'd move up again the following year at nationals and maybe win a medal. On the home front, things were great with Reuben and Wayne; I'd become a part of their family. My father wasn't doing so well, but he was hanging in there. George was home, and that was sure better than having him in jail. The only thing missing from my life was a boyfriend. And like an answered prayer, that's when I met a man I'll call Kurt. Unfortunately, it was the devil who granted my wish.

9

OUT OF MY MIND

Like most people, I expected that one day I'd fall in love and live happily ever after. Up until this point in my life I'd had only two real crushes—Johnny Rivera, my childhood crush, and Greg Louganis, whom I'd watched on television at the 1988 Olympics. I thought he was this wonderful combination of cute, gorgeous, sweet, and gentle, but I just assumed he was straight and had all kinds of girlfriends. I can't believe how wrong I was.

My newest infatuation was named Kurt, and now that I wasn't worried about Carole Yamaguchi looking over my shoulder and judging me, I pursued him with all the intensity and naïveté of an adolescent in love. But I was twenty-three years old, and hardly an adolescent, so I couldn't use that as an excuse for my stupidity.

Instead of pursuing Kurt, I should just have taken my whole life and flushed it down the toilet. That would have been easier on everyone, including me. But I obviously had some lessons to learn about life off the ice, and as usual, I had to learn the hard way. Maybe from reading about my experience you won't have to make the same mistakes in your relationships, straight or gay.

I met Kurt right after I got home from nationals. He was at the rink watching a guy who was taking a private lesson—I learned later that they were boyfriends—and we just started talking. While I thought he was attractive, he wasn't my type. He had light brown hair and he was a few inches taller than I am. He was really lean, all muscle but not built up. He also had a great voice and a sly personality. He had this straight-guy swagger that I thought was very appealing. I liked the fact that he was masculine and took charge of things. I instinctively knew he was gay.

If I'd thought for a second that Kurt was a potential boyfriend, I could never have called him up to ask him to go out with me. I've never asked anyone out for a date, ever, even to this day. I'm just too afraid of being rejected. But I thought of Kurt as a potential friend, that it would be fun to go out with him to a club. I could have gone out with Reuben and Wayne, but they were like a married couple; it wouldn't have been as much fun. So I called Kurt and asked if he wanted to go up to San Francisco one night to a bar called Badlands. He said yes.

I was all excited getting ready, putting on a new pair of jeans and a skintight T-shirt, waiting for Kurt to get to the house. You have to understand, Reuben and Wayne were really my only gay friends, and I'd never had a gay friend my age, a buddy, so this was something new for me.

Kurt picked me up in his broken-down old car. It was quite a contrast: this handsome young man dressed in a pristine white polo shirt and black jeans, sitting in a car that was so rusty I couldn't tell what color it had been. I opened the car door, which felt as if it would fall off in my hand, and we drove to the Castro, which is San Francisco's predominantly gay neighborhood.

We sat down at the bar, ordered a couple of vodka tonics, and talked. That's when I learned about Kurt's boyfriend, who was set to leave in a few days for a new job halfway across the country. After a while I noticed that Kurt was nursing his drink, and I asked him if he wanted a fresh one. He said he didn't have much money and couldn't really afford another drink. Kurt was a singer and worked one night a week at a sit-down bar; that was his only job, he said, but he was looking for more work. I told him not to worry about the money, that I'd pay. I was acting like I had money to burn because I wanted to impress him. The truth was, I had a little money in the bank from helping some of Laura's students with their jumps and spins and also some grant money from the USFSA for my skating. One too many drinks and I'd be broke, too. But I didn't care. If this was the cost of having a friend to hang out with, I'd spend the money. It was a whole lot better than being lonely all the time.

So Kurt and I started going out a couple of times a week. We'd drive up to San Francisco or go out in San Jose, have a lot to drink, then drive home. Choosing a designated driver was not a concept that ever crossed our minds. We were having too good a time to care. I thank God we didn't kill anyone or get killed ourselves. We even got stopped a couple of times by the police in San Jose while I was driving, but they recognized my name and just told me to be careful getting home. At the time, I thought I was lucky that I was never arrested, but in retrospect I think it would have been better if they'd hauled me in and locked me up for the night. That was obviously a lesson that still needed learning.

I can't tell you how it happened or why, but after the first few times we went out together, I fell in love with Kurt. Nothing had changed about him. He seemed to like me, but he hadn't given me any reason to think he was in love with me, and given his frequent reports about how his boyfriend was doing at his new job and how much they missed each other, I had every reason to think he had no interest in me beyond friendship. But that didn't matter. I had to be with Kurt or I'd go out of my mind.

Every time we went out, I tried to find some evidence that Kurt's feelings for me were changing. Sometimes he seemed to flirt with me or he acted kind of jealous if I commented on someone I thought was attractive. After a night out drinking, he always wanted to stay over at my house, and I let him, but the fact that he slept in his T-shirt and shorts and never even tried to kiss me should have been a hint that his level of interest didn't rise much above my wallet. While he slept beside me, I'd think about how I could get him to fall in love with me. I convinced myself that if I spent enough time with him, if I bought him enough drinks, his feelings would change and he'd want to be more than friends.

As much as I wanted to be with Kurt, I couldn't always go out when he wanted to, because I had to skate in the morning. It was still early in the year, so I could get away with not being 100 percent every day, but one night we got very drunk and stayed out really late, and it was nearly impossible for me to drag myself out of bed in the morning for my lesson. I managed to get myself onto the ice, but I was useless and couldn't do any of my jumps.

If Kurt called to invite me out but I couldn't go because of my skating, he'd ask if he could come over to get some money. Because I wanted him to like me, I always said yes. Other times, he'd call just to ask for money so he could go out with his friends—without me. He'd drive over to the house, I'd give him the money, and then he'd tell me I had to stay home, and I obeyed him as if I were his pet dog. It was pathetic. *I* was pathetic, but I was so caught up with being in love with him, or at least the idea of being in love, that if he told me to walk off a bridge, I would probably have told him, "Whatever you say."

Kurt liked to go to a club where his friends, whom I'll call Scott and Anne, sang. I liked Kurt's friends, and after they were finished performing, we'd all hang out together until three or four in the morning. The evening always ended with the same routine. Kurt would ask to stay over with me at Reuben and Wayne's, and I'd let him. But despite my hopes, there was never any physical intimacy other than my cuddling up against him. I thought it was better than nothing.

My frequent absences from the house and my new gay buddy didn't go unnoticed by Reuben and Wayne. They didn't like that I was out to all hours, and they didn't like Kurt—not one bit. So they started arguing with me about how much I was going out and the late hours I was keeping. It wasn't just Wayne who objected. Reuben really got on my case, too, telling me how I needed to be more serious about my skating and that I couldn't be carrying on all the time and expect to get out on the ice and win. I know I must have really tried their patience. After a while they gave up fighting with me because, after all, I was legally an adult and I was going to do what I wanted. So things quieted down for a while, at least until they found out I was doing drugs.

Even though my brother, George, had been heavy into speed and cocaine and God knows what else, and despite all the drugs in our neighborhood and at school, I had never tried anything. No cocaine. No marijuana. No speed. Nothing. Just cigarettes and different kinds of alcohol, which were bad enough. I really had no interest in anything other than alcohol and cigarettes, at least until Kurt and his friends suggested I snort some speed.

It was really late at night, after one of those evenings when we'd gone to listen to Scott and Anne sing, and we were sitting around their little apartment talking and talking. I fell asleep at about three-thirty, and they woke me up and said I should come with them into the kitchen. On the counter, this white powder was lined up, like cocaine. I asked them if that's what it was, and Scott said it was speed. He put a straw up to my nose and told me to snort it, but I hesitated and asked if it would burn. He said it would, a little, but that I'd like it. Kurt was encouraging me, saying, "Just do it, Rudy." He took my hand, and that was all the encouragement I needed. I didn't think about how drugs had messed up my brother's life. I didn't think about my skating. I didn't think about what Reuben and

Wayne would say. All I thought about was Kurt holding my hand, and if snorting speed made him happy, I'd snort speed or anything else they put in front of me. So I did it and it burned like nothing I'd ever experienced before. I was jumping all over the kitchen holding my nose for two or three minutes trying to get the burning to stop, and then the drug kicked in.

This is not an advertisement for drugs—I'll describe the downside a little later—but the feeling in that moment was incredible. Everything was great. I had all this energy. These people were my best friends. Kurt was my lover. I wanted to talk, talk, talk. Life couldn't be better.

When I stopped jumping around, I noticed they were all staring at me, wanting to know if I liked it. I said, "This stuff is good," and then they couldn't get me to shut up. They snorted some, too, and we talked all night about singing, skating, boyfriends, the state of the world.

I was awake for the next four days. Four days! And I still had to skate. I remember that first night, I stayed at Scott and Anne's apartment until 6:30 A.M. before going back to Reuben and Wayne's house to get ready for skating. I walked in and they said, "Hard night, huh?" They had no idea I was high and they teased me about being out all night. I took a shower, got into my skating clothes, and went to the rink. I had so much energy I could have skated all day.

That first time I did speed with Kurt was the first time he told me that he loved me. I'd been waiting a long time to hear those words, and I didn't care if it took a little speed to get him to say it. All I cared about was what he said. He loved me, and stupidly I thought that if I bought him drugs, Kurt would become my lover. I never even got a kiss, but before long, we were drinking and partying three or four nights a week with Scott and Anne.

On a typical evening out, we'd go hear Scott and Anne's act, then we'd hang around the bar drinking until the manager threw us out. We'd go back to Scott and Anne's apartment, line up the drugs, and stay up talking all night. After that, Kurt and I would go back to the house so I could get my skating things, and I'd take him with me to the rink. I'd show off for him while I did my lesson, then we'd go back to Reuben and Wayne's. We'd lie there in bed all day, trying to sleep, but our hearts were pounding so much from the drugs that we couldn't even close our eyes. Sometimes Scott and Anne would come over to the house for the day, listen to music, and snort speed; we'd all trip out. A lot of times we'd listen to skating music, trying to pick out something new for my programs.

By the end of the day, they'd head back home, and I'd shower, get dressed, and be raring to go out again just as Reuben and Wayne were coming in the door. They never said anything. At that point, I think they were giving me as much rope as I needed to hang myself.

All of that partying was expensive, and who do you think was paying for most of it? My bank account was empty in no time, so I lied and schemed to get money for drugs. I called one of my fans and told him that I needed money for skating boots. I also called friends of Laura's and asked them for money to have new practice outfits made. Then I used the money for drinking and partying. I felt guilty, but I was so out of control that I didn't feel guilty enough to stop.

Scheming and lying weren't the only bad parts of my new life. All the drugs I was snorting had some pretty awful side effects, like making it impossible to sleep for more than a couple of hours at a time and killing my appetite. Speed also eats away at your muscles, so you can end up looking and feeling pretty ragged. I thought I looked fine, but in pictures from that time you can see how gaunt and crazed I looked.

I was the most wired when the speed was wearing off. Coming down—crashing—was the worst. You zone out. You get depressed and withdraw from everyone. You want to eat, but you can't. Your stomach is hurting for food, your body is hurting for sleep, but you can't eat and you can't sleep. And then there were the muscle spasms. One night I did so much speed I couldn't walk because the spasms were so bad. I soaked my feet in the bathtub thinking that that would get rid of the pain, but nothing helped. Also, I got really paranoid: I imagined that everyone knew I was doing drugs, and that I'd be found out and sent to jail. Sound like fun? After a while it didn't matter whether or not I was having fun, because I couldn't stop. I was hooked.

I was so involved in going out, partying, and doing drugs that when Laura called one evening to tell me that Dad had had a heart attack, it took me a minute to figure out what she was saying. Somehow I pulled myself together and headed for the hospital. Driving there, I couldn't help but imagine my father hooked up to all kinds of machines and tubes. Between my drug-induced haze and the tears, I had to be careful to stay on the road.

Laura, Mom, and George were already there, and my dad was in pretty bad shape. The doctor made it clear that Dad wasn't going to make it this time and asked Laura what the family wanted to do in the event my father needed life-support machines. Dad had always been clear about not being put on machines, but I begged Laura to let them put Dad on life support, to please tell the doctors to do everything they could to keep him alive. It didn't matter that my father and I didn't have the closest relationship. He was the only father I had, and I wanted him to live long enough to see that his youngest son wasn't a complete failure, to live long enough so that I could pay him back for all the sacrifices he'd made for my skating. But my hysterical begging didn't have any impact. For a change, Mom took a firm stand. She wanted to do what Dad had wanted. Laura agreed. George just stayed silent through the whole thing, and I could do nothing but fold myself into a chair in the waiting room and cry.

Dad lived for a few more days, and I was at the hospital every day, sitting by his bed for hours on end. Mom and Laura were there, too, and a couple of times George came by for a short visit. Dad was completely conscious but he was very weak and emaciated. During past stays at the hospital, whenever the nurses poked at him, he'd joke with them and say, "Owwww!"

But now he was like an emptied-out sack. He just lay there. Once in a while he and I would talk quietly. He said, "I don't know if I'm going to be around to see you make it in skating." I told him that he was a strong guy, that he'd outlive all of us. I didn't cry in front of him because I didn't want him to know how bad things were. I thought if I gave him hope then maybe he'd pull out of it. He always had in the past, and I refused to believe he couldn't do it this time. I needed my father. He couldn't die now, not before I brought home the gold medal from nationals for him to hold in his hands.

The last time I saw my father was the day he died. We talked about nothing more consequential than the weather and my skating. I stayed only for a little while, not knowing this would be the last time. Before I left, I put my hand on top of his, leaned over, and gave him a kiss on the cheek. He gave me a little wave as I left the room, and I waved back.

That night, at midnight, George called me at Reuben and Wayne's. He was crying as he said, "Dad passed away." I don't know why I was shocked, but I was. It just didn't seem real. Thankfully, Reuben and Wayne were there to comfort me while I rocked back and forth on my bed, mumbling to myself that he couldn't be dead, that it was just a bad dream.

I took my dad's death hard, but I didn't really break down until I saw all the people hovering over his open casket at the wake. From a distance I caught a glimpse of him. He looked so good, better than when he was in the hospital. He looked like the dad I knew from before he was sick. That's when it hit me that he was gone, and I lost it. A couple of my relatives had to help me from the room. They sat me down on a couch in a waiting room and I couldn't stop crying.

After the wake, I stayed over with Kurt at his uncle's house. I'd never felt so down as I did that night, so when Scott and Anne came over with some speed, I didn't hesitate. We lined it up and snorted it. In moments, they were flying high again. For me, the speed just numbed the pain I was feeling over my father's death. I didn't do too much speed because I didn't want to be shaky at the funeral, especially since I was a pallbearer. Unfortunately, I did just enough to get spasms in my feet, and I had trouble walking the next day. I blamed it on my shoes, but it was the speed.

The funeral wasn't as hard for me as the wake. Maybe the speed took the edge off. I don't know. But I liked hearing people say nice things about my dad. That made me feel better.

Neither Kurt, Scott, nor Anne came to the funeral. They didn't offer, and I never asked. I was afraid people would be able to tell they were on drugs.

The whole time, I couldn't wait to get back to Kurt, and as soon as the funeral was over, I went to see him. Despite how he used me, I found comfort in his company. And after my father's funeral, I wanted comfort, which I found in Kurt's arms. Still, my crush on Kurt remained unrequited, and that, of course, made him that much more desirable.

At home, the relationship between Mom and George went from bad to worse. Mom cried nonstop. She was inconsolable, and George had almost no patience with her. He yelled at her all the time, telling her to get over it, that crying wasn't going to bring our father back. I thought he was being cruel and told him so, but he just ignored me.

I don't really know how George felt about Dad's death, because he never said a word about it and hardly interrupted his routine of going out to the bars, partying, drinking, and picking up anyone who would have sex with him. You would have thought that being HIV-positive, George would have taken better care of himself. I was always afraid that something would happen, and about a month after Dad passed away, it did.

George's first crisis happened on a weekend when Kurt's boyfriend was back in town for a few days. I was on my own and feeling angry and jealous, so to get my mind off Kurt, I called up Laura and asked her if she wanted to drive up to Santa Cruz for the day to hang out and visit. We spent most of our time talking about Dad's death and how hard Mom was taking it. So before we went our separate ways, we decided to stop at home to check in on Mom and to try to cheer her up.

When we walked in, George was sitting on the couch. He was an awful bright red color. He told us he'd gone to the park with a friend and that they'd fallen asleep in the sun for three hours. All of a sudden he started having convulsions. We didn't know what to do and for a few moments we just stood there in shock as George slid off the couch and onto the floor. He was shaking like a leaf, then his eyes rolled up into his head. I'd pretty much convinced myself that this was the beginning of the end, but then George sat up and told us he was okay. Well, he sure didn't *look* okay, and we called 911. The ambulance was there in no time and took George to the hospital. Laura, Mom, and I piled into Laura's car and followed the ambulance.

I called my friend Chris Miller, who's a nurse, and asked her to meet us at the hospital. I was glad to have her with us because we thought George would die right then and there. Chris was able to talk calmly with the doctors and then reassure us that he was all right. It was basically heatstroke, with some complications related to HIV. They kept him in the hospital overnight on an IV drip and then sent him home the next morning.

For about a week, George was fine, but then he started deteriorating. He lost his appetite, began losing weight, was tired all the time, and he seemed to be having problems with his memory. I was still living at Reuben and Wayne's, but for the first two weeks after George was released from the hospital, I stayed at home with him and my mom. That was when George told Mom that he was infected with HIV. She cried a little bit, but that was it. I don't think she realized until later what the full implications were of what he'd told her.

They didn't really need me around full-time, but I made myself useful and took George to see the doctor, did the shopping, ran errands, and made sure George got plenty of rest. He wasn't going out and partying because he didn't want anyone to see how skinny he was getting. So it wasn't difficult making sure he stayed at home.

After two weeks, George seemed to be doing well enough to be on his own with Mom, so I went back to living with Reuben and Wayne and back to partying with Kurt and his friends.

Around this time, I decided to confide in Reuben that I was doing drugs. I don't know what I was thinking, but the drugs made me stupid and I thought it would be easier if Reuben knew. I wouldn't have to sneak around so much and worry about him finding out.

Reuben was surprised, and I was surprised that he was surprised. He hadn't realized I was doing drugs. And neither had Wayne. But once they knew, that was it. They told me that speed was going to ruin my health, that I wouldn't be able to skate, and on and on. They told me, "No more late nights. No more Kurt. No more drugs."

Reuben and Wayne wanted to control me, but I wasn't about to be controlled. They'd make sure I was in bed when they went to bed, and as soon as they were asleep, I'd sneak out my bedroom window. Kurt would be waiting for me down the street, and we'd do more drugs. Then I'd make sure I was back in bed before they woke up. If I brought Kurt back with me, I'd get him out through the window before dawn.

Reuben and Wayne weren't stupid, and early one morning Reuben busted into my room while Kurt was still there. He started screaming at Kurt, "Get out of my house. I don't ever want to see you here again." I started screaming at Reuben, and it turned into one of those soap-opera scenes, not so different from what I'd seen on television over the years. I was yelling at Reuben that he couldn't talk to my friend like that, how we weren't doing anything wrong. And Reuben was telling me to shut up and telling Kurt to get his things and get out. I yelled at Reuben how he'd regret this. He said, "I don't care. I told you not to bring him here, and I want him gone by the time I leave for work." He walked out and slammed the door behind him.

I don't know how I had the guts to threaten Reuben because it was his house and I was his guest. I'm surprised he didn't throw us both out. I guess I could have gone back to my mother's house, but I didn't want to. I liked having their house to myself when they were at work. Looking back, I can see that I'd turned into the teenager from hell.

Of course, that big blowup with Reuben wasn't nearly the end of it. A few weeks later, Kurt came over to get money so he could go out bowling with some of his straight high-school buddies. I was sick of lending him money and then staying home while he went out, so I told him I was going out shopping. He said no, that I had to stay home, that he didn't want me going out. We got into this huge wrestling match. I broke away and called Reuben at work and told him that he had to come home right away, that Kurt was holding me prisoner in the house. By the time Reuben got home from work, Kurt was gone.

You can imagine how angry Reuben was, and I promised not to let Kurt in the house ever again. Of course, I broke my promise, because I had to be with Kurt. I was in love with him, whatever that meant, and I had to see him. So, just as I'd done in the past, I'd sneak out of the house and sneak Kurt back in.

After one more major incident, I was finally scared into making some major changes. Kurt and I came home one night from a bar, flying on speed. We'd been drinking, too, but with the speed, we didn't feel drunk. We wanted to go to sleep and not be awakened by the light in the morning. Kurt always liked the room dark, and my windows had no shades. So I went and got a hammer and nails and started nailing a blanket over the window. This was at three in the morning. I was so out of it that it didn't occur to me that Reuben and Wayne might hear the pounding. Sure enough, Reuben threw open the door, and he was furious. I was in such a haze that I don't remember what happened, but the next thing I knew, Kurt was gone and I was getting a lecture. Now I was scared, because I thought Reuben and Wayne would really throw me out.

I wish I could say I decided to stop seeing Kurt, but Kurt decided to stop seeing me. He got tired of having this lovesick lapdog around. He also probably got tired of being thrown out of the house. I could have pursued him, but I didn't. Skating had a lot to do with that. Reuben and Wayne kept telling me how I'd better pull things together because I had the Olympic Festival coming up in San Antonio, Texas. They told me I had to stop seeing Kurt and I had to stop taking drugs.

So it was skating that finally saved me. Reuben and Wayne forced me to acknowledge the toll all the running around and the drugs had taken on my stamina, and I certainly didn't want to make a fool of myself in Texas. That's when I decided to stop snorting speed and, once again, start getting serious about skating. Reuben and Wayne helped me realize that skating was still the most important thing in my life, and that realization made it possible for me to give up drugs and even Kurt.

Deciding to quit drugs was easier than doing it. When I was feeling okay, it wasn't so bad being without the drugs, but when I got depressed, the cravings were terrible. I'd tell Reuben and Wayne how I needed it, and they'd say, "No, you don't." I'd want to go out to the club and get some and they'd tell me I couldn't leave the house. It's funny, if I was having a craving, they'd tell me to have an apple. I liked apples, but it wasn't exactly the same thing.

I have to really thank Reuben and Wayne for taking control of my life for me, because I'm not sure I could have quit without their reading me the riot act and offering me encouragement. And over time, the cravings passed.

My cravings for Kurt, however, didn't go away as quickly. I never called him again, but on a couple of occasions I drove to the bar where Scott and Anne sang to see if he was there. I'd see Kurt from a distance, but I never spoke to him. Stupidly, I still wanted him, but I knew that getting mixed up with him again could ruin my life. Thankfully, after a few months I was able to see the true nature of my relationship with Kurt. What I wanted and needed was a boyfriend I could love and who loved me in return. Given how Kurt treated me and took advantage of me, he wasn't even my friend. And I was an idiot. I have no idea whatever happened to Kurt. I'm just glad I haven't crossed paths with him again.

I look back now and can't believe what I did during the first half of 1993. And I can't believe that Reuben and Wayne put up with all of my antics. But they stuck it out, and like the best parents, they helped me over one of the roughest spots in my life. I hope they know how grateful I am.

10

1994 NATIONALS

After all the months of craziness with Kurt and all the drugs and partying, I was surprised by how quickly life returned to normal at home with Reuben and Wayne. Within a couple of months, it was back to the way it had been before I met Kurt. They even began trusting me again and let me use their new Mazda Miata to go out on Friday nights. But that was my limit. One night out a week. And no driving drunk. I didn't dare break their trust again.

Back on the ice, with only a month to go before the 1993 Olympic Festival in San Antonio, I got serious about my training again. Rick had me concentrate on building my stamina and getting my jumps consistent, and it paid off. The night of the competition, the arena in San Antonio was packed to the rafters with thousands of people. I did all my triples, and my triple axel was flawless. I came into the long program in fourth place after the short, and my long program was so good that I finished in second place overall, earning a silver medal. I was thrilled to have done so well, especially after only a month of real preparation.

Because I'd placed fifth at nationals, I expected that in addition to the Olympic Festival I'd be competing in at least two top-of-the-line internationals. I was selected to go to Germany for the Nations Cup, and I was first alternate for Skate America, which is the most prestigious of the international skating competitions held in the United States each year. In 1993 it was set to take place in Dallas in October.

As first alternate for Skate America I was sure I'd wind up going, because at least one skater always drops out before the competition. And that's exactly what happened. But instead of sending me, the USFSA chose to send Todd Eldredge, who'd placed sixth at nationals and wasn't even on the list of Skate America alternates. An official from the USFSA called Rick and explained that Todd had more international experience, that he had been a national champion and therefore had more of a track record. I was furious. I thought they should play by the rules and send me. Why even bother to name a first alternate if you're not going to honor your commitment? But there was nothing I could do, because it was within the USFSA's rights to pass me over, which they then did a second time when another skater dropped out. And that time, the USFSA didn't even try to explain its decision.

Whatever their real reasons for ditching me, I knew the USFSA would never reveal them. The closest they came was saying that their decision was "subjective." Rick was pretty well convinced it had everything to do with the fact that they didn't want an effeminate gay man representing the United States at Skate America. It was no secret that the USFSA tried to project an all-American image, one in which the women were feminine, not the men.

Rick had heard from more than one judge that I needed to be more masculine, that my hand movements were "too girlish." In one newspaper interview he said, "Sometimes Rudy will hit two triple axels and the judges will say, 'The hands bothered me.'" Did they really think I was *trying* to be effeminate? That's who I am!

Now that I've had a few years to think about it, it's possible that the USFSA had other reasons for passing over me. I was developing a reputation for buckling under pressure, which I'd done at a number of national competitions. I had a temper, which I didn't make much of an effort to hide. Still, I wasn't the only one who had problems with pressure in competitions. And I certainly wasn't the only skater who ever threw a tantrum. So it's hard not to come back to the "effeminate gay man" issue.

Whatever the reasons for keeping me out of Skate America, the USFSA still chose to send me to Germany for the Nations Cup in November, where I placed fourth in a very competitive field. I should have been able to hold on to third place, but I was too cautious in my long program and turned one of my two planned triple axels into a double, so I dropped to fourth. First place went to Viktor Petrenko, the 1992 Olympic champion from Ukraine. Scott Davis, the U.S. national champion, was second, and Sebastien Britten of Canada was third.

I left Germany feeling confident that I could do well enough in the upcoming 1994 national championships in Detroit to place in the top five. Thinking ahead, I imagined earning a medal in 1995. Then, in 1996, when the nationals would come to my hometown of San Jose, I imagined winning the championship. And after that, the 1998 Olympics. But first I had to do well in Detroit.

For the third year in a row, I went to nationals with a win at the Pacific Coast sectionals under my belt. At sectionals in Redwood City I had no trouble landing any of my jumps, even my combinations. That gave me hope that I could do the same at nationals, as long as I could keep those negative voices in my head from getting to me.

People were really nice to me at nationals. Even though it had been several months since my father's death, everyone was coming up and telling me how sorry they were. I wanted to tell them not to remind me about my father's death because I was doing a good job of burying all of my feelings about what had happened. I didn't want to think about Dad's being gone, so having to talk about him just made it hard for me. While I was away, I even avoided talking to Laura, Mom, or George, because I knew the subject would come up.

In the days leading up to the competition, I was skating great in practices, although I was on antibiotics for a bad case of bronchitis. People were again telling me that I was going to make the world team, which meant I'd have to place in the top three. I would have been happy with fourth or fifth, especially given that I was sick. The bronchitis wore me out, and I couldn't breathe. So even though everyone said I looked great on the ice, I felt sluggish and was having trouble catching my breath. The antibiotics helped, but they left me feeling a little unsteady.

All I had to do was get past my first combination jump in the short program and I knew I'd have a chance of coming close to meeting my goal for the year. As I stepped onto the ice, I had these two voices both going in my head. One was saying, "Okay, don't miss it. You missed it last year, but it was a stupid mistake. You can do it. You know you can." And the other voice was saying, "You're going to miss it. You're going to miss it."

The voices were really battling it out as I skated into my approach for the combination jump, but I tried not to listen to them. I took off into the air, did three and a half revolutions, and landed smoothly. Right from there I took off into the double toe, and another smooth landing. I did it! With the audience cheering me on, I was really pumped and couldn't wait to do the next jump.

Now all I had to do was watch for that big hole I'd made in the ice during the warm-up when I practiced my third jump, the triple flip. This was a really easy jump, and I never fell on it. So I skated around, spotted the hole in the ice, took an extra second to skate past it, got into position, took off into the jump, and bam! I was concentrating so hard on missing the hole that I screwed up on my timing and wound up doing an extra half-revolution, landed forward, and fell on the ice.

I guess I didn't do a good job of maintaining my enthusiasm as I skated the rest of the program, because both my technical and artistic marks were really low. I wound up in ninth place. It was humiliating and, as usual, I was furious.

Just as the year before, I came back from blowing the short program and aced the long. I got a standing ovation for the second year in a row, one of only two ovations during the entire men's singles competition. But despite a fabulous performance, the judges weren't generous with my marks. I don't even think they were fair. After my poor showing in the short, they probably weren't expecting much, and they scored me according to their expectations instead of how well I did. No one ever said this wasn't a subjective sport. I placed seventh in the long and seventh overall. It was a terrible disappointment.

Whatever my own experience at nationals in Detroit, it completely paled in comparison to what happened to Olympic bronze medalist Nancy Kerrigan. As everyone knows, Nancy was clubbed on the knee by a paid attacker whose trail eventually led back to rival Tonya Harding's ex-husband. But it was days before any arrests were made, and by then Tonya had skated to a national championship, while Nancy recovered from the brutal assault.

I don't have any firsthand, behind-the-scenes stories to tell about the attack on Nancy Kerrigan. I was in the stands at the time it happened and was just as shocked and horrified as everyone else. But in the aftermath, I was also shocked at how surprised the public was to learn of the intense rivalries between skaters. It was hardly news to any of us. Skating is a highly competitive, subjectively judged sport, where every skater is out for himself or herself. Given the time and money it takes to become a competitive skater with any hope of ever getting to the top, you have to be. And given the huge amounts of money to be earned at the top, you're going to do what you have to—well, usually within reason—to stay ahead of anyone who threatens your position.

You don't have to be nasty about it or share your feelings about your rivals with reporters, but behind the scenes people say and do all kinds of things, from making nasty remarks and whispering put-downs to obvious efforts by skaters and their coaches to psych out the competition. It's hardly uncommon.

Up until the attack on Nancy Kerrigan, the USFSA managed to preserve a facade of good manners and civility. That all came crashing down at the '94 nationals. But you don't hear anyone at the USFSA complaining about it with any sincerity, because the attack, the nasty remarks, the intrigue, and the rivalries resulted in huge numbers of new television viewers who couldn't seem to get enough of competitive figure skating. And that, of course, translated into enormous profits for the USFSA from fat new contracts with the television networks. Women's figure skating is now the second most watched sport on television after NFL football. Thanks in no small part to the Tonya Harding affair.

Will we ever see another incident like the attack on Nancy Kerrigan? Who knows? Maybe that's part of the reason why so many people are glued to their television sets, watching.

11

—

TIME FOR A CHANGE

Having blown it at nationals yet again, I was pissed, and in no mood to accept responsibility for having done badly. It was the bronchitis. It was the hole in the ice. It was the prejudiced judges. It was Rick's fault.

I couldn't do anything about the bronchitis, the hole in the ice, or the judges. That left Rick, and I could do something about him. He kept telling me that there was always next year, and all I could think was if I came back for another year, it wasn't going to be with him.

I went home from Detroit feeling really depressed and frustrated. For the first couple of weeks, I spent a lot of time thinking about quitting competitive skating. The only problem was, I didn't know what I'd do if I didn't skate. I could turn professional and try for one of the skating shows, but I wasn't quite ready for that. If I was going to retire from competitive skating, I wanted to do it after winning a national champion-ship. At least then I'd be in a position to make a decent living. I could also have quit and started coaching full-time. I liked working with kids and they really liked working with me, but I couldn't imagine being behind the scenes all the time.

So in the end, I decided I wasn't ready to bow out just yet, and after talking over all my options with Reuben and Wayne, I decided to give it one more shot. But first, I needed to find a new coach.

To justify finding a new coach, I convinced myself that I felt trapped by Rick. I didn't really think about what I wanted in a new coach. I just knew that I didn't want a coach who handled every aspect of my skating. I wanted to be able to work with an outside choreographer. I wanted to have my music professionally recorded. I wanted to work with a costume designer to pick out my costumes. And the way I saw it in that moment was that Rick would never allow me to do any of that, so I had to find a new coach.

I never stopped to think exactly how it was that what I saw as Rick's possessiveness contributed to the problems I was having with my skating, but that's what I focused on. Maybe I should have thought more about what the specific problems were— such as my shaky self-confidence and my difficulties with pressure, for example. But I wasn't interested in doing a major self-evaluation. What I wanted was a quick, easy fix, and changing coaches was relatively quick and easy. Or at least I thought it would be.

After talking things over with Reuben and Wayne, I decided to go with their advice and call a top coach in Los Angeles who trained one of the best women skaters. They thought I should sound him out before deciding what to do about Rick.

Making the call on my own was a big step. This was the kind of call my sister usually made for me, so I was really nervous doing it myself. My heart was pounding as I punched in the numbers, and he answered on the second ring. I introduced myself and told him that I was thinking of changing coaches. Right off, he started telling me what I had to work on and how I had to change my programs: new choreography, new costumes, new everything. And I was going to have to train a lot harder: work, work, work! I wanted to compete, but what he was describing was more like army boot camp than figure skating. It hadn't occurred to me that a coach would have his own ideas about what I needed.

After we talked for a while, he told me that if I was interested in training with him, I should call him back after I fired Rick. But I knew before I hung up the phone that he wasn't the one. Besides, working with him would have meant moving to Los Angeles, and I was nervous about going far from home. In the months since George got heatstroke he'd started developing some AIDS-related illnesses. It wasn't too serious yet, but I thought it wasn't a good idea to move far away, because someone would have to take care of him when he got really sick. I knew that would be more than Mom could handle on her own, and Laura, as I said, was so disgusted with George that she could hardly bring herself even to talk to him. The only one left was me.

The next call I made was to Rick. At that point I knew I didn't want to work with him, so I thought I'd better get it over with. This wasn't easy, because even though I blamed Rick for what had happened in Detroit, deep down I really liked him. Also, I wasn't all that confident in my ability to make my own decisions. What if quitting Rick wasn't the right thing to do? Nonetheless, I made the call. I was pretty direct and told Rick that I needed a change. And he said, "Okay, babe"—which is what he always called me—"who are you going to train with?" He sounded so calm and casual that I was kind of shocked, but as we talked more, I could hear that his voice was a little unsteady, as if he were trying not to cry, which made me feel terrible. I told Rick that I was still looking for a coach, that I hadn't yet decided. It was just a casual conversation, or so it seemed, which ended with Rick saying, "It's been great working with you." Then I thanked him for everything, including getting me to internationals, and we said good-bye.

So now I was free. By then I'd decided I had to have a coach in the Bay Area because I didn't want to be far from home in case George started getting really sick, so the coach in L.A. was out. That's when I hit on the idea of working with Julie Zusman. She worked at the same rink as Rick, so I'd gotten to know her during the three years I'd trained at Belmont. She'd always been nice to me, really positive. From talking with her over the years, I knew she'd be supportive of my working with choreographers and that she'd let me have my music done professionally.

I called Julie, and we had a long talk about Rick. I wanted to make sure that working with me wouldn't be a problem for her, since I knew they were friends. She told me not to worry, that she was sure it would be okay, and we made an appointment to meet at the rink two days later.

It didn't turn out as I'd expected. I had in mind that Julie had the same easygoing personality as Rick, but I was wrong. As soon as I was on the ice, she made me do all my triples, including my triple axel, and she made me do them ten times each. "Okay! Again! Again! Again!" And if I landed a perfect triple, it still wasn't good enough. "Nice job, but I want to see it again! Again! Again!" In no time I was exhausted, and I tried taking a break. She told me to get back on the ice. "You're going to have to do this and this and this." She'd always been so nice, but now that she was my coach, her whole demeanor changed. She turned into a drill sergeant. I was in shock, and all I could do was pretend that I was enjoying the lesson. I didn't know what else to do.

That first day with Julie taught me an important lesson about what I didn't want in a coach. I didn't want someone who was going to change the way I did things. I already knew how I liked to train. I already knew how to do all my triples. I just wanted someone there for support. And I didn't want to be driven to exhaustion. Julie may have thought I needed to work that hard to win, but I didn't think so.

The whole first week I couldn't figure out how I was going to get out of working with Julie, and I went along with whatever she wanted to do. We listened to music for my new long program and picked out a classical version of "Firebird." I'd been using the disco "Firebird" for years, and it seemed like a good time to change. I should probably have ditched the disco music years before, but it was fun skating to it.

Once we had a rough cut of the music, we started laying out where the jumps were going to be. The music is strong, so it was easy to figure out where to put things. For example, you start out with the most difficult triple, because you want to do that when you have the most energy. Then you go to an easy jump and then build to the other more difficult ones as the music builds. You also want to do the biggest jump somewhere in the middle of the program at the peak of a crescendo. You fit the spins in where it sounds like they should be. And through-out the program you have to find your resting points so you don't get exhausted.

Once we were done laying out the jumps, Julie had me go through the whole program, doing doubles where the triples would eventually go. Now, this was just the bare bones of the program, no choreography, just the jumps. It was really hard, and by the time I got through the four and a half minutes, I was tired. I was ready for a break, but Julie insisted I go through the program again, and toward the end she wanted me doing triple jumps instead of doubles. Then I had to do the whole program *again,* but this time she wanted the triples all the way through. It was too much. After the first week and a half I started making excuses and not showing up. I'd tell Julie I had to go down to San Jose to help take care of my brother, which was a lie, but I had to get away from her and figure out what to do. I felt especially guilty because Julie was really nice about it and told me to just make sure that I practiced while I was away. And she added, "Tell your brother I said hi, and that I hope he feels better."

The new Ice Centre had recently opened in San Jose, three miles from my mom's house, and that's where I practiced while I figured out my escape. It's a beautiful facility, with side-by-side Olympic-size rinks, but the best part about skating at the Ice Centre was that Laura was there teaching her young students. So I got to spend a lot of time with her and I met her best friends, John Brancato and Kevin Peeks, who also taught there. They worked as a team; Kevin is the jump expert and John does choreography. Kevin has auburn hair and John has brown hair. And both were in their early thirties.

I had a really good time getting to know John and Kevin, and by the end of the week I was thinking maybe I'd start training with them at the Ice Centre. I talked to Laura about it, and she thought it was a great idea.

In the meantime, Julie was calling me every day, asking how my skating was going. And I'd tell her everything was fine. At the end of the week she asked if I was coming back the next day, and I made up some lie about George not doing well and my needing to stay another day. She said, "Okay, just give me a call when you know you're coming back. I hope he feels better." I let another whole week go by and didn't call her.

I loved being back in my hometown, skating at the new Ice Centre and having Laura watch me while I practiced and make suggestions on how to improve my jumps and spins. I was starting to get really motivated about my skating, and that's what helped me make the decision to leave Julie and start working with John and Kevin. Everything about being in San Jose seemed right.

I should have called Julie and told her I wasn't coming back, but I took the coward's way out and waited for her to call me, and by then she'd heard through the grapevine that I was skating with John and Kevin. She was furious. I tried to tell her that it was best for me to be in San Jose because my brother was sick, which again was a lie, but I was trying to save myself. It didn't work. Julie said I could have trained with her and commuted, which was true. I should have just told her the truth, but that didn't cross my mind until it was too late to salvage even a friendship.

Ironically, John and Kevin ended up driving me even harder than Julie had done, but by the time I found out how tough they were it was way too late to back out. It all started with a meeting at Reuben and Wayne's house. Laura had talked to John and Kevin about working with me, and they suggested we get together and talk about it. So Reuben and Wayne had a little dinner party—I was still living there, despite what I'd said to Julie about moving home to San Jose to be with George—and Laura, John, and Kevin came over. We had a really nice time, mostly talking about skating, and then after dinner they put me in this little chair and told me what they thought I needed.

Do you know how on those television police dramas they put the suspect in a chair and grill him? Well, that's what it felt like, except instead of asking me questions, John and Kevin lectured me. They sat me down and told me that I needed a total makeover: conservative outfits, great choreography, cut the feminine moves, shave the beard, get rid of the earring, new shorter hairstyle, new publicity pictures, and professionally recorded music. They were making all these comparisons to how I did things in the past and how things were going to be different in the future. No walking around in jeans and a T-shirt at competitions. I could only wear the best, most conservative clothes whenever I was off the ice. And the whole time they're throwing all this at me, Laura and Reuben and Wayne were nodding in agreement, saying, "Yes, we agree. You're right!"

I couldn't believe what was happening, but I didn't dare say anything because I knew Laura really wanted me to work with John and Kevin. So I decided to let them take over. They all seemed to think this was what I needed, so why argue? But I wasn't convinced that changing the package was going to make all that big a difference with the judges. As long as I kept giving them obvious reasons to give me low scores—such as crashing into the ice instead of landing on my feet—no new haircut or conservative costume was going to make any difference.

As skeptical as I was, the repackaging still made some sense. John and Kevin didn't want to give the judges any reason not to award me the scores I deserved. It was no secret that the judges were capable of marking you down if they didn't approve of the way you looked and acted on or off the ice. So if the judges didn't like the long hair, cut it. They have a problem with the earring? Get rid of it. They want the skaters to look like young ladies and gentlemen? Dress for the country club instead of the hood. They want the men to skate like men? Stop skating like a girl. Well, there wasn't a lot I could do about that. There was no pretending I wasn't gay, and there was no hiding the fact I was feminine. John and Kevin never suggested I try acting more masculine because they knew I wasn't that good an actor. No one's *that* good an actor. I am who I am and the world would just have to live with that.

Once John and Kevin had me on the ice, I discovered that superficial repackaging wasn't all they had in mind. They believed I needed better programs and that I needed to work much harder if I was going to land all my jumps and win. That meant a brutal training regimen on and off the ice. On the ice, John and Kevin worked me harder than I'd ever been worked in my life. And off the ice, they set me up with a trainer who put me through a punishing hour-and-a-half weight-training and aerobic program, five days a week.

Kevin did the choreography for my long program. We used the same classical version of "Firebird" that Julie Zusman and I had chosen, and Kevin pretty much kept all the elements I'd worked out with Julie, although he threw in two more triples. "Firebird" is tough enough to skate to; now John and Kevin had me doing eight triples without a single stop during the program. Normally you have two or three stops at points where the music changes, so you can catch your breath. John and Kevin were adamant: no stops, and push like hell the whole time. With the long program you have the option of going ten seconds under four and a half minutes or ten seconds over. They wanted me on the ice and going, going, going for the full 4:40.

I liked Kevin's choreography, but it was very intricate. And right from the start they had me doing full run-throughs with all the choreography. The first few times they gave me a break and let me do the program with double jumps instead of the triples. Then they had me do the whole thing with triple jumps in the beginning, doubles in the middle, and triples at the end. After two weeks I was doing full run-throughs with all the triples. I thought they were trying to kill me.

I was not a sport about being driven so hard, although I tried to put on a good front because I wanted to please Laura, especially since she was paying for everything. But as I said, I'm not a good actor. So more often than not John and Kevin would get out on the ice with me when I wasn't giving it my all, and they would literally push me, or they'd skate along-side me and yell, "Push! Push! Push!" John and Kevin would be screaming at the top of their lungs at the arena, embarrass-ing me in front of all these other skaters. I couldn't stand it, but because they were Laura's friends, all I could say whenev-er she asked how things were going was "I love it." In fact, I *hated* it!

Laura was paying for everything out of her own pocket with money she earned from coaching. She wrote checks for John and Kevin, for the professional trainer, for the photographer, for the hairstylist, for practice outfits, for costumes, for profes-sionally recorded music, for the trainer. I have this memory of Laura writing check after check after check. I felt guilty, but there was no other source of support. I had hardly any USFSA grant money, and with all the training, there was no time to do any coaching work on the side. So if not for Laura's generosity, I don't know what I would have done. As much as I didn't like being driven so hard, with Laura investing all that money in me, there was no way I could let her down.

Then in the middle of being driven by John and Kevin to what I thought was my absolute limit, George got really sick. Mom asked me if I could come home to help her because George was too weak to do much for himself, and she needed help. That night Reuben and Wayne helped me pack, and two days later I was back home in my old bedroom. But with Dad gone and George sick, home was nothing like it had been before. Without Dad there, the house seemed empty, and with George sick in the next room, it was a struggle to sleep at night without wondering what nightmares awaited all of us under that roof.

12

LIFE IN HELL

The next three months at home with George were like a descent into hell. At first it was no big deal. I was mostly going to the bank, shopping for groceries, or going out to buy George's favorite foods from Jack in the Box. He was supposed to be on a special low-fat diet, but just like our father, George loved all that greasy stuff, and it was about the only pleasure left in his life. Running around and doing all those things made me feel useful. I was really making a difference in someone's life, instead of just focusing on my own.

Within a few weeks of my moving home, George's condition declined precipitously, and Mom and I were dealing with all the realities of taking care of someone with late-stage AIDS, and that's when things got difficult. There were all the doctor visits, trips to the hospital when George was really feeling sick and needed emergency treatment, and making sure he was taking the various medications that were keeping him alive.

The worst was the intravenous treatment George had to get

at home every other day. He had developed a viral infection in his eyes, so he had a permanent catheter surgically implanted in his chest. That way, he could get an infusion of medication without having to puncture a new vein every time. People from a service came in to hook up the IV, but George hated them. Sometimes he'd call them up and tell them not to come, that "Rudy and my mom will take care of it."

From watching the home health care people do George's IV, we managed to figure it out and do it ourselves, but it was complicated. First, Mom and I would put on latex gloves. Then we had to flush George's catheter with saline solution. Then everything had to be swabbed with alcohol before we inserted the needle into the line. You had to do the whole thing just right and make sure no air bubbles were trapped in the tube. George would get so mad if there was one little bubble. You'd be trying your best and he'd be screaming that you were trying to kill him.

George was always yelling and cussing at us, but we never screamed back at him, ever. We knew he was dying and so did he, so being angry seemed like a normal thing. Sometimes he'd apologize and tell us what a tough time he was having, but he never said thank you. A thank-you would have been nice, but George couldn't bring himself to say it. That's just how he was.

While George was still well enough, I took him to church once a week. This was his idea, not mine. I believe in God, but organized religion was something I never liked. I don't think George was all that interested in church either, but one of his friends went to this place, and I think George was looking for some sort of hope. If I were in his shoes, I would have been looking for hope anyplace I could find it, too.

The church was one of those television-evangelist-type things, with a thousand people in the audience. The minister was dressed up in a fancy suit. His wife was in the front row, wearing a beautiful hat and diamonds. When they sent around the collection plate, it didn't seem to occur to anyone that what they put in the plate was going right to the minister's wife to pay for all her fancy clothes and jewelry.

George's favorite part of church was when the minister did his "heal the sick" routine. I couldn't stand it, but George always wanted to go up and get healed. I didn't want to ruin it for him and say, "Yeah, right, George, he's going to cure your AIDS," so I stayed in my seat while George went to get healed. When George got to the front of the line, the minister put his hand on George's head, said, "Bless you, child," and theatrically pushed him over into the arms of a couple of congregants who were waiting to catch him. I know George got a kick out of that—he loved the drama of it all—but it did nothing to keep him from going downhill fast.

Before long, George needed help to get from his bed to the bathroom. Then, to make it easier for him, we put a toilet right next to his bed. At first he managed it himself, but after a couple of weeks I had to lift him out of bed and put him on the seat. He was like a dead weight. Then I'd wait while he sat on the toilet and didn't do anything. So then I'd put him back in bed, and as soon as I was out of the room, he'd mess his sheets. "Rudy!" I'd go back into his room and pick him up off the bed, and Mom would clean and dry him. Then I'd put George in a chair, and Mom would change the sheets. After that happened several times, we decided he needed diapers.

I hated changing George's diapers, but it had to be done. Mom and I usually did it as a team. I would undo his diaper and lift him up, while she slid the diaper out from under him. Then we'd roll him over on his side, which he hated because it hurt him to have all his weight on his bony rib cage. Mom would wipe his butt and dry him. Then I'd lift him up and she'd slide a new diaper under him. I'd fasten the diaper and cover him up, and we'd leave the room. A minute later he'd mess his diaper again. "Rudy!" Most of the time he went through five diapers a day. Some days it was more.

We kept George as clean as we could with sponge baths, but when he started to stink, we'd put him in the tub and give him a bath, which he didn't like. He was always a very clean person, always took showers, but once he was sick, he didn't care anymore and didn't like the bother of being washed.

Bath time was an ordeal. Our house was big for a trailer, but it was still a trailer and the bathrooms were pretty small. Getting George around the sliding glass door and into the tub required planning. You'd have to get his feet in first, then twist around and get him to slide in. I'd scrub his back and Mom would wash his hair. If you handed him the soap, he'd wash whatever he could reach, but slowly, like a little child. Then he'd sit there in the tub while we poured water over him to rinse off the soap. It was so sad looking at my big brother, who was just skin and bones.

Once we were done, we'd have to get George out of the tub and dry him. I'd hold George up while Mom quickly dried him. Toward the end he was down to barely a hundred pounds, but a hundred pounds is still a hundred pounds.

All of this wasn't close to the worst of it. George's brain disease almost drove us all crazy. He'd scream because of the pain in his head. The screaming was unbearable, and it usually happened at night. I had this medication the doctor gave me to spray on his skull, which helped kill the pain. But first it made him scream even more before he began feeling better.

Sometimes George would holler and carry on for God knows what reasons. He had dementia and would wake up screaming, not knowing where he was or what was chasing him. My room was right next to his and I'd hear him talking nonsense, which was usually followed by screaming and banging on the walls. I'd get up and go into his room, and his bed would be empty. I'd find him hiding behind the curtains, cowering, like I was an ax murderer out to get him. At moments like that, he'd have no idea who I was and I'd have to convince him I wasn't going to hurt him. Eventually, I'd get him back in his bed. And just as I'd start drifting off to sleep, it would start all over again.

A couple of times I couldn't decide whether to put a pillow over my head so I could sleep or put a pillow over George's head to smother him. He suffered so much I thought maybe he would be better off dead. And at times I thought I'd be better off if he were dead. It's hard not to have those feelings, but it made me feel terribly guilty.

Maybe if all I'd been doing was taking care of George, I could have handled it better. But I was also training harder than I ever had in my life and I was at the ice rink starting at six in the morning, five days a week.

Let me give you an idea of what one of my days was like: It's five o'clock in the afternoon, and George calls me into his room. He's shaking and sweating or having some kind of convulsions. I don't want to call for the ambulance, because it's too expensive. So I get George out of bed, and Mom and I put him in his beat-up old car—the Trans Am was, by now, long gone. I always brought a bag with us in the car, because you never knew if George was going to throw up. We learned that lesson the hard way.

I drive to the hospital, hoping the whole way that the car isn't going to break down. When we get to the hospital, they put him in a bed in the emergency room, and we wait for them to run tests to figure out what's wrong. The worst test was the one where they had to take fresh blood right out of an artery. They'd take this huge needle and carefully dig under the veins in his wrist, looking for an artery. That just freaked me out and I'd have to walk away. Unfortunately, even in the waiting area I could still hear George screaming in pain.

After staying with George for three or four hours—until it became obvious that they'd be keeping him overnight—I'd tell him that I was going home, that I'd see him in the morning. It was so nice to come home to a peaceful house knowing that I could get into bed and go to sleep without having to worry that George was going to have a fit in the middle of the night. But then the phone would ring at 3 A.M., and it was the hospital calling, saying that they were releasing George and I should come get him. This happened a number of times, and I'll never understand why they couldn't just let him stay the night. So I'd get up, get dressed, and drive to the hospital. They'd leave George in the lobby waiting area, slumped in a chair. He wasn't having convulsions or anything, so I guess he was better, but I didn't think this was the most humane way to treat a patient.

I'd have George put his arm around my shoulder and I'd put my arm around his waist, and we'd walk slowly out to the car. When we pulled up to the house, I called out to Mom to come help, and we got on either side of George and walked him up the stairs. We put him to bed, and by then he was so completely exhausted, he usually fell right to sleep.

There was no time for me to sleep, because I had to be at the ice rink at 6:00 in the morning. So I'd take a shower, get my skating clothes on, and drive over to the Ice Centre. To warm up, I did all of my jumps from 6:15 to 6:45 A.M. Then Kevin would say it was time for my lesson, which was a full run-through of my long program, with Kevin skating alongside me, telling me, "Push! Push! Push! Do this! Do that! Don't stop! Keep going! Faster! Push!"

A lot of times, I'd say I couldn't go on, and Kevin would grab my arm and demand that I keep going. Sometimes he screamed at me at the top of his lungs, "Keep going, goddammit!" And then I'd walk through the rest of the program, but I had to do the jumps. A lot of times I fell, but he wouldn't let me stop. By the end of the long program my heart was pounding so hard it felt like it would explode.

My lesson would go until 7:15, but John and Kevin kept me on the ice practicing my jumps and my long program—doing doubles instead of triples—for another hour. And whenever I slowed down or tried to stop, I'd hear their mantra again: "Push, Rudy! Push!" Finally, at 8:15, there was a fifteen-minute ice cut, and I got to rest. But not for long, because then I had another hour of skating, during which I did the short program and had another half-hour lesson.

From the Ice Centre I went to the gym to work out with my personal trainer, and I was out of there at 11:15 A.M. and home by 11:30. The rest of the day was spent running errands, going shopping, and looking after George. In the afternoon we'd bring him out to the front room and set him up on the sofa in preparation for his IV treatment, which was around 5:00 or 6:00. I'd go make dinner, and we'd try to get George to eat, but the IV would make him sick, so he was always throwing up. By 9:00 P.M. we got George into bed. If we were lucky, he slept. If we weren't, he'd start babbling nonsense to himself and start screaming. It was a nightmare, but worse, because we were awake.

The weekend was such a relief. I was so happy not to have to get up in the morning to go skating, which meant I could go out if George was having a good night. I'd give my mom the telephone number of the club I was going to and tell her to call me if she needed me. It was never hard to find me, because I was just sitting at the bar drinking. I knew that drinking as much as I did wasn't good for me, but I didn't care. It made me forget what was going on at home.

Drinking on the weekend wasn't always enough, and sometimes during the week, when George was asleep, I'd go out as well. But then I'd have to deal with John and Kevin in the morning. If they smelled alcohol on my breath, they'd give me a lecture and then punish me by working me even harder than usual. They knew George was sick, but I didn't want to tell them everything that was going on at home because I knew they'd think I was making excuses and then they'd push me even harder. At least that's what I thought would happen.

As much as I drank, the alcohol wasn't doing enough to help get me through, and I started doing speed again. With speed, I didn't have to worry about being tired. I could be up all night taking care of George, wrapping his head in towels to stop the pain, changing his diapers, whatever, and I could go right to the ice rink and still have enough energy to skate. The downside was that the drugs made my heart pound even harder than it usually did, which was terrifying. But I didn't dare tell John and Kevin to ease up. They might have quit being my coaches, and that would have been worse than anything. Without that daily routine at the arena, I would probably have lost my mind.

For the several weeks I used speed, before I ran out of money, it was great. I'd snort some speed and I'd feel as if the world were wonderful, that I could do no wrong. Sure, George was sick, but I was taking care of him. I was getting things done. On the other hand, I was wired, I couldn't eat, and even when I felt tired, I couldn't sleep. Also, even though I was feeling up, it's not like I was really happy. I don't know how to describe it, but speed is a depressing up. Clearly, this was not the permanent solution to my life, but in the short term, I thought it helped.

The real answer to being overwhelmed was to get someone to help us with George. I don't know why I thought it was my responsibility to do everything myself, but at the time that's how I felt. I went so far as to tell Laura that I didn't want her helping because I didn't want her to see George waste away. Given her less-than-positive feelings for George, I didn't have to work hard to convince her. No one else stepped forward to offer help. George had a lot of so-called friends at the bars, but not a single one of them ever came to see him. The only person who ever came by to visit was an old high school friend, who brought his wife and kids along.

Finally, what pushed me to get help was an upcoming trip to Vienna. It was September 1994, I had this competition to go to, and I knew Mom couldn't handle George on her own. I called Laura and told her she had to get me some help, and within a week we had one nurse from 8:00 A.M. to noon and then another nurse from 2:00 until 5:30 P.M. Of course, except for having to change his diapers, George would be great during the day, sleeping most of the time. But as soon as the nurse was out the door, he was up and screaming and banging his head against the wall. It was like living in an insane asylum.

During the last month before I left for Vienna, George got weaker and weaker. During the day he couldn't do anything for himself. He could hardly move. But at night—I don't know where he found the energy—he'd still scream and bang on the walls. Eventually, he'd tire himself out and then was so quiet that I found myself checking in on him just to see if he was still breathing. On the one hand I'd hope he was gone, but on the other I'd hope he was still breathing.

By the time I was preparing to go off to Vienna, it looked as if George could die any day. He didn't recognize me or Mom and he'd stopped talking. If you asked him something, you were lucky to get a blank stare. I remember the morning of the day I was leaving. I was in my room, packing my things and crying. I was thinking that maybe I shouldn't go, that maybe George would die while I was gone, but I needed to go. I'd been training really hard and I was skating great. If I was going to do well at the '95 nationals in January, it would help for me to place in the top five in Vienna, to show that I could compete at an international level. I feared I was being selfish, but I told myself that George would want me to go.

Laura came over to the house to drive me to the airport, where I was to meet up with John and Kevin. Before I left, I went in to say good-bye to George. He was completely out of it, but I always liked to think that the real George was still in there, that he just couldn't communicate with us anymore.

I went over to the bed and put my hand on his hand, which was cold and really limp. He was just skin and bones, and it made me uncomfortable to touch him. I said, "George, can you hear me?" He kind of looked at me. I told him, "I'm leaving for Vienna now. I'm going to compete and I'm going to try to win this one for you. You're in good hands. I love you." No response. But as I turned to leave, my brother said, "I love you, too, Rudy." And he said it in his old voice, as if he'd never been sick. I was so shocked that I laughed. I went back to the side of his bed, put my hand on his again, but by then he had disappeared back into semiconsciousness. Later, Laura told me that he never said another word after I left.

As the plane took off, I was overwhelmed with both a sense of relief and regret. I was relieved to have the responsibility of caring for George lifted from my shoulders, even if only for a few days. I felt regret, because George had just recognized me and I didn't want to leave him. I was especially fearful that he would die before I got back. I wasn't there when my father died, and I wanted to be there for George at the end.

Given what I'd just left behind at home, I don't know how I managed to do so well in Vienna. Right from the beginning I was doing great in the practices, even in comparison to the often unbeatable Russian skaters. I got second in the short program, placing just behind Ilia Kulik, a young, up-and-coming Russian skater who had an arsenal of powerful triple jumps. In the long program I moved ahead of Ilia and won the gold medal. I was so excited that my worries about George momentarily slipped from my mind.

Back at the hotel, I went to the front desk to ask if there were any messages for me. There weren't. I thought it was really weird that no one had called. Laura always called to see how I'd done in a competition. That's when it hit me, and I turned to Kevin and said, "I think George died." Kevin, who had already talked to Laura, said that he had.

Of course I'd known it was coming, but there was no way to prepare for the news that George was gone. I ran down the hall crying and called Laura from my room. She told me that George had died peacefully in his sleep and that she was making funeral arrangements. We didn't talk for long, and once we hung up, I cried for most of the night.

I found out later that Laura had called John and Kevin an hour before we left to go to the arena for the short program to tell them that George had died during the night. She told them to wait until after I did the long program the next day to say anything to me. I couldn't do anything to change things, and Laura knew I'd never get through the long program if I knew that George had passed away. She was right.

The day after I learned of my brother's death, on my twenty-fifth birthday, John, Kevin, and I left to go back to California. It was a long trip home, and the whole way I was thinking about what the funeral was going to be like, who would come, what people would say.

George had wanted a really nice funeral with a fine wooden

casket and everything. He'd been saving the disability money he'd been getting from the government, but only a thousand dollars was in his account by the time he died. And Laura had spent so much money on my father's funeral the year before that there just wasn't enough money to do what George wanted. So we had to have him cremated, which left some money for renting a room at the funeral home and flowers.

We had the funeral at the Chapel of Flowers, the same place where we had my dad's funeral, but in a smaller room next door. Instead of a casket, there was just a framed picture of George from before he got sick, and it was surrounded by flowers. The room was packed with people, but other than George's one high school friend and his wife and children, not a single one of his friends came. None of the bar crowd. Not one. Everybody who was there came for me and Laura. They were all skating people. It made me feel good that they cared enough about us to be there, but I felt sad for George that so few people who were there even knew him. That more than anything made me cry.

All the time I was taking care of George, I never forgot that I could just as easily have been the one dying of AIDS. I didn't run around the way George did and I wasn't promiscuous. But you don't need to be promiscuous to get infected with HIV. All you need to do is have sex with an infected partner and either not know enough to protect yourself or, for whatever reasons, not take the proper precautions.

When I had sex for the first time, I didn't know I needed to practice safe sex. Given that this was in the late 1980s, you might find that hard to believe. But I was completely immersed in my skating. I never picked up the newspaper to read about anything much, and I would change the channel when the television news came on. AIDS also wasn't something my parents talked about at home, and it wasn't something I learned about in school. I wasn't in school past the eighth grade, and even if they had taught us about AIDS before high school, I was only going half-time, so there was only a fifty-fifty chance I would have been there to hear about it.

I don't want to give the impression that I was completely ignorant. I knew what AIDS was, but I didn't know enough to think of it as something I had to worry about. Until my early twenties, when I started paying more attention to the AIDS epidemic and its impact on gay men, it didn't occur to me that I needed to take any kind of precautions.

Fortunately for me I'm okay. But I worry about the young skaters today, who, like me, often don't learn about AIDS in school or from their parents, and don't know enough to protect themselves from this preventable plague. This is where I think the USFSA can make a huge difference. Every year, the top competitive skaters go to sectionals and nationals. These are the skaters who are most likely to have missed learning about AIDS because of their demanding training schedules. Why not bring in someone from the skating community who is infected with HIV to talk about it? And to be sure everyone attends, make the presentation mandatory for both male and female skaters. If you don't come to the presentation, you don't skate. Plain and simple. Nothing will make more of an impression on these young skaters than hearing from someone who is part of the skating community.

In an ideal world, this wouldn't be a job the USFSA would have to do. But we don't live in an ideal world, and the USFSA owes it to its young skaters to give them the education they're not getting at home or in school. Even if it saves just one life, it would be worth the effort.

13

1995 Nationals

Once the funeral was over, I tried not to think about George. It was just like I'd handled my dad's death and Jim Hulick's death. I had to block it out or I would have been overwhelmed by my emotions. While that may not have been the best way to deal with these losses, that's what worked for me, or at least it's worked so far. It wasn't that I forgot about George, Dad, and Jim; I remembered them in my prayers every night. I just didn't dwell on it. I couldn't, not if I wanted to go on living.

After I returned from Vienna, there was no letup in my training schedule. John and Kevin were determined to get me into even better shape for sectionals and the 1995 nationals. I hated how hard they made me work, but I had to admit that they were making me a better skater. I just wasn't having any fun doing it.

In November, I went to the regional competition in nearby Redwood City to watch some of my sister's students. I wasn't there to compete, because I'd done well enough the year before to skip over regionals and go right to the Pacific Coast sectionals. My old coach, Rick Inglesi, was there and he gave me a big hug. He looked great, so I was surprised after regionals to hear that he'd been in the hospital. Someone told me that Rick had AIDS and wasn't doing well. I knew that Rick's partner had died the year before from AIDS, but it never occurred to me that Rick would get sick, too. Perhaps, I was naïve, or maybe it was just wishful thinking.

I called Rick and made a date to come visit him in the hospital. It was odd to see him there because he looked just as he always had. We talked for a while and he seemed perfectly normal, but then all of a sudden he got things all mixed up, and he started talking nonsense. I didn't want to ask, but I figured he had some sort of brain disease, like George. But he looked so good that I was sure it would be a long time before he died. I stayed with him for a couple of hours. Before leaving for home I gave Rick a kiss and a hug and said, "I'll see you when you get home. I'll come visit." He said, "I love you." And I added, "I love you, too."

A few weeks later, before I'd had a chance to talk to Rick again, Laura drove me over to John and Kevin's house for our trip up to Oregon for the Pacific Coast sectionals. I walked into their kitchen, and John said, "By the way, did you hear that Rick passed away?" I was in shock and I grabbed the back of a chair to steady myself. I didn't say a word on our drive to the airport, and during the whole flight to Oregon I thought about Rick and all that he'd done for me. I didn't know how I was going to compete, but I couldn't just go home. Once again, I had to block out everything, and by this time I'd become an expert at that, so much so that by the time we got off the plane I felt completely numb.

Despite how emotionally dead I felt, I skated great all week at practice in Oregon. My short program that year was choreographed to music from the movie *Strictly Ballroom*. I was skating to a Spanish piece, and I had a costume to match. I wore black pants, a bolero jacket over a black vest, and a white shirt with a little red tie. The whole program had a Latin feel to it.

In addition to all the required moves, the program had a lot of intricate choreography. I opened with a triple-axel, double-toe-loop combination. Then I went into a flying change sit spin. I skated around for the easy triple flip, which was followed by my straight-line footwork. After that I skated around and did another required spin, two sets of circular footwork, and then a required double axel. I finished with my traveling spin.

When it came time to do the program in competition, I felt really confident. I knew there was no way I'd miss my opening combination. I went into the jump and I did a single axel—a single axel! I was stunned, but in the split second after I landed, I figured I had better do a triple toe loop to try to make up for it, and I landed that fine. But still, I couldn't make up for having blown the triple axel, and for the rest of the program I was thinking that I'd just given away my Pacific Coast title. I should have been concentrating on the program instead of beating myself up, because at the end of it I stepped out of the double axel, which was a really easy jump.

As I skated off the ice, I could see the disappointment on John's and Kevin's faces. They didn't say much of anything, and we all walked together down the hallway back to the dressing room. I was kind of curious to see what my marks were, but I was too embarrassed to wait around at the edge of the rink. My technical marks were really low, around 3.6, but my style marks were mostly 5.6s. It would be next to impossible to win the Pacific Coast title for a fourth year in a row.

My main competition was standing nearby when the marks came up, and I could hear his coach say, "You're going to win this! You're going to win this!" And then he went out and made the same mistakes I did. Because my style marks were so high, I beat him and placed first in the short program. I felt very lucky.

My long program was again choreographed to "Firebird," and even before I got on the ice I was thinking about how exhausting a program it was going to be. But with the exception of two-footing the landing on a triple lutz, I made no mistakes. I won first place again and got a standing ovation from the small crowd in the stands. John and Kevin were ecstatic, and I was mostly relieved.

I wish I could say that I had a great attitude going into the 1995 nationals in Providence, Rhode Island, but I didn't. Despite my win at sectionals, I felt like I'd be fighting an uphill battle with the judges at nationals, who I figured would never let me win even if I skated well. I convinced myself that what they really wanted were those all-American, masculine skaters, and as hard as I worked with John and Kevin, and as much as we worked to repackage me, I was still far from that ideal. What made it even more difficult for me was that for a second year in a row I came down with bronchitis just as we were leaving for the competition. John and Kevin didn't pay attention to my complaints and pretended they didn't hear me coughing.

I also wish I'd been able to turn my attitude around and stop blaming everyone and everything. What I needed to do at nationals, if I was going to get through both the short and long programs without falling, was to chase away those negative voices, to really believe in myself. I'd trained hard and skated flawlessly in practice after practice. I just needed to do that again during the competition.

At the first official practice session in Providence, all eyes were on John, Kevin, and me. People wanted to see how I was going to do with my new coaches. This wasn't trivial. A lot of the judges come to the practice sessions to get a sense of how well the various skaters are doing. They start forming their opinions about the skaters well before the actual competition, and what they think of how you skate during practice can have a big impact on the scores they give.

Despite how lousy I felt—I was sure I had a fever—I went out and skated a clean short, including a triple axel, triple toe loop. But it wasn't good enough for John and Kevin. They were furious: "How dare you skate that slow!" I tried explaining to them how hard it was to breathe, but they wouldn't hear it. They ordered me to get back out on the ice and skate my short without the music, and this time they wanted me to do it fast. I told them I couldn't do it, that I was too congested. They wouldn't take no for an answer and forced me to go out and skate, which I did, but this time I wasn't just slow, I missed some of my jumps. They were so mad that they ignored me for the rest of the practice.

As soon as I got off the ice, I went to the health center to see a doctor. I was determined to prove to John and Kevin that I wasn't faking it, that I was really sick. I didn't tell them I was going, but they tracked me down and found me there. The doctor explained to them that I had bronchitis and a fever, and he put me on antibiotics.

John and Kevin played down the whole thing and said I'd be better in no time. We still had three days before the competition began. I thought they could have been a little more sympathetic, but they weren't cutting me any slack. And over the next three days at practice, even with packed audiences, they were yelling at me to push, push, push! I can still hear them yelling, "Push, Rudy!" It was so humiliating in front of my skating peers that I wanted to kill them. Instead, I just missed all my jumps, substituting doubles for triples. It wasn't that I didn't try, I simply had no energy.

By the time the competition began, I was in fact feeling a lot better. The antibiotics had done their magic. I opened my short program with a beautiful triple axel, double toe, and the crowd went crazy. I did my flying chain sit spin, and as I came out of it, I remember thinking, "I'm doing great!" The only thing I had to worry about was getting through the easy triple flip that I'd missed the year before. This time, I was determined that nothing was going to ruin my program. I came around, did a double flip, and fell. I have no idea what happened. I just know that as I dragged myself off the ice, all I wanted to do was go hide.

I finished the program, doing all the arm movements like I didn't care. My performance was lifeless, and that was reflected in the marks. Both my technical and style marks were low. I guess it was obvious to everyone that after my fall I'd given up. Again, John and Kevin didn't say anything, but I could tell they were disappointed. You can guess what I did next, because it was becoming something of a routine. I went back to the hotel and cried my guts out. By now, I was an expert at feeling sorry for myself. And by this time I felt really sorry for myself. I'd worked so hard, Laura had paid so much money, and I'd blown it on an easy jump. All I could think was, "What a waste."

We had one day to practice before the long program, and it was a complete disaster. My trainer had emphasized that the day before a performance you never do a full run-through. John and Kevin knew this, so I went to practice thinking I'd only have to do a few jumps and spins. But during the practice, some of the other skaters did full run-throughs, and as I was warming up, John and Kevin pulled me aside and told me they wanted me to do the whole thing. I said, "I can't." And I'm sure I said it with attitude. In my mind I wasn't prepared to do a whole run-through, and there was no way I was going to do it.

John and Kevin tried to stay calm and explained to me that many people were watching, including a lot of judges, and that it was important for them to see me do my long program and to see me do it well. I looked at them and said, "There's no way I can do it." You could see the steam coming out of their ears, and I quickly backed down. I gave in and said that I'd do it.

When my name was called, I went out and did my program. I missed everything. I told myself it was because I wasn't prepared, that I'd thought I wouldn't have to do the whole program. But in truth I was mad at John and Kevin, and by skating so badly in front of all those people, including the judges, I was punishing them. I wanted to embarrass them. Of course, no one was hurt more by my lousy performance than I was, but that didn't occur to me at the time. I was too focused on being mad and getting even.

When I finished my program, John and Kevin called me over. As soon as they started criticizing me, I skated off. I didn't want to hear it again. I'd had enough of them. And apparently they'd had enough of me, because by the time I turned around, they were walking out of the coliseum. I couldn't believe it, because no coach ever leaves a student on the ice during that kind of practice session, not with everyone watching. But given my attitude, I guess I had it coming.

What I should have done was chase them down the hallway and apologize for my infantile behavior, but unfortunately I wasn't through acting like a four-year-old. I had my sister brought down from the stands by one of the security guards, told her what had happened, and said that I'd never work with John and Kevin again. I told Laura that I wanted her to stand at the side of the rink where the other coaches were standing and to finish the practice session as my coach. I know she was reluctant, but Laura did what I asked.

With Laura at the side of the rink, I actually had fun. In contrast to John and Kevin, she was very reassuring and supportive, never raising her voice. When I was wobbly on a jump, she said, "Oh, that was a close call. Try it again, Rudy. Go and show them what you can do." I wanted to please her, so I went out and did my best.

After the practice, on our way back to the hotel, I told Laura I didn't want John and Kevin standing at the side of the rink during my long program. I wanted Laura to replace them. Without thinking, I'd put Laura into a really difficult spot, because they were her close friends, and I was her temperamental brother who was on the verge of a meltdown.

After some back and forth, Laura convinced John and Kevin not to quit, and she convinced me that it was best to finish the competition with them as my coaches. She said she was too nervous to put me on, and that it wouldn't look good to the judges if John and Kevin suddenly disappeared. I gave in because I wanted to make my sister happy, but I wasn't happy about it.

The next day, backstage at the arena, I was still mad at John and Kevin, but I tried not to show it. It wasn't easy. They kept telling me that I needed to push, push, push. I needed to go fast, fast, fast. I was thinking, "Oh, brother, just let me worry about my jumps." They finally stopped talking to me as we walked out into the arena, but right before I got on the ice, they told me one final time that I needed to push. And I thought to myself, one final time, "Just land your jumps."

I took my position on the ice and took a couple of deep breaths, and the "Firebird" music started. I skated into my first jump and did a huge triple axel, double toe. It was beautiful. I went for the triple lutz and landed it great. Then the slow part started and for some reason my energy just drained out of me. I went for the triple flip and landed smoothly, but then I slipped off the edge of my skate and fell. I hadn't fallen on my long program in a competition in years, so I was stunned. I got back up and went for a triple loop: It was flawless. Then the fast part started and I skated into a triple salchow. I landed it, and the crowd reacted with a cheer. Then I slipped off the edge of my skate and fell again.

I thought John and Kevin would be furious at me for falling, but they were happy that I'd pushed. It didn't feel like I was going fast, but I guess all the training kicked in, and my skating had a lot more speed than usual, which is what the judges like.

My scores were okay, but my competition was strong that year and included Scott Davis and Todd Eldredge. By the time all the other skaters had finished, I found myself in eighth place in the long program. Laura and I were sitting in the stands when the final results were posted. I was eighth overall.

After all that work and all that money, I'd gone nowhere. Laura turned to me and asked, "What are you going to do this year? Do you still want to compete? Do you want to turn professional?" I didn't know what I wanted to do. Going into Providence I'd thought I'd hang on through 1996 because I wanted to compete in San Jose. But now that I'd placed about as low as I'd ever been after working so hard, I wasn't sure. I'd have to think about it. Maybe it was time to quit.

14

AT A CROSSROADS

After Providence, I had nothing to do. I didn't have my sick brother to take care of. There were no international competitions to train for, not after my terrible performance at nationals. There were no coaches yelling at me to push, push, push—I was through with John and Kevin and they were apparently through with me. There were no training grants from the USFSA—I'd done a good job of proving that I wasn't exactly a good investment. There was no Laura telling me what I needed to do—she wanted me to make my own choices. For the first time in my adult life, I was on my own and free to do whatever I wanted. So I sank into a state of total despair.

The way I saw it, I had every reason to feel sorry for myself. I was twenty-five years old, which is getting up there for an athlete. My skating career was pretty much over—how many more years could I keep spending Laura's money and trying and failing to make it to the top? I felt like I had no friends. I had no money. I had virtually no education. I had no boyfriend and had never had a real relationship. I was living with my mother in a trailer park in East San Jose. My father was dead. My brother was dead. My two coaches were dead. I didn't even have a car that worked. So for the first several weeks after I got home, I just hung around the house and tried to make myself feel better by watching *All My Children*. No matter how bad I thought things were in my life, it was nothing compared to what Erica Kane went through every week.

The last thing I needed to do when I was feeling so down on myself was watch the world championships, but of course that's exactly what I did. In years past, when I watched worlds, I always felt like I was just as good or better than the top skaters. I felt like I deserved to be on the U.S. team. But not this year. Everyone was pushing the envelope by doing more and more jumps. And these were the difficult jump combinations that I hadn't even been practicing. Watching them, I thought there was no way I could compete against these skaters and win. So even if I ever made the world team—which at that moment seemed like a pretty remote possibility—I wouldn't have a chance against the best skaters in the world. I figured that I was finished.

I know that Laura and her new boyfriend, Andy Black (whom she later married), were very worried about me, because they kept encouraging me to go see a counselor. I was so withdrawn and depressed, they were afraid I might kill myself. But as miserable as I felt, suicide wasn't something I considered. Some nights I went to bed thinking it would be easier if I didn't wake up, but I never did anything about it.

Despite Laura and Andy's encouragement, I didn't think I needed therapy, but I figured if I agreed to go one time, I could get them to stop bothering me. So I went, but not with an open mind; I didn't think talking to anyone could help me with my problems, whatever they were. That was something I felt I had to work out on my own.

I don't remember what I talked about with the counselor, but my attitude was "I'm fine. I don't need this." No counselor will drag you kicking and screaming into therapy, and this counselor was no different. She left it up to me. So I told Laura and Andy that the counselor said I was fine and that I didn't need to come back. Whether or not they believed me, they didn't mention it again.

Normally, after a monthlong break following nationals, I'd be back out on the ice by late February or early March, doing what I'd done every year since I was eight years old: practicing my jumps, learning new programs, and skating, skating, skating. But I didn't know what I was going to do, so there was no point getting a new coach and going back out on the ice without a definite goal. Besides, I was having too good a time wallowing in self-pity to do anything useful, so I just stayed home and watched television.

After a couple of months of *All My Children* and feeling sorry for myself, I decided I'd better do something or they'd wind up coming for me with a straitjacket. So one afternoon I went down to the Ice Centre to talk to the director about getting my old job back. I'd worked with Laura's students on and off for the past few years, and I thought it would be constructive to do it again while I figured out my life.

On my way through the arena's lobby, I noticed a poster announcing the 1996 nationals, which were set to take place at the nearby San Jose Arena in January. I stopped to look at the poster and got caught up in a daydream about how much fun it would be to skate in my hometown in front of all the hometown fans. I remembered from my years of skating that hometown skaters always got incredible ovations—even if they came in twentieth. But I stopped myself in the middle of the daydream. This wasn't why I was at the Ice Centre. I was there to get a job and earn some money.

I went upstairs to talk to the director and told her that I was interested in coming back to work with Laura's students. It wasn't like I thought she'd say no, especially since I knew it was okay with Laura, but it was really nice that she was so positive about it.

A week later, I was back on the ice, but in a different role. My

178

My first coach, Colleen Blackmore, and me at the hotel for the "Oktoberfest" competition in 1977 in Marysville, California. Some last-minute sewing on my costume.

(Collection of the author)

It's my eighth birthday! That's my brother, George, on the left in a matching Mickey Mouse party hat.

(Collection of the author)

Having fun with Dad and Laura after a local competition in Visalia, California, in 1978.

(Collection of the author)

You can see how proud Dad is of my first-place win as a novice skater
at nationals in Indianapolis in 1982. From left: Jim Hulick, Colleen
Blackmore, Mom, me, and Dad.

(Collection of the author)

My dad, the cowboy, in one
of his many cowboy hats at
the Mission Valley Skating
Club annual picnic in the
early 1980s.

(Collection of the author)

Another proud moment. First place in 1985 at the "Arctic Blades" competition in Los Angeles.
(William Udell)

Kristi Yamaguchi and me.
(Collection of the author)

My family on the porch of our
mobile home in 1992: Laura,
Dad, Mom, me, and George.
(Collection of the author)

At the Dublin Arena for "Skate
St. Moritz," a local competition,
in 1994. That's Joan Cristobal
on the left. She's one of Laura's
students, and I choreographed
her program. Next to Joan are
Laura, Rick Inglesi, and me.
(Collection of the author)

In front of Laura's car with
Mom in her driveway in 1995.
(Collection of the author)

Taking a breather after doing my long program during practice in December 1995 at the San Jose Ice Centre.
(Steve Keegan)

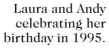

Laura and Andy celebrating her birthday in 1995.
(Collection of the author)

At the San Jose Arena on January 18, consulting with Laura during an official practice for the 1996 nationals.
(Collection of the author)

I was out of my mind with excitement right after completing a perfect short program at the 1996 nationals in San Jose.

(Anna Marie Remedios/ *San Jose Mercury News*)

My famous "shotgun" spin at the end of my long program at the 1996 national championships. You can see from the smile on my face that I knew I'd done a perfect program.

(AP Photo/Craig Fujii)

My best friends, Wayne Leonard and Reuben Jenkins, in 1996.

(Collection of Wayne Leonard and Reuben Jenkins)

Clowning around at practice with Joan Cristobal at the San Jose Ice Centre in 1996.

(Collection of the author)

Right after winning the 1996 nationals. We couldn't be happier. My former coaches, John Brancato and Kevin Peeks.

(Lynn Noto)

Laura's wedding day! Me, Laura, Andy Black, and Andy's father, Judge Tom Black, at Judge Black's home in Aptos, California, August 10, 1996.

(Sara Black)

Traveling on the bus to the next city on the Campbell's Soup Tour of World Figure Skating Champions with Olympic medalist from China, Chen Lu, me, and Laura, April 1996.

(Collection of the author)

Official photo of the 1996 United States world team. Top row, from left: Jason Dungjen, Kyoko Ina, Renee Roca, Gorsha Sur, Todd Sand, Jenni Meno, Michelle Kwan, Rudy Galindo, Tonia Kwiatkowski, Elizabeth Punsalan, Jerod Swallow. Bottom row, from left: Brian Wells, Tara Lipinski, Dan Hollander, Todd Eldredge, Shelby Lyons.

(Paul Harvath)

day began like it always had when I was training. I was up at 5:30 A.M. and in the car for the short drive to the arena by 5:55. It was thanks to Laura that I even had a car to drive; she paid to have my broken-down car fixed. At 6:15 I was on the ice, but instead of practicing my jumps and learning new choreography, I was working with all these little six-, ten-, and fourteen-year-old girls on their spins and teaching them new choreography.

After more than three hours of work, I headed for the gym to do my hour-and-a-half routine. Even for teaching, I needed to be in top shape. Following the gym, I went home, had a nap, then went back to the Ice Centre to teach from 3:00 to 5:30, and some days until 7:30 P.M.

I really liked teaching and I was good at it. I'd learned so much from all my different coaches about what to do and what not to do that I instinctively knew how to give each student exactly what she needed. Each kid is different, so you have to know how much to push and when to ease off. Some kids love to be pushed, so if you're tough with them, they excel. I had one student, little Joan, who loved to be pushed. In coaching her I'd say, "I don't want to see another fall like that." Or, "That leg is bent. I didn't teach you to do it like that. Don't ever skate like that again. I want to see you jump the way I taught you."

With other kids, if you push too hard or you're too critical, they rebel and don't work as hard. That's the kind of skater I always was. If you try to have more fun with them and make light of their mistakes and use humor, then they try harder. For a student like that, who needs a reassuring coach, if they missed something, I'd say, "Oops! You fell on your butt." Or, "That sure was a loud fall." Comments like that would make them laugh, and then I'd explain how to do it differently the next time.

Another key to being a good coach is knowing how to explain to a student what she's doing wrong. When I see a skater fall, after she lands on the ice I replay in my head what just happened, and I can see exactly what she's done, split second by split second. Then I break down each element and explain it to her so she can understand and use what she's learned to improve her technique. My emphasis is always on how to correct the problem, not on what a skater's done wrong.

Going to work was the best thing I could have done. It got me out of the house. It made me feel productive—I was earning my own money for a change and learning to appreciate the value of a dollar. I really loved working with the kids. And best of all, the kids loved working with me—I knew this because they were always hugging me.

I also loved when parents would come back from competitions and show me videotapes. The programs I choreographed almost always came in first or second, and I could see the smiles on the faces of my students when they did well. The feeling I got from that was almost as good as when I was up there receiving an award myself. I was really proud of my students and proud of the job I was doing with them. Then I started getting calls from other arenas from people asking if I could choreograph their kids' programs. That made me feel even better, because it meant I was doing a good job—a better job than the other coaches. As you can imagine, all that positive reinforcement helped lift me out of my funk.

The whole time I was teaching, people kept asking me, "When are you coming back?" "When are you going to start training for nationals?" My standard answer was "I haven't decided." At first, I really didn't know what I wanted to do, but as the months passed, I realized some things about my skating that helped me make a decision.

Working with all those kids at the Ice Centre, and seeing how much fun they had learning new things and how much they enjoyed expressing themselves through their skating, I rediscovered why I loved skating so much in the first place. In the years since the breakup with Kristi I'd forgotten that I once loved skating for the same reasons my students did. It was a way to express myself emotionally and artistically. And it was fun.

In the aftermath of the breakup, it felt like skating was all I had, that without it I'd have nothing to do with my life. It also became a weapon, a way to prove to Kristi, Carole, and the whole skating community that I could be a champion on my own. But those were the wrong reasons to skate, and they ruined skating for me. After taking a break, after working as a teacher and having had a chance to reflect, I realized that I still wanted to skate, but for the right reasons—the very same reasons my students were on the ice every morning at 6:15.

Even though I knew by midsummer that I wanted to compete in nationals, I kept it to myself. I didn't even tell Laura. I just didn't want the pressure of everyone's expectations. But keeping it secret didn't stop me from beginning work on my long program. I started listening to lots of different classical music, trying to pick out what I was going to use for my long program. One of the CDs I bought was a recording of *Swan Lake* by the French Canadian Orchestra. It was so beautiful, and I played it over and over again, piecing together the parts I was going to use for the program. It was perfect skating music. It was really powerful at the beginning, with a horn fanfare, and it had lots of crescendos throughout, which are the perfect places to do the jumps. It had a great section for the slow part of the program. And the ending was totally uplifting. You think it's going to end, but then it builds to another crescendo. I thought it would be perfect for my closing spins.

It got to the point where it was hard for me to sleep, and I'd play the CD over and over again. I'd get so excited listening to it that I'd get out of bed, turn on the light, and work out some steps to the music in my little room. In the past I'd always plotted out my programs with a coach, but now I was just doing what felt right to me, and I was doing it all by myself.

By late September, Laura was really pressing me to make a decision. She told me that she didn't care if I wanted to compete, join an ice show, or teach, but if I wanted to compete, I needed to make a decision fast because time was running out. She was afraid that if I waited much longer, I wouldn't have enough time to get everything done in time for sectionals, which were coming up in December. She said that if I wanted to compete, she'd pay for everything, including a top-ranked coach.

Laura was right: If I was going to compete, I had a lot of work to do. I knew that picking out the music for my long program and laying out the jumps and spins was just the beginning. So I told Laura that I'd decided to train for nationals. "But," I added, "I don't want you paying for anything." Laura had spent too much money on me over the years, and I didn't want the pressure of knowing that if I bombed one more time, I'd be wasting her money all over again. And I added, "But there is one thing I do want from you, Laura. I want you to be my coach."

Laura thought I was kidding. She gave me this look and said, "Yeah, right, you want me to stand at the rail with all the top-name coaches." But I was serious. I didn't think anyone could be a better coach for me than Laura. She's a great coach, she knew how to handle me, I trusted her, and I knew she'd love me no matter what happened at nationals. This last part wasn't an insignificant thing. Knowing that Laura, as my coach, would still love me took some of the pressure off, which helped a lot.

For my whole life Laura was always there when I needed her. When we lived with my aunt Cindy in East L.A., Laura never let me out of her sight. When we moved home, she protected me when Mom would go off and have her tantrums. When there was no one to drive me to practice in the morning, Laura took me. I think about it now and I can't believe that a thirteen-year-old got behind the wheel of a car and drove me to practice at six in the morning. When there wasn't enough money for both of us to take lessons, Laura gave up competitive skating and went to work to help pay for my coach. For years I'd turned to Laura for advice about everything from music to choreography to costumes. And we just knew each other so well. So to me it felt perfectly natural to have Laura as my coach.

I could understand why Laura might have had her doubts or be nervous about putting me on the ice. It wasn't that she thought she couldn't do it. Laura was an experienced coach. But usually at nationals you have a top-name coach putting you on. Laura would be standing there with all the famous pros. She was afraid the judges would look down on that and lower my scores. I told Laura that everyone would just love her, and after thinking about it for a few minutes, she said she'd do it.

It was so much fun working with Laura. I'd go to the Ice Centre at my normal time, so I was practicing on the ice by 6:15. While Laura was teaching her students, she'd keep an eye on me and offer suggestions when I needed them. At 8:30, when she was finished teaching, she'd spend fifteen minutes to a half hour working with me on my jumps and my program.

One of the best things about working with Laura was that she was so encouraging, always building up my confidence, but she didn't tell me what to do. For most of my skating career, people had told me what to do. They made decisions for me, and I may not have liked it, but it saved me from having to decide for myself. Do this competition. Wear that costume. Hold your hands this way. Cut your hair. Skate faster. Jump higher.

In the past, Laura had been one of the people I counted on to tell me what to do. I'd ask her and she'd tell me. Not anymore. At practice, the first time I asked her if I should go through my program, she said, "It's up to you. You're twenty-six years old. I'm not going to stand here and tell you what you have to do or chase you around the arena. If you want to win, you have to be here and you have to work. That's your choice." After that one time, Laura didn't have to say anything. I wanted to please her, and that meant trying to do my best.

No matter how I did, Laura never got mad. She was always calm and always happy, which was a lot like my old coach Jim Hulick. If I was having a bad day, she didn't yell at me or tell me I needed to work harder. Instead, she'd comfort me. She knew what was best for me.

A lot of times Laura and I didn't need to talk to each other when I was on the ice, because unlike anyone else I'd worked with, she could communicate with me just by looking at me. We knew each other so well that each of us could tell what the other was thinking with just a glance. And when we needed to talk, it was always in shorthand. Other people had no idea what we were talking about, because we used so few words.

I loved it that Laura let me be myself. She never tried to change me or my skating style. She didn't tell me to shave off my beard or cut my hair. She never said I had to be less balletic and more masculine. She knew the best thing was to let me be who I was and to make my own stylistic and artistic choices. That meant I got to decide my own music and costumes, and when I asked about going to a choreographer for my long program, Laura helped me find someone who would complement my style.

After describing to Laura the type of long program I had in mind, with modern movements to classical music, she suggested I go to Sharlene Franke, a local jazz-dance teacher at a place called Dance Attack. Sharlene had choreographed a program for one of Laura's students, and I really liked what she did. It was freestyle movement with high kicks and leaps—the kind of thing you see on MTV. I also liked that except for working with Laura's one student, Sharlene had no experience choreographing for figure skaters. That meant she wouldn't have any expectations of what I could and couldn't do. She would come to the situation with a completely open mind.

I made an appointment to meet Sharlene at her studio. I showed her the layout of the long program, with all the jumps and spins, and then with the music playing she choreographed all the moves in between. Instead of doing the typical ballet arm positions to my *Swan Lake* music, she had me do jazz-funk movements. It took four or five one-hour sessions to work out the whole program.

Laura was with me for all of the sessions with Sharlene, and she sat there with this big smile on her face. When I asked her, she'd say what she liked and didn't like. We agreed on almost everything.

Around the same time I was putting together my new long program, my car died. For weeks, I'd been having problems with it overheating, so I was using it only to drive to and from the Ice Centre. But then one morning it just wouldn't start. I called one of the ice-skating moms and asked if she could pick me up on the way to the arena. When I got to the Ice Centre, I told Laura what had happened. She said we should take it in to get it repaired. Just a few months before, Laura had put $1,500 into the car to get it running again. I didn't think either of us should spend another penny on it. It wasn't worth it, so I told Laura to forget it, that I'd ride my bike to the arena instead.

I hadn't had my own bike, but I'd inherited George's bike when he passed away. It's a really beautiful, pink and purple, top-of-the-line mountain bike that he'd planned to use for exercise. But he was already sick when he bought it, and after he brought it home, he never used it. I felt lucky to have it, because I wound up using it a lot. Every day I rode my bike three and a half miles from the trailer park to the Ice Centre. Then it was another four miles farther to the gym and then nearly eight miles home.

I know some people at the rink felt sorry for me that I had to ride my bicycle to practice every day, but the truth was I felt really good about being so independent and not taking money from Laura to fix the car. There was also a huge side benefit to riding my bike nearly sixteen miles a day. It really helped build up my stamina. I was already working on my aerobics at the gym and doing complete run-throughs at the arena. The bike riding just added to that.

I didn't have a lot of time to worry about how tough life was without a car. I had only three weeks to go before sectionals, and I still didn't have a short program. I hadn't even chosen the music. So I quickly went through all my CDs and decided to use the Canon in D by Johann Pachelbel. I'd always liked Pachelbel's Canon, but in the past I'd been afraid to skate to something that no one had used before. It's a slow, classical piece, and almost everyone chooses fast music for the short program. But I decided that with the exception of Laura, I didn't care what other people thought. So I played Pachelbel's Canon for her and she thought it was beautiful.

Despite the falling-out I'd had with John and Kevin, I decided that I wanted John to choreograph the short program for me. I liked his style of choreography and knew it would be perfect for the music I'd chosen. Since I'd started teaching at the Ice Centre, I'd seen a lot of John and Kevin, and we were getting to be friends again, but still I was afraid to ask. So Laura asked for me and John agreed to do it. We made an appointment for the next day, and within a week I had a new short program.

My short program was basically the same as the year before, but this time, instead of doing a triple flip, I decided to do a triple lutz. It's a harder jump, but I didn't want to have to worry about falling on the triple flip again, which I'd done two years in a row at nationals. I also decided to drop my traveling spin and do a normal camel sit spin instead because it takes less time. That gave me more time to do interesting choreography.

After I finished working with John on the choreography, I had to get my costumes done. The woman who'd made my costumes in the past had moved away, so I went to Julie Rose, a local costume maker whose work I really admired. For the long program, I told her that I wanted a one-piece costume made out of black cotton Lycra. I wanted the costume to be tight-fitting, with points on the sleeves and a high neck. The only decoration would be white trim around the neck and points and two buttons at the end of each sleeve. My plan was to add airbrushed swans on the front later.

I wrote Julie a check for $120, which was incredibly inexpensive for a costume, and she promised to have it ready for me in a few days. It was really satisfying to me that I paid for the costumes and for John's and Sharlene's choreography with my own checks. I'd had a checking account for a long time, but I'd only used it for deposits and to withdraw cash. I'd never written my own checks before, so it made me feel like a grown-up to take care of these things with my own money.

Three days later I had the costume, and I couldn't wait to try it out on the ice. When you get a new costume, you always have to see how it feels, find out if it moves freely enough for all your jumps and spins. When I stepped out of the dressing room, everyone started telling me how classy it was. I mentioned to a few people that I was thinking of getting it airbrushed with pictures of swans, and everyone said to leave it just as it was. Of course, that only made me want to get the swans even more.

Laura took me to a store that specialized in airbrushing. I described to the guy what I had in mind and he said he could do it, but he warned me that because the fabric was so tight-fitting, he couldn't guarantee that the paint wouldn't flake off as it stretched. I couldn't risk it, so I reluctantly gave up on my idea.

Julie also made the costume for my short program. I had her do black pants with a ruffled, cream-colored shirt. It was really flowy and the sleeves came way down on my hands, so we didn't need points. And I wore a maroon velvet vest over the shirt. I'd wanted Julie to do something classically romantic to fit the music, and that's exactly what I got.

Before I knew it we were on our way to southern California for sectionals, which were being held at the Pickwick ice rink in L.A., the same arena where Kristi and I competed as a pair for the first time. To save money, we stayed with Laura's boyfriend's sister, Kathryn, in Ventura. On a good day that was about an hour-and-fifteen-minute drive from the arena.

Andy's sister was really great and she had this cute little house. It was so much nicer to be staying in someone's home than at a hotel. It was very comfortable, so I thought I'd sleep better. No chance. I was so excited that I could hardly close my eyes. I couldn't wait to get up in the morning and go to practice and show everyone that Laura was my coach and that I was skating really well. We were a great team, and I wanted all the other coaches and skaters to know it.

I was up before everyone else and I had my practice outfit all ready to go. I'd learned a lot from John and Kevin, so I had a simple practice outfit. It was just black pants and a red, short-sleeved mock-turtleneck shirt. But despite what John and Kevin had suggested—and maybe it was in spite of—I kept the goatee, put my earring back in, and did my hair in a spiky, flattop style. I did what made me feel comfortable, and if the judges didn't like that, well, I'd pay the consequences.

I put on my practice outfit and told Laura, "Let's go! Let's go! Let's go!" I'm surprised she didn't just smack me. At that hour of the day, when I was completely hyper, I could be very annoying.

We drove to the arena, and the place was filled with a lot of coaches and their skaters, about seventy-five people in all—no spectators. Sectionals aren't organized the way nationals are, with everyone having an assigned practice time. Instead, you buy ice time and then it's first come, first served as far as who gets to have his or her music played. A lot depends on how aggressive your coach is in getting your tape to the person who handles the music. Laura's tiny, but she didn't let any of those big coaches get in her way. From where I was standing, I could hear her: "Rudy's going next. Rudy's going next." And sure enough, I went next.

At the practice session, all the other skaters are on the ice as well, so when you're doing your program, you have to be careful not to fall over anyone. I took my opening position for the long program, and the music started. I did my first combination, a triple axel, triple toe, and I heard some applause. Then I skated around to my triple lutz, triple toe. At that point I could see people beginning to gather at the rails; the coaches were pulling their students over to watch. Then I did a triple flip, triple loop. I still had a minute and a half to go, and by then I was all by myself on the ice. Everyone else had stopped skating, and they were all watching me.

I did a clean program, from beginning to end, and when I finished, I went right into doing laps around the rink. Everyone was patting me on the back and telling me how incredible the program was. I could see Laura smiling by the rail. I knew she was proud of me, and I was proud of what we'd accomplished together.

The next practice wasn't until that night, so we drove all the way back to Kathryn's and then back to L.A. that evening for my short-program practice session. It was just like the morning practice. Everyone stopped skating and watched, and at the end I got lots of praise and applause.

For three days in a row at practice I did clean programs. I know a lot of people were surprised that I was skating so well after taking off eight months. They didn't expect me to come back skating better than I'd ever skated before, especially with my sister as my coach.

Finally, the competition began. We got to the arena with plenty of time for me to get warmed up. As I walked in, everyone was coming up to me to wish me luck. That's when I started getting nervous. John told me later that Laura was so nervous she was shaking, but she never let me see that. When I was doing my stretches and people were trying to come up to me, Laura calmly kept everybody away. And whenever I looked at her, she just gave me this warm, reassuring smile. Everything was going to be okay.

After doing my stretches, I went to change into my costume. All the other skaters were super nice to me, asking me about my programs and when I was going to practice the next day. I was polite to everyone, but I was trying to stay focused on what I had to do when I went out on the ice, so I said as little as I could.

I walked out of the dressing room and found Laura, and then I took her hand and we walked over to the ice for the men's six-minute warm-up. There were only six men, and they announced us in the order we were set to compete in. I was fourth. I got out on the ice and did my jumps, and every time I landed, the audience cheered. That was nice, especially since I wasn't a local skater—usually, the skaters from out of the area don't get much of a reception.

After the warm-up, I got off the ice and walked partway down the corridor underneath the arena. I didn't go too far because I wanted to hear how the crowd reacted to the programs of the first three skaters. Usually I didn't listen to the crowd because you can tell if the skater is doing well and that makes you nervous.

It was a mistake to listen, because sure enough I got very nervous and started doubting myself because the three guys who went before me did really well. I was afraid that I might be out of the running. By the time the last of the three finished, I was squeezing Laura's arm so hard I'm sure I was cutting off her circulation.

Then it was my turn, and they called my name. It's a tiny rink, so the stands can fit only a few hundred people, but they all applauded enthusiastically as I skated out to my starting point. As soon as the music began, I suddenly felt calm. In fact, I felt incredibly light, like I could almost fly. I skated into my first triple combination—and landed smoothly. *Yes!* Every jump after that was just as good. The whole program was clean and fast. Not a single mistake.

Laura was waiting at the side to give me a big hug as soon as I got off the ice. Then I put my arm around her as we waited for the results. I was expecting 5.3s and 5.4s. I was wrong. My technical marks were mostly 5.6s and 5.7s, and I got three 5.8s in my style marks. I'd never received such high marks before. Laura and I were so excited, and as we were walking out, all these people, including some of the judges, walked by us and told us what a beautiful program it was. It was also a good-enough program to land me in first place after the short.

The next day we had another practice session, and the following day was the competition for the long program. By the time I stepped onto the ice to do my long program, I felt pretty confident, although my muscles were achy. I'd overdone it at practice the day before.

I got into my opening position, the music started, and I

skated into my triple axel, triple toe. It was perfect, and the crowd went crazy. I skated around, and as I was going into the triple lutz the audience was still screaming and applauding from my last jump. I wanted them to quiet down because it was making me nervous, but they never quieted down through the whole program, and when I finished, they got even louder.

All my marks were 5.7s, 5.8s, and 5.9s, which is unheard of at sectionals. No one scores that high, and no one else scored as high that night. I won!

I guess you could say that winning sectionals was nothing new for me because this was the fourth time in a row that I took first place. But after an eight-month break, with a whole new attitude, and with Laura as my coach, this was a new beginning for me. The doubts were gone, the anger was gone, I felt confident, and I felt loved. And for the first time in years, skating was fun again. With only one month to go until nationals in San Jose, you'd think I'd be nervous. I couldn't wait!

15

1996 NATIONALS

Laura and I had one goal during the month between sectionals and nationals: consistency. Given how well I skated at sectionals, it was pretty clear that I was already in peak form, so all we had to do was maintain that level of performance with my normal daily practice session and hour-and-a-half workout at the gym. Laura made it clear that she didn't want any drama or histrionics out of me—just calm and deliberate work as we counted down the days to nationals.

The only threat to our simple plan came two weeks before the competition. I started coughing. I tried to ignore it, but as soon as Laura heard me cough during practice one morning, we went straight from the ice to the doctor's office. As if I had intentionally got sick, Laura said, "You're not doing it again this time. No excuses. We're going to the doctor. You're going on antibiotics. You're getting better." And after a few days on medication, I did get better. I didn't want any excuses either.

One potential disruption to our calm routine that we didn't

have to worry about was the media. The Bay Area newspapers each published an article about me and how I was competing in my hometown, but I'd been such a nonstory for so long that I didn't exactly have to fight off the national press. I felt a little hurt, but given how much trouble I have with pressure, it was also a blessing not to be the focus of attention. I have to thank the USFSA in part for keeping me out of the spotlight; they didn't include me in their printed guide for the media. I can't really blame them for leaving me out. In their eyes, they had no reason to draw attention to me, because I was a has-been.

Despite the USFSA's low expectations, I had my own ideas about what I thought I could accomplish. Based on how well I did at sectionals, I figured I could finish fifth or sixth, in which case I'd continue competing as an amateur to maintain my Olympic eligibility. If I placed any lower than that, I'd turn professional and probably get a job skating in one of the ice shows for skaters who never made it to the top.

The real focus of attention in the upcoming nationals was on the anticipated battle between Scott Davis, Todd Eldredge, and Aren Nielsen. Scott had won two national championships. Todd, who'd placed sixth behind me at the 1993 nationals, was now the reigning national champion. And Aren had won a bronze at the 1995 championships. All three had been to the world championships at least once; Todd won a silver in 1995. And both Todd and Scott had competed at the Olympics. Their formidable combined records squashed any fantasies I might have had about winning a medal at nationals, because barring any last-minute disasters, they had the first three spots locked up. If nothing else, they'd earned them.

The week prior to nationals, I had two official practice sessions a day. Normally, during that final week before a competition, I'd be quiet and withdrawn, so much so that I could hardly have a conversation with anyone. People would ask Laura what was wrong with me, and she'd tell them nothing was wrong. Silence was just my way of dealing with the pressure. I'd screen everything out and retreat into my own world.

This time, without the pressure and with my new-old attitude toward my skating, I felt relaxed; I could carry on a conversation and answer questions like a normal person. And as the competition neared, instead of becoming increasingly withdrawn, I became more and more focused, calm, and confident. It helped that I hardly missed a single jump during the practice sessions all week and was doing clean run-throughs.

It was so much fun having nationals in my hometown. I could sleep in my own bed and be at home with my mom, instead of at the hotel with all of the other competitors. Laura's boyfriend, Andy, took the whole week off, and during the day, between practices, Laura, Andy, and I went to the Valley Fair Mall to hang out and have lunch.

Best of all, having nationals at the San Jose Arena meant Mom could come to nationals. She hadn't been to any of my competitions in recent years because we were afraid the travel would be too much for her nerves. Her medication kept her mental illness under control, but she was still fragile. Now, with the competition just a few miles away from home, there was no reason for her not to come.

Mom even surprised me by coming to a couple of the official practice sessions during the week. But after watching me, and knowing my history of blowing it in the short program, she decided it would be too stressful for her to come see that part of the competition. Besides being nervous herself, she didn't want me to worry about her worrying in the stands. I appreciated her concern, but I made her promise she'd be in the audience for the long program.

The week flew by, and finally it was the night before nationals. I went to bed early, around 9:30, because I had a 5:30 practice the next morning. As I always do, I prayed before I went to sleep, but this time, in addition to asking God to bless all of my loved ones, I prayed directly to my father and brother.

I said, "Dad, George, please help me do a clean short program. I really need to do well this year in front of my hometown."

Before drifting off to sleep, I visualized doing my short program. I started out with a nice, easy triple axel, then did the entire program without missing a thing. In the visualization, by the time I finished my program, the audience was on its feet cheering and I felt happy. It was like a dream, and maybe it was, because the next thing I remember is my alarm going off at 4:30 A.M.

After so many years of getting up well before dawn, I didn't mind it, but I also wouldn't have minded being in one of the practice groups in a later time slot, especially since the competition wasn't until six that night. But I didn't have a choice, so I got up, showered, and put on my practice outfit. I was too nervous to eat anything so I just headed over to the arena in Laura's car, which she'd lent me for the week.

The arena was virtually empty, just the six skaters in my practice group, our coaches, and a handful of onlookers. My good friend Wayne snuck up from behind me and surprised me with a big bear hug. I thought he was crazy to drive the half hour down from Belmont at that hour of the day, but he said he wanted to be there to support me, and I was glad he was there. As much as I'd complain in my down moments that I didn't have friends, here was Wayne, standing with Laura at the side of an ice-cold rink at five-thirty in the morning, giving me a big smile every time I caught his eye. If that isn't a friend, I don't know what is.

The practice was only twenty minutes long, so it was really just a chance to warm up my jumps. I ran through all my triples and my triple-triple combinations. I did a few spins and ended with my traveling camel spin. Everything felt solid, my spins were fast and tight, my jumps had great height, my landings were clean. I felt better prepared and more relaxed going into nationals than I had since the early days with Kristi.

After practice, Laura, Wayne, and I went out to breakfast. I was starving and ate a big breakfast of eggs and bacon, potatoes, toast, and orange juice. Wayne and Laura just watched me eat. I didn't know it, but Laura was so nervous, she couldn't eat the whole day. When we finished, Wayne went to work, I dropped Laura off at her place, and I drove back to my house.

The rest of the day was totally uneventful, which is how I wanted it to be. Since I had Laura's car, I took Mom to the Fairview Mall and we walked around for a while before sitting down for lunch. We hardly talked at all, but Mom doesn't really talk much on most days, and I know she was feeling nervous for me, so she talked even less. After lunch we walked around some more, and then we stopped at the grocery store on the way home.

When we got home, I took a two-hour nap and woke up at about 4:00 P.M., an hour before I had to leave for the arena to arrive there in time for me to do my floor exercises, put on my costume, and get on the ice for my warm-up. The competition was set to begin at 6:00, and I was scheduled to be the eleventh of seventeen skaters.

Before leaving the house, I tucked in my teddy bears and kissed my cats for good luck. I have these two stuffed bears that Kristi gave me one Christmas. I named them Boo Boo and Goo Goo, and I tucked them under the cover on my bed and positioned them with their heads on the pillow, side by side, as if they were sleeping together. Then I kissed them both and said, "I love you, Boo Boo and Goo Goo. Give me some good luck."

Finding my three cats, so I could kiss each one of them on the forehead, was easier said than done, because my newest cat, Sky, liked to hide. George's cat, Trucker, who is a Siamese mix, was standing in the middle of my room looking at me, so I knelt down and kissed him. Star, who is also a Siamese mix, was on the living room couch sleeping and didn't stir when I kissed her. Sky, my new cat, whom I rescued from the street, was still a kitten. She was this tiny black cat, and she was easily frightened, but I managed to find her under the bed in what had been George's room.

After kissing each of the cats good-bye, I said good-bye to my mom, gave her a kiss, and told her not to worry, that I would do fine. Then I drove over to Laura's house to meet her and Andy, who was going to drive us over to the arena. In the car, I don't think any of us said a word. As much as we tried to be casual, we were all feeling pretty tense. Andy dropped us off at the back entrance, gave us each a hug, wished us luck, and drove off to the parking lot. He would be up in the stands watching.

Backstage before a major competition like nationals, it always feels like a giant pressure cooker. All the coaches stand next to their skaters while they warm up, which is exactly what Laura did with me. John Brancato, my former coach, who choreographed my short program, met us there and stood with Laura. They looked really sharp together, with John dressed in Ralph Lauren everything, and Laura in a long Oriental-print skirt and jeans vest.

As I did my stretches and air turns, Laura was completely focused on me. Every time I looked up, she was looking at me, nodding, reassuring me that I was doing the right thing. She didn't say a word. She didn't have to, because we'd established that line of silent communication.

After about fifteen minutes, Laura nodded in the direction of the dressing room. It was time. I nodded back and headed for the dressing room to put on my costume and skates. It took only a few minutes to undress and put on my costume. Then I put on my skates, which were about a year past retirement age. Normally I got new skates twice a year, but these were the same skates I'd used at the 1995 nationals. A new pair costs around $600, which Laura had offered to pay, but I'd wanted to do everything on my own. Unfortunately, by the time I'd saved up the money, there wasn't enough time to break in the new skates, so I wound up using my old ones. I finished lacing them up, put on the guards that protect the blades when you're off the ice, and walked out of the dressing room.

Laura was waiting for me just outside the door with John, and we all walked down the hallway that leads out to an open area adjacent to the ice. As we were walking, I went through my whole range of not completely unconscious tics. I cleared my throat, brushed back my hair, rolled my shoulders, and tugged at the waistband of my pants. I'm sure it was unconscious when I first did these things, but over time I became aware of them, and now I was afraid if I didn't do them, it would be bad luck.

We stood near the boards waiting for the warm-up group of six skaters to be called, and as we waited, I did knee bends, holding on to Laura's forearms—she had her arms folded across her chest. I was feeling really good, and confident, but a little impatient. I wanted them to call my name for the warm-up so I could hear how the audience of 9,500 would respond. What kind of welcome would I get?

We waited only a few minutes, but it seemed like forever. Finally they started calling our names in the order in which we were scheduled to skate. Scott Davis was called just before me, and the crowd applauded. Then they announced "Rudy Galindo!" and the crowd went crazy! I mean, it was a deafening roar. For a second I got scared because the sound just about lifted me out of my skates, but it was also unbelievably exciting.

I stepped out onto the ice, did a back spin, and then skated over to the boards where Laura was standing. I had a sip of Coke, which Laura had been holding for me, and I asked her if I should do a triple lutz. She told me to do whatever I felt like doing. It was up to me. So I did a triple lutz, which was perfect, and I looked over to Laura and she gave me a little nod. Then I went through each of my triples and triple-triple combinations, and with each landing the crowd cheered. It was such an incredible feeling to know they were with me, focused on my every move, just like Laura. Some of the guys teased me later in the locker room that I could have done a simple waltz jump and they would have cheered for me. But it was my hometown and it would have been the same for any of them if the competition were held on their home ice.

After doing all my jumps, I skated over to John and Laura to rest, and Laura put her hand on my arm. I was watching the five other skaters on the ice when the announcer said, "One minute remaining." I decided I'd already done everything I wanted to, and I got off the ice and went backstage.

Scott Davis skated right before I did, so while I was backstage doing some final stretches, I could hear the crowd cheer when he landed his triple-axel, double-toe combination. I listened for the applause for his triple lutz, and from the sound of it, he nailed that jump, too. And then it was time for me to head back to the ice. As I walked down the brightly lit hall with Laura and John, I shook my head back and forth to simulate what it's like when I do my spins, just to get used to the way it looks when I'm actually doing them.

Right as we got to the ice, I looked out at Scott skating. He was just landing his double axel, and he put his hand down on the ice as he landed to keep from falling. The audience gasped. That's one of the required moves, so that was an automatic two-tenths-of-a-point deduction. I was relieved it wasn't me out there putting my hand on the ice. But before the self-doubt had a chance to creep in, I blocked the thought. I was going to skate a clean program. That's what I'd visualized. And that's what I fully intended to do.

As they were announcing Scott's marks, I stepped out onto the ice to do a waltz jump next to the boards—just a little warm-up jump. The audience was quiet while they were listening to Scott's marks being announced, but when I stepped on the ice for my quick warm-up, you could hear people yell from different parts of the arena, "Go, Rudy! Go, Rudy!" I smiled and looked down at the ice. It was kind of embarrassing, but I loved all the attention.

I went back to the edge of the ice next to Laura, and she put her hand on my arm again. The arena was quiet for a moment, and then the announcer said, "Skating to selections from Canon in D by Johann Pachelbel, representing the St. Moritz Ice Skating Club in Berkeley, California, Rudy Galindo!" As the crowd cheered, I leaned over and gave Laura a kiss. She said,

"Stay tough. Stay tough." What she was saying to me was "Don't let those little demons inside your head get to you. I know you can do it."

With Laura's final words, I skated out to my starting position as the audience settled down. I never just skate out to my starting point. I circle around until I feel ready, which was a good thing, because as I circled around, my right skate slipped on something, which is no big deal when you're just skating, but when you do a jump, a little slip can mean the difference between a perfect landing and landing on your butt. As soon as I was in position, I lifted up my skate and brushed off some dirt from the blade that I must have picked up as I stepped from the rubber mat onto the ice.

I adjusted my costume, put my hands down at my sides, held up my head, looked out to a cement wall in the stands, focused on it, and waited for the music to start. In those few seconds, I calmly thought to myself, "Just lean into that circle, dip your right shoulder into that first triple axel, and when you land it, just do the triple toe."

The music started, and I headed for my first triple-triple: stroke, stroke, stroke, jump. In that split second when I completed three-and-a-half revolutions in the air, Laura was at the side of the rink, hands clenched, holding her breath, pressing against John, and as I landed, I could see out of the corner of my eye that she jumped up. Then I went right into the triple toe, and as I took off, Laura's shoulders went up with me. And she did that with me throughout the entire program, counting with me, concentrating on the takeoff, jumping up with each clean landing. John later told me that midway through my program, he had to remind Laura to breathe.

From the time I landed my first triple axel, I had a smile on my face. With each jump, and as the cheers from the crowd grew louder and louder, my smile got bigger and bigger. It was the kind of smile that you can't take off your face, even if you want to. And I had no reason to do anything but smile, because I didn't miss a move, and I was having so much fun.

200

I headed into my third and final required triple, the triple lutz. As I came around on the ice, I thought to myself, "Do a double, do a double." I wasn't actually going to do a double, but when I think of doing a double, it keeps me from "prerotating"—that's when you're so eager to do a jump that as you're getting ready to tap the ice with the tip of your skate to launch into the jump, you begin rotating your upper body ahead of your lower body. I said to myself, "Don't prerotate, just blend it all together."

I tapped the ice, took off into the air, rotated three times, and nailed the landing, for a perfect triple lutz. As I headed into my final double axel, which is an easy jump that I'd blown on more than one occasion, Laura told me later that she was thinking, "Oh, God, this is an easy jump. Keep those freaking demons out of your head. This is your last jump. Just do it, Rudy!" I jumped, whipped off two-and-a-half revolutions, and landed on a cushion of air. As I went into my next move, a spiral, I caught Laura's eye, and I could see her smiling, holding her clenched fists in the air, and saying to me, "You did it!"

I was home-free and it showed on my face. The audience knew it, too, and as I did my final footwork and skated into my last combination spin, the crowd was on its feet screaming and cheering. It was a huge ovation, unlike anything I'd ever experienced before in my life, and when I finished my spin and came to a stop, I threw my hands into the air and jumped up and down. That moment was one of the real high points of my life, and for a few seconds I just stood there and soaked it up.

When I finally composed myself, I took a quick bow, then skated off as fast as I could, jumped off the ice and into Laura's arms. I did it! I did it! I did a clean short, and I did it in front of the home crowd. It was a moment of delicious vindication after all those years of failure.

Laura and I sat calmly in the kiss-and-cry booth waiting for my marks to come up. I thought to myself, "Maybe I can get that fifth spot, maybe I can do it." I just wanted to make the fifth spot, because that would mean I'd make the ABC Sports cut—they subsequently broadcast the performances of the top six skaters.

As the technical marks came up, before I even had a chance to take them in, the crowd started booing, and the whole time the announcer was reading the marks, the boos got louder and louder. The marks were mostly 5.7s and 5.8s, which I thought was good considering that I hadn't had a clean short program in years. In skating, the judges tend to take into account how you've done in the past, and I had a consistently bad track record in competition.

My style marks came up, and they were slightly higher, and the crowd still booed. My scores put me in third place, behind Todd and Scott. Clearly the audience thought I deserved to be higher, but I was thrilled to be in third place, and Laura and I hugged as we headed backstage.

At the press conference after the short program concluded, the reporters asked me if I thought my marks should have been higher, especially since I was the only one of the top three skaters who'd done a triple-triple combination. Scott and Todd both did triple-doubles, and Scott put his hand down on his double axel. But I was so delighted to be in third place, which was two places higher than I'd allowed myself to imagine I'd get, that I could honestly say that I was glad to be in third. And to finish third overall would be absolutely fantastic, because that would mean I'd be on the world team, the first time since the breakup with Kristi. But something no one was saying— and that I wasn't even thinking—was that being in third place put me within striking distance of first. The short program is only one-third of your total score. If I finished first in the long, I'd win the gold medal. But everyone knew Todd was going to win, so that thought had yet to cross my mind.

There was plenty of speculation in the press over the next couple of days regarding the scoring in the short program. Jere Longman of the *New York Times* wrote that I "received what appeared to be artificially low marks." He also said that my performance was slow and "lacking in creative footwork," which I, of course, disagree with. But he noted that people in the skating world speculated that what held me back were other things, like my goatee, the fact that I didn't have the titles that my competitors did, and that in journalist Christine Brennan's new book about figure skating, I'd said I was gay. I can't imagine that such a disclosure came as a surprise to anyone, but in the skating world, if you're gay, you're expected to keep quiet about it.

Fortunately, I generally avoid reading whatever is written about me, so I didn't see any of those clips until months after nationals. The last thing I needed to do in the time between the short and long programs was to get caught up in all the gossip, rumors, and speculation.

Right after the press conference, Laura and I went down the hall to draw numbers for the long program. Our arms were full of flowers that fans had brought for me, and we were laughing as we struggled not to drop any or bump into anyone.

At the draw, which was held in one of the arena's meeting rooms, the top five skaters in the short program drew last for the final five spots—thirteen through seventeen—in the long program. Because I placed third, I got to pick third, and I reached in the bag and accidentally grasped two slips of paper. I held on to the one that was closest to me and let go of the other one. I withdrew my hand from the bag and unfolded the paper. I drew seventeen, the last spot, and I wasn't happy about it. I like to be the first or second skater out, right after warm-ups, and I don't like to wait around, trying not to hear how everyone else is doing. Laura tried convincing me that skating last was a good thing, because the judges typically save the highest marks until the end, in anticipation of needing them for the best skaters. I wasn't convinced, but I wasn't going to let the draw kill the excitement I was still feeling as we left the arena and got in Laura's car to go back home.

When I got home, I told Mom how well I'd done, and she was relieved. I felt terrible that my skating made her so nervous, but I could do nothing except reassure her that everything would be okay no matter how I did.

We had a full day between the short and the long program, which was scheduled for Saturday at 4:00 in the afternoon. That's a lot of time to think about what had already happened and to anticipate what was to come. While I was at home on Friday, I received several phone calls from local and national newspaper reporters asking me how I felt about placing third and what I thought would happen in the long program. Laura had reminded me on the way home the night before not to count my chickens before they were hatched, so I gave everyone the same answer, which was, "A lot of things can happen, and whatever happens, happens." Of course, in my own mind I was thinking specifically of what could happen. Above all, I hoped to hang on to third, but I reminded myself not to get greedy, because fourth or fifth would have made me very happy just the day before. I simply needed to focus on doing my best and enjoying myself and not on how I was going to place. It was a struggle.

The only bad thing about placing third was the pressure that went along with it to do equally well, if not better, in the long program. Now people had expectations of me. What if I didn't do as well as people expected? What if they were disappointed? I had to stop myself midthought and remind myself that none of that mattered. What mattered most was that no matter how I did, my family and friends would still love me. And the hometown crowd was going to love me because I was out there skating for them.

We had practice first thing that morning, and then I hung out for most of the day with Laura and Andy. That night, before going to sleep, I prayed as I always did, and I thanked Dad and George for looking out for me. Again, I asked them to watch over me, and to help me skate a clean program.

I had a hard time falling asleep, so like I did the night before the short program, I visualized doing a perfect long program, getting a standing ovation, and taking my bows. By the third replay of that scenario, I was sound asleep. After all the excitement and not getting much sleep the night before, I needed the rest.

The next morning at ten o'clock, Laura and Andy picked me up for a final practice. On the way over to the arena, I tried to maintain the attitude that this was a practice just like any other practice, as if there weren't any competition coming up later that day. Laura stood at the side of the ice, holding my lemon zinger tea—with lots of sugar—and a can of Coke. John Brancato came for practice that morning and Laura had him hold my water bottle.

At some point during practice I looked down at my hands and noticed a hole in my right glove. I know this sounds ridiculous, but I almost lost it. In a state of panic, I skated over to Laura and showed her the glove. "There is a hole in my glove!" Laura looked at me. I looked at Laura. And in that moment I realized I'd gone off the deep end. Okay, so it wasn't a practice like all other practices. I was under a lot of pressure, but just because I had a hole in my glove didn't mean that the day was going to be a disaster. It wasn't a bad omen. It was just a hole, nothing more.

After fifteen minutes, having done all my jumps, I got off the ice and packed up my things to go home. Before we went our separate ways, I asked Laura what she planned to wear for the long program. She said, "I don't know. Just something casual and professional." I thought professional was fine for the other coaches, but I wanted Laura to look professional *and* beautiful. So I asked her to wear her black dress, which looks fantastic on her, and she said she would.

Andy took Laura home so I could borrow Laura's car again, and on the way home, I drove by the cemetery to visit my father's grave. His plot was easy to find, because it's on the edge of the cemetery, where the new graves are. There was just a temporary marker there with his name, and birth and death dates. We didn't have enough money to do the headstone right away.

I stood by my father's grave, and I said, "Please, Dad, help me stay on my feet tonight. It's time for me to give something back to the family." I know my father would have wanted me to take care of my mom and Laura. And I knew if I did well at nationals, that I'd be in a better position to pay Laura back for all that she'd invested in me and to help Mom move to a nicer house.

On Dad's grave I placed a single red rose, which I'd brought from home that morning from the pile of flowers I'd been given after the short program; then I went back to the car and drove home. I wished Dad had lived long enough to be at the rink with me that afternoon. He would have been so proud.

I had only a few hours at home before I had to leave to pick up Laura to go to the arena. Andy would be coming by a little later to pick up my mother, and the two of them planned to sit together, with Reuben and Wayne, during the competition.

As usual, before leaving the house, I tucked in Boo Boo and Goo Goo, then kissed my cats good-bye. Only, this time I couldn't find Sky, and I wasn't leaving the house without giving Sky a kiss. I looked everywhere and finally found her nestled in the pile of flowers on the kitchen table, sleeping. I picked her up, gave her a kiss on her forehead, and she licked my nose. I think that was her way of wishing me luck. My mother saw me to the door, I kissed her good-bye, and before I got in the car, I said one last prayer to Dad and George: "Please let me do a perfect long program."

I drove over to Laura's place, knocked on the door, and when she opened it, she simply took my breath away. She had on the black dress I'd asked her to wear, and her hair was up in a sexy French twist. We got in the car and we hardly said a word on the short drive to the arena. When we talked about it the next day, we discovered that we were both thinking the same thing, that all I had to do was hang on to third and I'd make the world team. Neither of us would allow ourselves to think about what would happen if I fell to fourth. And we didn't dare fantasize about my doing any better than third. We didn't want to jinx the whole thing.

At the arena, Laura and I went through the same warm-up routine as two nights before. After I did my stretches I headed to the dressing room to put on my costume and skates. I met Laura outside the dressing room and we walked side by side toward the ice.

At the side of the rink I held on to Laura's arm and did knee bends. I was really calm, and then they called my group to warm up. That's when I got nervous.

Despite my feelings, I had a great warm-up. Unfortunately, because I was skating last, I had a forty-five-minute wait before I was called to do my program. So I went backstage and took off my skates. I borrowed Laura's Walkman, tuned it to a rock station, and turned it up really loud to drown out the crowd. I didn't want to hear how they reacted to the other skaters' performances. I sat down in a corner, closed my eyes, and pretended I was in my room at home.

With two skaters to go, Laura came over and told me it was time to put my skates on, which I did, and then we walked toward the rink. And again, I went through my routine tics, clearing my throat, rolling my shoulders, running my hands through my hair, and adjusting my costume.

Todd Eldredge had skated before me, and they were still announcing his marks when I stepped onto the ice to do a quick warm-up. After a couple of waltz jumps, I came back to where Laura was standing, looked up at Todd's marks, chuckled, and said, "Yeah, right." Todd didn't do any triple-triple jump combinations, and did only five triples overall, but he skated a clean program that earned him marks that were so high I knew I'd never even come close.

Just before they announced my name, I noticed that Laura had her coat on, so no one could see her dress. I asked her to take off her jacket and give it to me, which she did, and I put it down on a chair. She looked spectacular, and I was so proud to have everyone know that she was my coach and my sister.

Fortunately, before stepping onto the ice, I didn't know where the other skaters had placed, because it would have been intimidating. Todd was in first, and Dan Hollander, a twenty-three-year-old from Michigan who was known for his powerful jumps, had come out of nowhere and vaulted into second place after doing seven triples, including one triple-triple combination. And Scott Davis, who'd had trouble with his triples, had slipped to third.

As I waited for them to introduce me, I was thinking, "Just hit that first jump combination, and then you can relax, just a little." I was getting pretty nervous by the time they announced my name: "Skating to selections from the ballet *Swan Lake*, and representing the St. Moritz Ice Skating Club in Berkeley, California—Rudy Galindo!" The audience roared; it was the biggest roar I'd ever heard in my life. I thought, "Oh, my God, I'm going to have to skate well because this crowd is waiting for an awesome program."

I took Laura's hand. She told me to stay tough and gave me a kiss, and I skated out onto the ice to take my opening position. As I skated out, the cheering got even louder. I wanted to say, "Shush." The people in the stands were making me so nervous that my legs were shaking. I looked up, and I could see that my mom was frozen in her seat and that Andy was already crying.

As I made my way toward the center of the ice, I felt like I was dreaming, except if I'd been asleep, the noise from my pounding heart would have awakened me. It seemed even louder than the crowd.

I skated around toward my starting point, and I could see the judges to my left, but I looked just above their heads. I didn't want the added pressure of seeing the expressions on their faces. I stopped at a point on the ice that lined up with the end of the judges' table and a concrete pillar. I tried to slow my heart rate by taking a couple of deep breaths, because I didn't want to use up valuable energy that I was going to need during the four-minute-forty-second program.

I took my opening position, which is supposed to be evocative of a swan, with my arms behind me, my left leg in a bent position—almost a lunge—and my right leg stretched back.

My back was arched and my head was turned so that I was looking over my left shoulder.

It's only five to ten seconds between when you take your starting position and when the music starts. And in that time I was thinking to myself, "When is the music going to start? Now? Is it coming? Hurry up, because it's hard holding still." Suddenly, the music started. I took a final deep breath and thought, "Here goes."

I was feeling confident as I started skating, but as I did my initial footwork, I went back on my heel and almost tripped. No one could see it, but I could feel it in my blade. I caught myself and thought, "Nothing is going to stop me this time." I was determined not to fall. So as I skated around for the approach to my first triple axel, I bent my knees more than usual, to be even more solid over the blades. As I approached the takeoff point, I lifted my arms and jumped. Three and a half revolutions and a split second later I landed smoothly, facing backward, then took off again on the toe of my skate for the triple toe loop—spin, spin, spin. The audience roared so loud I could hardly hear the music. As I landed, I thought, "This is way too easy." And apparently it was a flawless triple-triple, because I heard later that the announcer, Dick Button, just about yelled, "That's the best moment so far in this men's competition!"

With a huge smile on my face, I did another triple-triple combination: a triple lutz, triple toe loop. I was the only skater in the competition who did two triple-triples. It was so odd, because I didn't feel like I was working hard and I was getting great speed and height and landing cleanly. Part of it had to do with how hard I'd trained, so I had lots of stamina. But there was something else. I know it sounds crazy, but whenever I skated into a jump, I felt like I was being lifted off the ice from above, as if George, my father, and my coaches Jim and Rick were reaching down from heaven and helping me with my jumps. It truly felt as if they were the wind beneath my wings.

Dad, George, Rick, and Jim were there with me for the rest of my program. I didn't even have to think about getting height, because I was lifted off the ice as if I were in a harness. It was an amazing feeling. And every once in a while I'd catch a glimpse of Laura at the side of the rink, doing every move with me.

With each jump, the roar of the audience got louder and louder until it just about blew me off the ice. Toward the end of the program I felt I wanted to land another jump just to show all eleven thousand people in the stands what I could do and to hear them roar; it was intoxicating.

With less than a minute to go, I had one triple left, my eighth, and then I would be finished with my jumps. I was feeling so relaxed that as I skated by the judges' table, I actually made eye contact with one of the judges, something I hadn't done in years, but I was feeling so confident that I did, and the judge smiled at me. Then I spotted one of Laura's students in the first row, and as I skated past her at one end of the arena, I waved to her. I never, ever did that in a competition, but it felt like the natural thing to do. Then I did my last triple, nailed it, and headed for my final combination spins.

At this point I was flying across the ice, riding high on the roar of the crowd and my own elation, because by then I felt sure that I'd at least made the world team. I went into my final combination spin, holding all of my muscles tight, fighting the incredible centrifugal force, barely able to breathe, and I listened for my cue to finish. But as I spun on the ice, too fast to see, I had trouble hearing the music. Nothing was wrong with my hearing or the audio system. It was the audience. They were all on their feet applauding and cheering like crazy, and they were so loud that I had to strain to hear my final cue.

I was already crying when I finished my spin and went into my final position. I wrapped my right arm around my waist and reached to the heavens with my left arm. I looked up to the rafters, and while I couldn't see my guardian angels, I knew they were there. I crossed myself, took my bows before the thousands of people applauding in the stands, and looked over to the side of the rink where Laura was standing. I could see she was crying, and I skated over as fast as I could, stepped off the ice, hugged her, and yelled over her shoulder and into the air, "Thank you, Dad! Thank you, George! Thank you, Jim! Thank you, Rick!" I couldn't have done it without them.

Laura and I walked over with John Brancato to the kiss-and-cry booth, where we waited for my scores to come up. Sitting there between Laura and John, holding Laura's hand, and knowing now how the other skaters had placed, I figured the best I could possibly do was second. I felt certain the judges wouldn't score me ahead of Todd.

The technical marks came up mostly 5.9s and I squeezed Laura's hand. These were fantastic marks, but I was sure they'd knock down my style marks. I held my breath in anticipation of the style marks, and in that moment, the crowd started chanting, "Six! Six! Six!" It was Reuben who started the chant. I looked at Laura and kind of chuckled and thought to myself, "Yeah, right." There was no way any judge was going to give me a 6.0, especially since I'd never gotten one before.

Usually, they announce when the marks are coming up, "Rudy Galindo's marks for competition and style are . . ." and then they come up on the computer screen as the announcer reads them off. I don't know why, but the numbers just came up without any announcement, and there they were: two 6.0s! The audience erupted. These were the first 6.0s awarded to a skater at nationals since 1988! I was in shock, and before I could react, the final standings flashed on the small video screen in the kiss-and-cry booth, showing me in first place over Todd. I screamed and jumped up and down, and Laura, John, and I hugged each other. In another couple of seconds the final results flashed on the arena scoreboard, and when they did, it was pandemonium. I thought the roof would fly off the building from all the noise.

We hugged and cried some more and then walked out of the kiss-and-cry booth (not for no reason is it called the kiss and cry), and we were met immediately by a couple of Laura's skating parents. They were there working as volunteers, and as volunteers they were supposed to be very professional, but they grabbed us and hugged and kissed us as we all jumped up and down. There aren't too many moments in life that you can describe as pure joy, but this was one of them for me.

As we walked backstage, Olympic figure skating medalists Peggy Fleming and Debi Thomas came up to me, and Peggy said, "Welcome to your new life." Debi added, "Nothing is going to be the same." I wasn't sure what they were talking about, but I didn't have a moment to think about it because I was swept along through the hallway to the room where the final press conference was about to begin.

The press conference was held in a small room underneath the arena, just down the hallway from where the skaters come off the ice. It had room for about one hundred people, but it seemed a lot more packed than that with all the USFSA officials, the judges, television cameras, and all the local and national reporters. As I walked into the room with Laura, the whole atmosphere was electric, as if everyone there had brought the excitement of the competition with them from the arena. I know Laura and I were still flying.

At the front of the room was a long table on a riser. I was seated at the center of the table with Laura next to me, and Todd Eldridge and Dan Hollander were seated on either side of me with their coaches. Dan was as excited as I was, but given the expectations everyone had had for Todd and the expectations Todd must have had for himself, it was no surprise that he was subdued.

Most of the questions were for me. "How do you feel?" "What are you thinking?" "Did you ever imagine this would happen?" "Is it a dream come true?" "How does it feel to win in your hometown?" It was so much fun fielding all the questions. "It feels like a dream . . ." "I'm still in shock . . ." "Yesterday I visualized doing a clean program and getting off the ice with the crowd standing and cheering . . ." "My jumps seemed so light and easy. I don't know if it came from extra training or from above . . ."

One reporter asked how it compared to winning the nationals with Kristi, and I said, "It's a lot sweeter doing it on my own." I also got a question about money, and what I was going to do with it all. As the national champion, there would be all kinds of opportunities to earn money. Even before we got to the press conference, Laura and I saw Harris Collins, one of the people who ran the annual Tom Collins Campbell's Soup Tour of World Figure Skating Champions, a premier skating tour. He told us not to sign anything without talking to him.

In response to the money question, I said, "I guess I can pay for my ice time next year. I won't have to be out on a corner holding a sign, 'I'll work for food.' " I was asked a follow-up question about how I'd supported myself during the last year, and I explained, "I had to teach classes and I put money aside to pay for the choreography and my costumes. And, of course, my sister is free." Without missing a beat, Laura said, "Not anymore." Everyone laughed, including me.

During the press conference, it hadn't occurred to me that anyone would ask me about being gay, but as Laura and I were trying to leave the conference room, we were surrounded by a few reporters who still had questions, and that's when I was asked how I felt about being the first openly gay national champion. I hadn't thought about it. Two things flashed through my mind: I don't know what I'm supposed to say, and the last thing I want to do is talk about anything that's going to get me in trouble with the USFSA. So I said, "No comment." I figured there would be time to deal with that later.

Right after the press conference I was taken down the hall to be drug tested, which is standard procedure. I went into the room, and I was handed a little cup in a wrapper. You have to pee into the cup, which was quite a challenge. Given all the excitement, I really had to concentrate and keep my hand from shaking.

After the drug test, I walked with Laura and John out to the side of the ice where we waited with Todd and Dan, and Scott Davis, who'd placed fourth, for the awards podium to be put in place at the center of the ice. Dan and I were like little kids with our noses pressed to the candy store window, looking at the medals, which we could see by the side of the rink. We were so excited. I tried saying something to Todd, but he was deep in thought and apparently didn't hear me.

Once the awards podium was in place, they rolled out the red carpet—literally—from the edge of the ice to the base of the podium. Then the four young girls who carried the medals stepped out onto the ice and skated over to the podium. They were dressed in black uniforms with multicolored vests, and each carried a medal on a little pillow.

Besides the four girls with their little pillows, someone was standing by the podium holding a big silver plate, which I didn't notice at first, but Dan pointed it out and said, "Oh, you're lucky, you get the big plate." I could hardly believe it, but if I harbored any doubts that I'd really won the national championship, the announcer took care of that:

"Ladies and gentlemen, our gold medal winner, the 1996 national men's champion, from the St. Moritz Ice Skating Club in Berkeley, California—Rudy Galindo!" And once again the crowd was on its feet cheering. Dan just about had to push me out onto the ice. It's one thing to do a performance, but I felt embarrassed going out to take my position on the podium. Don't get me wrong. I was thrilled to win, and I was proud of what I'd achieved. But in that moment I felt a little shy.

From where I stood at the edge of the ice I waved to the crowd and bowed to one side and then the other. Then I skated out to the podium, went behind it, and climbed the steps to the number one position. I stood there all by myself, acknowledging the people in the crowd, smiling and waving to everyone. As I waved, I was thinking to myself, "Please hurry up and call the other kids. I don't want to be out here by myself."

As the other skaters were called, I started thinking about how much it had taken to get to that point, and what a long time it had been since I'd been honored in this way at a national championship. It was a familiar feeling, but standing there by myself, instead of with my pairs partner, I was just about bursting with a sense of pride and accomplishment for having done it on my own. Then I thought of my father, and how proud he would have been, and that brought tears to my eyes. I wanted to go home and show my dad the medal the way I always had in the past. He'd be sitting in his chair, waiting for me to come through the door.

During my last years with Kristi, when Dad was too ill to come to competitions, we had this routine where before I left for a competition he'd say, "Let the golden star above shine on you." And whenever I came home with a medal, he'd say, "I told you that golden star was shining on you." His eyesight was just about gone from the diabetes and he'd hold the medal really close to his eyes. Then he'd run his fingers over it, and he'd just smile. A couple of times I caught him talking to Mom and saying how proud he was of me. I tried to imagine that he was in heaven at that moment looking down from above, and that he was the golden star shining down on me that night.

I was so caught up in my reverie that I almost didn't notice when they started giving out the awards. Various officials from the USFSA actually present the awards, and as an official placed the award around my neck, he said, "Congratulations! Great job!" I said, "Thank you."

That night, after the awards ceremony, there was a competitors party. I'd planned to go, but I was so mobbed after the awards ceremony that Laura and I decided it would be more fun to go out and celebrate in a quiet corner at an Italian restaurant that she liked, not far from the arena.

We were just a small group: me and Laura, Andy, John Brancato and Kevin Peeks, Reuben and Wayne, and a couple of other friends of Laura's. Mom was so exhausted from the competition that after she had a chance to hug me following the press conference, Andy drove her home and then came to meet us at the restaurant.

They seated us in the back of the restaurant in a dark corner, but that didn't keep people from coming up to the table to congratulate me. The funniest remark was when someone said, "Thank you for putting San Jose on the map." I thought to myself, "San Jose is already on the map, what do you need me for?" Thank goodness I had the presence of mind not to say what I was thinking, and I smiled and said, "Thank you." I was smiling so much during that dinner that my cheeks were hurting, and with all the people coming over to the table, I could hardly get a piece of ziti in my mouth without being interrupted. But it was a small price to pay for all the adulation and support. I could always eat something when I got home.

After dinner and all the hugs good-bye, Andy and Laura drove me home. We pulled up in front of the trailer, and the whole side of it was covered with gold balloons and a big banner that said, "Congratulations!" One of the coaches from the Ice Centre, a close friend of Laura's, had run around after the competition getting all the little kids who take lessons to sign the banner. Then she raced over to the house, put up the balloons, and hung the banner.

Mom stepped out of the trailer. "Look at all these beautiful balloons!" she said. I told her that I could hardly miss them, and we went inside. She gave me a kiss, and she was so exhausted from all the excitement that she went right back to bed.

It was such a wild day that it was weird being home all by myself. I went into my room and got undressed, and before getting into bed I put on a CD that Reuben had given me before nationals. It was the sound track to the movie *Waiting to Exhale*, and it came with a "Good Luck" card in which Reuben had written out the lyrics from one of the songs, "Count on Me," which is about friendship. I cued up the song, turned it up really loud, and as I listened to the lyrics and thought about what good friends Reuben and Wayne had been to me, I started to cry. After a day like the one I'd just had, I thought I was entitled to a good cry. And for a change, these tears had nothing to do with sorrow, loss, or disappointment.

After the song was over, I turned off my CD player. I kissed my bears good-night and I prayed. I thanked Dad and George for giving me the strength to win, and for being my guardian angels. Then I asked God to bless all my friends and family, the cats, and Boo Boo and Goo Goo. I ended with, "I love you, God. Amen."

I don't know why I thought I would sleep, because after the evening I'd had, I couldn't even keep my eyes closed. So I thought about the long program, and I imagined doing it again and the audience giving me a standing ovation. I thought about how far I'd come since the breakup with Kristi, and how lucky I was. And I also thought about the larger meaning of the gold medal's being awarded to someone like me: an effeminate gay Mexican-American. I thought that my winning proved that whatever discrimination there is—or was—in skating, it didn't keep me from winning as long as I gave a winning performance. As Morry Stillwell, president of the USFSA said in an interview at the arena after my win, if "peripheral" issues decided skating competitions, "you wouldn't have the judging panel doing what they did today." He added, "There are a lot more weird people in this sport than Rudy." That's for sure!

16

—

FAME

The two months between nationals and the world championships in Edmonton were a metaphor for my life. There were incredible highs and surprising lows and not a lot in between.

First, some of the lows. If I had any fantasies of living happily ever after following my win at nationals, those hopes were dashed during my first week as national champion, because I found myself at the center of a media frenzy and was completely overwhelmed. The phone never stopped ringing, and not just my mother's phone and Laura's phone. There's some poor guy in San Jose, Rob Galindo, who's listed in the phone book under R. Galindo, and he got thirty phone calls that first day after nationals. All the national media were calling wanting interviews, and all kinds of people were calling to congratulate me, even people I didn't know. We even got a phone call from the president's office congratulating me and inviting me to the White House. The one call I really wanted to take was from

Kristi, but I was running from interview to interview, and we kept playing phone tag.

Laura and I had had no experience with this sort of thing. I'd gone overnight from complete obscurity to being a national news story, and it was more than either of us could handle. We didn't realize that I could have just said no to everything. Instead, we were trying to juggle all these requests, running from one place to the next, with barely a moment to stop for something to eat. I felt pulled in every direction, with Laura fielding the calls and then asking me to help decide which requests to accept and which to turn down. It was horrible.

It was clear from that first day that we needed to hire someone to handle all the media requests and appearance requests and to deal with the Tom Collins tour folks to negotiate a contract. They wanted me to join their winter tour for a three-and-a-half-week engagement and then their big seventy-six-city national tour following the world championships, and Laura and I couldn't negotiate that kind of deal on our own.

So we hired a well-known skating agent, Michael Rosenberg—and just in the nick of time, too, because Laura and I were at each other's throat by the end of the first week. We were both under so much pressure and so exhausted that we had a huge blowout over nothing in particular that ended with Laura bursting into tears and with me storming out of the restaurant where we were having dinner. I guess it was inevitable given the circumstances, but it was a hard landing after the high of winning nationals.

Even something as simple as going to practice became a big challenge. Before nationals I could go to practice without having everyone at the rink watch every single jump. But now there were parents, little league hockey players, beginning ice-skaters, reporters, and television news crews all focused on me. With everyone watching, I felt this incredible pressure to skate as well as I'd skated at nationals. Every jump had to be perfect, but with everyone watching, I became self-conscious. After an hour on the ice, I got off, thanked everyone for being there to support me, and left. All the attention was going to take some getting used to.

On the plus side, I was stunned and encouraged by all the support I got from people in San Jose. At the gym, I had these big guys coming up to me telling me how they had cried watching my performance and how proud they were of what I'd accomplished. A waitress at lunch one day came up and told me how touched she was that someone who had worked so hard had achieved his dreams and had made it. But despite the predictions of my friends—and despite my hopes—no one asked me out on a date!

Lots of people mentioned the world championships and said things like, "Skate the way you did at nationals and you'll be world champion." I knew I could never skate that way again. Everything came together at nationals in a way it never could again, no matter how well I skated. So having people telling me to do well at worlds, or saying, "Make us proud at the world championships," just added to the pressure I was feeling over having to prove that nationals wasn't a fluke, that I wasn't just a one-shot deal. Also, I didn't want to let down all these people who were counting on me to do well. How was I ever going to skate well with all that pressure?

Among the various events that were held in my honor those first couple of weeks, the one that overwhelmed me was given by the Mexican-American Community Services Agency in San Jose. As the first Mexican-American national figure-skating champion, I realized that some people who shared my heritage took particular pride in my accomplishments. After nationals, a lot of people came up to me on the street and congratulated me in Spanish and started talking to me. And all I could manage to say in Spanish was "Thank you, but I don't know anything." And I don't. My father's parents were Mexican, and like a lot of second-generation Americans, I'd never learned their native language. It made me feel like an idiot.

When we drove up to the Mexican-American Community Services Agency, which was on the east side of San Jose, there were police officers on horseback, and volunteers directing traffic and showing people where to park. They'd expected about two hundred people to come to the reception, but eight hundred people showed up.

I was taken to a waiting area adjacent to the gym where the stands were packed to overflowing. My mother and some of her relatives were waiting to greet me. I was glad they were there, and spending a few minutes with all of them helped me calm down. After a short while, I was introduced to the crowd, and as I walked into the gym and took a seat on the dais, people started clapping, stomping their feet, and whistling. It went on for several minutes before everyone quieted down.

A couple of people spoke before I did and talked about what my accomplishment meant to the community, and then it was my turn to speak. When I stepped up to the microphone, people applauded all over again, and the smiles on the faces of everyone in the room were incredibly uplifting and put me at ease.

Speaking before a large audience was something entirely new for me, so I kept my remarks short. I said, "I can't explain how incredible this feeling is to stand here in front of you and receive all of this love. I'd like to tell you that if you have a dream, if you want something badly enough, and you work hard, it will come true. Look at me, I'm proof!" And with that, they were on their feet again applauding.

Afterward, I signed more than three hundred autographs, and by the end my arm was killing me. But it was worth it, especially when teenagers in line told me that I'd inspired them to stay in school and pursue their dreams. I couldn't believe how many people were affected by what I'd done.

The most amazing thing was when my eighth-grade history teacher, Ross Jackson, asked me to sign an old yearbook from when I was his student. I still can't believe that my teacher wanted my autograph.

Another big high point was when Kristi and I finally got to talk. Since the breakup, we'd bumped into each other at events a few times, but we'd never just had a conversation one-on-one. She was incredibly gracious and congratulated me on my win. So we talked and talked and discussed what it was like to be a champion skater, and how weird it was to be suddenly famous. She told me that my life had changed forever, and that I should be sure to enjoy it.

Before we said good-bye, Kristi told me how proud she was of me, which meant a lot to me. I was glad we were back in touch with each other after so long.

One of the things I tried to enjoy was the financial rewards that followed my win at nationals. The first windfall was a substantial, no-strings-attached check that came from Tom Collins Productions, in advance of my signing a contract to go on their Campbell's Soup winter skating tour, to help with training costs.

When I opened the Federal Express package and looked at the check, I thought someone was playing a joke on me. But Laura was there, and she looked at the letter and the check, and it really was a very generous check made out to Rudy Galindo. For someone who was paying off a $300 doctor bill at a rate of $20 a month, Tommy's gift was a huge amount of money. It was breathtaking!

I'd lived for a long time on very little, so it's not like I even knew what to do with the money Tommy sent. So I gave the check to Laura to take care of, and the two of us went out and bought a new pair of sneakers for me, a video camera so I could tape my practices, and a leather jacket for Laura. I didn't have any credit cards, so Laura used hers and I paid her back once the check cleared. It was scary spending any money, because I thought I should put all of it in the bank, but Laura told me not to worry, that I could afford to spend a few dollars, especially given all the offers that were coming in and the anticipated income from the upcoming skating tour.

But that was all I bought, although I did test-drive a new car, which I thought would be fun. Andy knew from Laura how much I'd always wanted to have a Corvette, so he arranged for me to drive a loaner car for a day. It was so funny when we went to the dealership, because they asked for my insurance card. I didn't need insurance to drive my bicycle. So Laura took care of that by giving the dealer her insurance card, and he handed me the keys to a forest-green T-top Corvette. That's the kind where you can remove the roof panels, so it's like a convertible.

As Laura and I pulled out of the lot, I just loved the feeling of being behind the wheel, but then as we drove down the road, people started recognizing me and honking and giving me the thumbs-up sign. I started feeling self-conscious driving this really fancy car, and I started shaking. Once again, I was overwhelmed. I pulled over to the side of the road and turned off the engine. I was sweating, and I put my head down on the steering wheel. Laura asked me if I was okay. I wasn't. It was too much, too soon. I'd wait to buy a car.

The best thing about knowing that I'd be earning a lot of money was that I could pay back Laura for all she'd done and take my mom shopping at nice department stores and maybe even buy her a house. What made me sad, though, was that my father didn't live long enough for me to pay him back. He'd put so much into my skating, passing up the dream of owning a home, not taking vacations, and now that I could look forward to giving back to my family, my father was gone.

Once my agent, Michael Rosenberg, started negotiating the various offers that had come in, I asked Laura not to tell me how much money was involved, because it made me far too nervous. I was afraid even to get out on the ice. What if I fell and couldn't skate? So much was riding on every jump now that I was having trouble keeping my mind clear enough to focus on skating.

As much as Laura and I tried to get focused back on skating, so I could start preparing for the world championships in March, it was impossible to get clear of the ongoing frenzy. That was the primary reason Laura decided that it was a good idea for me to accept the offer to go on the Tom Collins

Campbell's Soup winter tour for three and a half weeks. That would get me away from home, and I'd still get back to San Jose in time to prepare for the world championships. And by that time, we expected that things would have quieted down.

The day before leaving on the tour, I wanted to get in some practice time at the rink. It had been several days since I'd had the chance to train, and I don't know what I was thinking, but I got on the ice without warming up and just started going through my jumps. So many things were going through my mind, from worrying about what I was going to bring on the tour to feeling the pressure of the upcoming world championships, that I wasn't concentrating on what I was doing.

When you're spinning through the air and landing on a quarter-inch-wide piece of steel, it's not a good idea to think about other things, especially when you haven't warmed up. And sure enough, I slipped off the edge of my skate after landing a triple lutz and fell. It wasn't until I started getting up that I realized I'd sprained my ankle. I didn't think it was a bad sprain, so I did a few more jumps and then went home. I didn't say anything to anyone about my ankle, in part because it didn't hurt that much, but I was also leaving the next morning on a flight to Pittsburgh to join the winter tour, and I was afraid if I said anything, I'd have to stay home and miss the tour.

By the time I got off the plane, my ankle was so swollen that I had trouble walking up the ramp into the terminal. And during my first practice, I couldn't do anything, not even a waltz jump. Fortunately, a physical therapist travels with the tour, and over the next several days, and then for the rest of the tour, he worked on my ankle, and every night he taped it so I could do my jumps. By the end of the tour, even with all the skating I was doing, my ankle was almost back to normal.

I had a blast on the tour, traveling with all of these famous skaters, from Brian Boitano to Oksana Baiul. More than once, I had to pinch myself to make sure I wasn't dreaming. I'd watched all of these skaters on television, always envious of their success, and now I was one of them, skating before sold-out crowds every night, soaking up the adulation like a sponge. And everywhere we went, we stayed in first-class hotels and were treated like royalty. As unreal as it all was, I didn't have a lot of trouble getting used to it, but I never took any of it for granted. After struggling for so many years, I wasn't about to forget where I'd come from.

Before going back to San Jose to train for the world championships, I had one more commitment. While I was away on tour, I was invited to go to St. Petersburg, Russia, for a major "U.S. vs. Russia" competition. It would be an opportunity to compete against the best Russian skaters, who were generally the best skaters in the world, in advance of the world championships. It would also be my first chance to demonstrate that I could compete at a world-class level.

Two days before I was set to leave for St. Petersburg, I was out shopping in Savannah, Georgia, with some of the skaters from the tour, and I stepped on a rock and wrenched my left ankle again. It was the first time I'd gone out walking without taping the ankle, and that was a big mistake. I dropped my bags and fell to my knees in pain. This time, I knew right away that I'd done damage.

Having hurt my ankle again, I should have withdrawn from the St. Petersburg event. With only three weeks to go before worlds, the most important thing was for me to go home and stay off my ankle for a few days. But I was under so much pressure to prove myself, and everyone around me was saying that I couldn't withdraw because it would look bad, as if I were afraid of having to prove myself against the best Russian skaters. It was a difficult decision to make, and I made the wrong one. I didn't withdraw.

By the time Laura and I got to St. Petersburg, the swelling was down, but in practice none of my jumps were solid, and because it was the left ankle that I'd sprained, I couldn't even attempt a triple lutz. The pressure of the takeoff was just too painful. I managed to get through practice and even did the short program, but I was in pain the whole time and I two-footed the landing on the triple lutz. By the end of the program my ankle was numb, and I knew I couldn't get back on the ice to skate the long program. I'd be lucky if I was well enough to skate at worlds. I withdrew from the rest of the competition and flew home. Besides the additional damage I did to my ankle, all I managed to accomplish in St. Petersburg was to give ammunition to those who said I was a one-shot deal.

17

THE WORLD CHAMPIONSHIPS

I returned to San Jose from Russia completely exhausted and emotionally shot, not exactly the condition you want to be in three weeks before a world competition. But fortunately, after a couple days' rest, Laura was quick to get me back into a daily training schedule, and at the same time I went to a wonderful physical therapist, Donna Burden, who worked on my ankle every day.

Although we'd hoped that things would quiet down, with the world championships approaching it was almost as intense as before we left. But we'd learned how to handle the frenzy a little better, and my agent was making sure that I wasn't overdoing it with the interviews. Still, I looked forward to my half-hour daily session with the physical therapist because it was the one time during the day when I didn't have to deal with fans, the press, the telephone, and decisions. All I had to do was sit there and relax as Donna massaged my ankle.

On the ice, Laura was careful to work me up gradually to

doing my full program and all of my jumps. Within a week, she had me doing everything but the triple lutz and triple flip. It was another week before my ankle felt strong enough to finally do those jumps, and when I did, you could see the relief on Laura's face. It only hurt a little bit to do them, and I knew in time the pain would disappear entirely. It felt great to do my full program again, and to do it confidently. With just a few days to go before we were to leave for Edmonton, I felt that I was back in top form.

The only real challenge I felt in the countdown to the world championships was staying focused emotionally. Over and over in media interviews and in comments from people who saw me at the rink or stopped me on the street, people were saying how if I skated the same at worlds as I skated at nationals, I was going to win the gold. I found myself explaining over and over that this was my first time at worlds in singles, and that all I hoped for was to make the top ten. No one goes to the worlds for the first time and wins a gold medal. It would be foolish of me even to think that I could do well enough to get any medal my first time out on the world stage.

Despite the pressure of people's expectations, in the days before leaving for Edmonton, I was in really high spirits. My ankle was better, my practices were going great, and I felt confident that I could do well enough at worlds to prove all the doubters wrong. To celebrate, Reuben and I decided to go up to San Francisco to a gay club that I liked. So I got dressed up in a nice pair of jeans and a pressed shirt, and we drove to the city. I was excited, because I hadn't been there since nationals, and I was curious to see what kind of reaction I would get.

Reuben and I walked into the place, and it was as if a cold wind had blown through the room. We walked over to the bar and I said hello to the bartender, who had always greeted me warmly in the past. In a chilly voice he said, "Hello, how are you doing?" It seemed odd to me, and then this guy I didn't even know walked by me and said, "Thanks a lot, Rudy, you asshole." We got out of there fast, and Reuben asked me if I'd said anything to insult the guy. I'd never seen him before in my life.

It was so confusing, because since nationals, wherever I went, straight people had always greeted me so warmly. I couldn't understand why my own community had turned its back on me, and I felt really hurt. I told Reuben I wanted to go home and we got back in the car and drove to San Jose.

What I didn't know at the time was that my "no comment" remark after the press conference at nationals, and my decision not to talk to the gay press, had led to a number of different articles in which I'd been condemned for trying to go back into the closet. I also discovered that people had expectations of me being able to speak out as a gay spokesperson, but what I think people didn't understand was that I had absolutely no background in the gay civil rights struggle and didn't have the vaguest idea of what I should say in response to "How do you feel about being the first openly gay national figure-skating champion?" I was just a skater who happened to be gay and didn't hide it, and in that moment after the press conference, I was too scared to say anything other than "No comment." Then when the gay papers started asking for interviews, I stupidly said no, thinking I should keep the focus just on my skating.

Thankfully, when I later learned what was going on, I was able to clear up the misunderstandings in a couple of different interviews that I did with the gay press. In the interviews I explained that I couldn't believe that people thought I was trying to go back in the closet. I wasn't in the least bit ashamed of being gay and had nothing to hide. I just didn't know what to say at first without getting myself in trouble, but because I didn't talk about it, trouble was exactly what I got myself into.

Very quickly, and in part after reading Greg Louganis's autobiography, I learned a lot about what an important position I was in as an openly gay competitive athlete, and how important it was for me not to appear as if I were in any way ashamed of or embarrassed by my sexual orientation.

Anyone who knows me knows that I believe that all gay and

lesbian people should be able to live their lives openly and without the threat of discrimination. I thought that went without saying. And if I can be an example of a gay person who's managed to be himself and still achieved his dreams, I'm happy to do that. I just hope that people aren't disappointed when I don't take the lead on gay rights issues. I'm a skater who happens to be gay, and I don't think it's fair for people to expect me to be an expert on anything other than skating.

So how do I feel about being the first openly gay national figure-skating champion? I should have said, "I'm proud to have won the national championship, and I'm proud of who I am. The fact that I'm out and still won proves that in the sport of figure skating there's no longer a need to hide. I hope my example inspires others to be themselves. It's a lot easier than hiding."

Since getting the opportunity to clear things up, I've been welcomed warmly by gay people all over the country. I was even invited to be the grand marshal at the 1996 Ft. Lauderdale Gay Pride Parade and to be the starter for the annual Front Runner's Gay Pride fun run in New York City. Unfortunately, I was on tour at the time and couldn't make either event, but I loved being invited and I look forward to when I can accept some of the many invitations I've received.

Laura and I left for the world championships in Edmonton a full week before the competition was to begin. We wanted to be sure I had enough time to get settled and to get used to the ice at the Northlands Coliseum, which was where Kristi and I had trained.

It was odd being back in Edmonton. It was as if my life had come full circle, but instead of being at one of the lowest points in my life, I was returning to Edmonton as the U.S. national champion. People on the street and at the coliseum were wonderful to me and treated me like a hometown kid. Everywhere I went people wished me good luck, patted me on the back, and requested autographs.

I tried not to think too much about everyone else's expectations of me. I knew some people believed I'd fail miserably, and some people were also talking about what a storybook ending it would be if I won the gold medal. I tried to put it all out of my mind, because to think about it would have been debilitating. I was in Edmonton to do the best I could, and of course I planned to skate for first place—but as long as I made the top ten, I'd go home satisfied.

To keep the pressure from getting to me and to calm my nerves, I took Laura, Andy, Reuben, and Wayne, who'd flown up to be with me at worlds, to the West Edmonton Mall to ride the Mindbender roller coaster. We did that on three different days. I know this may not sound relaxing to some people, but nothing helped me to unwind better than riding the roller coaster, over and over. Everyone was pretty green after the first few times, but I probably rode it ten times on the day before the qualifying round. And as a follow-up I rode the Zipper. To me it was like doing spins on the ice, and I just laughed as we went around and around. I'm afraid I was the only one laughing by the time the ride stopped.

The most nerve-racking part of being at worlds was the qualifying round. Skaters who had been to worlds the previous year and had placed in the top ten didn't have to compete in this round, so Todd Eldredge was exempt. But this was my first time out, so I had to earn the right to compete. I tried not to think, "What if I don't qualify?" But the thought kept creeping into my mind.

Several of the skaters and coaches who had been to worlds before told me not to worry about qualifying, that all I had to do was a couple of triple jumps and I'd have no trouble making the cut. But I wasn't taking any chances and planned to do my full program with all eight triples.

I was so nervous in the warm-up session that I missed two of my triples and wound up doing doubles instead. So by the time Laura and I were at the edge of the ice waiting for my name to be announced, I was gasping for air. I felt like I was going to faint, and I held on to Laura's hand just to stay on my feet.

Added to that, I was fighting an old battle in my head against those familiar negative thoughts. I had this one voice saying I couldn't possibly go out there and do a clean program after doing so badly in the warm-up, then I had this other voice saying, "You can do it. You know you can do it."

When they announced my name, I got such a warm welcome from the five thousand people in the stands that it helped break the spell, and I pushed back all the negative thoughts as I stepped onto the ice, took my opening position, and waited for the music to start.

I planned to open with my usual triple axel, triple toe, but I had trouble with the landing on the triple axel, so I cut the triple toe to a double. To make up for it, I added a triple flip, triple toe later in the program. I wasn't taking any chances.

I finished the program to a standing ovation and got the highest scores of anyone in my group of seventeen skaters. But even more important than coming in first in my group, doing as well as I did made me feel confident that what I accomplished in San Jose wasn't a fluke. I'd made it to the world championships because I *deserved* to be there. I could say good-bye to those negative voices once and for all.

The field of competitors at worlds was daunting, so I don't think I was wrong to say that I would have been happy as long as I placed in the top ten. The top contenders included Elvis Stojko of Canada, who'd won the previous two world championships; Philippe Candeloro of France, who had won the silver and bronze at the last two worlds; Ilia Kulik of Russia, who was only eighteen but had taken ninth at his first worlds in 1995 and won the St. Petersburg competition that I'd withdrawn from; Aleksei Urmanov, also of Russia, the Olympic gold medalist at Lillehammer; and Todd Eldredge. That I could possibly come to the world championships my first time and win the gold medal was clearly a fantasy, and I can tell you honestly that I was too much of a realist for it to be *my* fantasy.

I had hoped I wouldn't be nervous the night of the short program; my goal had been just to have fun. But when I walked out into the arena with Laura to do my warm-up and looked out at the sixteen thousand people in the stands, I got very nervous. I took some deep breaths and thought to myself that all I had to do was score in the top ten. But there were thirty skaters, and if I didn't do well, tenth place could turn out to be an unreachable goal. Fortunately, I didn't have much time to dwell on that thought, and before I knew it the warm-up was over, and the announcer was introducing me for the short program.

The audience gave me a warm welcome, and a big section filled with Americans, waving little American flags, stood up and cheered—that's where Andy and Reuben and Wayne were sitting. I took my position, and then the music started.

Other than cutting my second jump to a triple-double from a triple-triple, I skated a perfectly clean short, and I was rewarded with my second standing ovation of the competition. I just loved those standing ovations, but the good feeling I got from the audience that night didn't come close to what I'd felt in San Jose. I knew it would never be that way again, but it was hard not to feel a little disappointed.

The final results from the short were much better than I'd thought they would be. As fate would have it, Elvis fell on his triple-triple combination and placed seventh, and Candeloro did a single axel instead of his planned combination and wound up in sixteenth place. That eliminated both of them from a chance at a medal, and it left me in fourth place behind Ilia Kulik, Todd Eldredge, and Aleksei Urmanov. I was stunned, because now I had a shot at a medal. It always pays to have realistic expectations, because you can really enjoy it when you exceed them.

I spent much of the next day on the roller coaster, so by the time I got back to the hotel I was feeling totally relaxed and I had every expectation that I wouldn't be nervous at the competition that night. I'd already proved that what had happened in San Jose wasn't a fluke. I was even in a position to win a medal. But as I walked down the hallway from my hotel room on my way to the arena, with Laura and Andy at my side,

I was the most nervous I'd ever been. I was shaking and sweating. Here I was, my first time at the world championships as a singles skater, and I was skating in the final warm-up round with the best skaters in the world. I felt a little bit like an impostor and that any minute they'd discover they'd made a mistake and ask me to get off the ice.

I asked Laura if she was nervous, and she did a great job of lying and said no. I had no idea until later that underneath her perfectly cool and calm facade she was struggling to keep her legs from shaking. I don't know how she did it, but her calm manner helped me pull myself together once we got to the arena.

I went through my usual stretches and warm-up routine, and by the time they introduced me for the long program, I'd settled down and my heart wasn't jumping out of my chest. I gave Laura a kiss, she smiled and told me to stay tough, and I skated out to my starting position. As I skated around, getting comfortable, I looked up and saw that several people in the audience were holding up signs with my name: "Rudy!" And I spotted a couple of rainbow flags, which are symbols of gay pride. That really gave me a boost.

I took my starting position, and while I waited for the music to start, I reminded myself that I'd already proven myself, that I just needed to skate my best, and that Laura, my mom, and my friends would still love me no matter how I did.

I did great. I hit my first two triple-triple combination jumps without a hitch and didn't miss on any of my other jumps or spins. It was another clean program, and as I went into my final combination spins, the crowd was on its feet. It was amazing. But even more amazing was Laura's smile. You could see relief, joy, and pride all wrapped up in that smile, and she had tears coming down her cheeks. We just hugged and hugged.

My scores weren't quite as high as I'd hoped for, but it was over, and for the moment I was in first place. Since I was the first in my group to skate, we wouldn't know the final results until the last skater was through. So all we could do now was watch the other skaters. And now that it was over for me, it was actually fun watching the other skaters do their programs.

When the final results were calculated and the final order was flashed on the arena scoreboard, I couldn't believe my eyes. I grabbed Laura and we just screamed and jumped up and down. Todd Eldredge was in first place. Ilia Kulik was second, and as hard as it was to believe, I was third! It was the first time the United States had won two medals at the world championships since Scott Hamilton and David Santee finished first and second in 1981. It was a very sweet moment, and I was filled with a sense of accomplishment and pride.

For the first time in my life, I didn't have to imagine what it would be like standing on the podium at the world championships, while they played the national anthem. I stood there on the podium, looking out at the thousands of people in the audience, and I placed my hand over my heart. I looked over to where Laura was standing, and I could see her there crying. I thought of my dad and my brother, wishing they were there with us, and tears filled my eyes as well.

From the awards ceremony we went to the press conference, and after the press conference, before we left to go back to the dressing room, I took the bronze medal from around my neck and put it around Laura's neck. She deserved it as much as I did. Even more.

The next day we got an early start because we had to rehearse for what I suspected was going to be the most meaningful part of the world championships for me, the exhibition program. It wasn't a competition; it was an opportunity to do whatever we wanted on the ice without having to worry about our marks or our competitors. All the medalists were invited to perform on the final afternoon of the championship, and I planned to dedicate my program to George, Rick, and Jim.

Fortunately, I'd already been working with Laura on a new program for the upcoming Campbell's Soup tour, so I had something that was special and new. I was using music that George had helped me choose. Two years before, I'd had an exhibition to do, and George was too sick to go, so to make him feel that he had a part in it, I asked him to listen to different kinds of music and help me choose something to skate to. The one he liked best was an instrumental version of "Ave Maria." I thought it was beautiful.

For worlds, I was using a version of "Ave Maria" sung by the Fleet Street Choir at Stanford University. It's so spiritual and moving that the voices of the choir lift me to another state of mind, and it feels as if I'm floating. To match the music, Laura and I did choreography that drew from different kinds of spiritual imagery, but they were things from my own life, so I wasn't sure people would get it.

My costume was also part of the imagery. It was a black velvet, one-piece outfit, and around my neck I draped a six-inch-wide strip of red fabric in the shape of a big AIDS ribbon. It was my way of remembering the people I loved who had died from AIDS and conveying that to the audience. Most of the people there knew my story from the press reports, so they knew what a huge impact AIDS had had on my life. I could have worn one of those standard-size AIDS ribbons, but if I'd done that, the people way up in the stands couldn't have seen it, and they'd miss the point of what I was doing.

But before I knew it, it was my turn to perform. They announced my name and I skated out to my starting point on the ice and took my opening position. I placed my arms at my sides and looked down at the ice. In the moment before the music started, I thought, "Will they get this?" But once the music began playing, I was transported, and I let the music carry me.

As the music began, I looked up and turned around, facing the audience, as if to say, "Here I am." Then I took a couple of strokes and assumed the position of Christ on the cross as I glided across the ice. I simply raised my arms as if I were draped on the cross, then raised one leg, crossing it over the other, and I cocked my head to the side. To me that represented what the whole piece was about, how George and Rick and Jim were up in heaven and Jesus was taking care of them. And now they were looking after me. By assuming that position, I was trying to say to the audience that my loved ones were safe in heaven.

From there I skated around and did a double axel, then I glided across the ice and extended my right arm so that I could see the spotlights filtered through my fingers. And as I looked into the light, I imagined that I could see George. Then I skated around, did a triple loop, and once I landed, I stopped on the ice and reached out to the audience as if I were in pain. Then I clenched my fist, looked down at the ice, closed my eyes, and drew my fist back toward me, to show that I didn't want to let George go.

After that I did a spin and a turn and stepped forward, raising both of my arms to the heavens. I was sad that my loved ones were gone, but I was reaching toward heaven to show that I knew they were okay. Then I went down on one knee, wiped the ice smooth with my hand, and looked down and visualized four faces: my dad, George, Jim, and Rick. And I thought to myself, "I wish you guys were here, I love you." As I stood up, I did a backbend and watched the ice drip from my fingers.

I ended with a series of moves and spins. The final spin was my shotgun, which is where I hold my leg like a rifle in front of me and lean back, so I look like a spinning *Y* on the ice. Then I let go of my leg and collapsed to the ice, as if in death. But that wasn't the end, because as the music faded away and the light diminished to black, I reached for the sky, I reached for life.

The next morning I was on a plane to Boston to join the four-month skating tour. Debi Thomas and Peggy Fleming were right; my life had changed forever, and in ways I couldn't yet imagine.

POSTSCRIPT—
DECEMBER 1, 1996

It's been an amazing several months since I left for the first stop on the seventy-six city Tom Collins Campbell's Soup Tour of World Figure Skating Champions. Try saying that ten times fast. And then try imagining what it's like traveling to that many cities and performing that many times in four months. I had a blast, but what a whirlwind!

There was a lot to like about being on tour. First of all, everything was taken care of for us from travel and meals to hotels and physical therapy. The whole thing was a cross between a Broadway show, a Las Vegas revue, the Ringling Bros. and Barnum & Bailey Circus, and a traveling rock concert. This unbelievable operation consisted of more than thirty skaters, five support staff, and a crew of thirteen people who set up all the equipment in each city. Ten of the crew traveled in a crew bus along with four tractor-trailer trucks, and three of the crew flew in to each city in advance of the tour to prepare for the arrival of the trucks. I've never seen people work so hard in my life. As we were taking our final bows before the sold-out, cheering crowds, the crews were already packing up our workout equipment, the washer-dryer, the traveling offices, everything. And once the audience was gone and we were on our way back to the hotel, down came the lights, up came the runners, all the computers and sound equipment were packed into shipping containers, everything was loaded onto the trucks, and off they drove to the next city. There was no question who had the hard jobs on the tour, and it wasn't the skaters.

One of the things I liked best on the tour was meeting the other champion skaters and making friends. This amazing group of people included Brian Boitano, Michelle Kwan, Elvis Stojko, Chen Lu, Surya Bonaly, Nicole Bobek, Nancy Kerrigan, Oksana Baiul, Todd Eldredge, and Viktor Petrenko. On more than one occasion, while getting on the bus or waiting at a gate at the airport, I looked around at all of these famous skaters and thought, "What am I doing here?"

Most of the time, everyone got along well, especially considering that you had so many champions traveling together. Given all the egos, mine included, and traveling in such close quarters, it was a surprisingly congenial group of people with only the occasional moment of tension.

For the majority of the tour I hung out with 1995 national champion Nicole Bobek and Nicole's mom, Jana. Nicole and I share the same adolescent sense of humor and spent a lot of time in the back of the bus teasing each other, cracking jokes, and laughing at the most ridiculous things. I don't think all of our traveling companions appreciated the racket we made, but they were very tolerant of us.

One of the things I wondered about before leaving on the tour was how the other skaters would treat me now that it was so widely known that I was gay. I hoped there wouldn't be any problems, and there weren't; I was made to feel completely welcome. Some of the other skaters and a number of the support staff and crew would tease me sometimes, pointing out a guy and asking if I thought he was cute, which I thought was great. It was just the kind of teasing that let me know that people felt comfortable with who I am. If there were people who had a problem, they kept their thoughts to themselves.

I can't tell you how many times I was asked privately if any other gay skaters were on the tour. Of course there were, although I was the only one who was public about it, and none of the skaters who I assumed were gay ever confided in me. That said, if I were playing football and you asked me if there were any other gay players on the team, I'd also answer yes. The fact is, there are gay people in every sport, and in every walk of life. Are there more gay figure skaters than gay football players? Who knows, and what does it matter?

What matters to me is setting an example so other gay and lesbian athletes don't feel compelled to hide. I had hoped that my example would quickly change things, at least in skating, and that gay and lesbian skaters would feel more comfortable being themselves. That hasn't been the case, and it's taught me a valuable lesson. Deciding to be open about being gay or lesbian is a very personal decision, and it's one that I can't make for someone else. Given the history of how gay people have been treated in sports and in the larger world beyond, it's perfectly reasonable that gay men and women are fearful of coming forward, especially when they're at the top of their profession. I hope that my example inspires others to be themselves—it's a lot easier than hiding—but it's not up to me.

The toughest parts of being on tour for me, and I think for a lot of the other skaters, were being away from home for so long and the roller coaster of emotions that you go through almost every day. When you're competing during the regular season, you only experience a peak adrenaline high for one or two evenings every couple of months. But on the tour it was almost every night. Even though it was only an exhibition performance, as soon as the music started and they called my name, my heart started pounding and I could feel the adrenaline pumping through my veins. And it didn't stop until we took our final bows. A lot of times we'd get back to the hotel, and instead of going right to bed, because I knew I'd never fall asleep, I'd go to the hotel bar and have a few drinks just to get calmed down. And on my days off, I went out with some of the other skaters and invariably had more than a few drinks.

Looking back, I can see that I was drinking too much, and I can also see that I wasn't drinking simply to relax after a performance. Despite the fact that everything was going so well in my life, I still found myself fighting off those all too familiar dark moods. I worked really hard to stay up, to always be joking and having a good time, but no matter how much I tried, I couldn't stop from feeling bad. The only thing that seemed to help was going out and having a few drinks.

The saddest moment on the tour was when Harris Collins, Tommy's brother and the producer of the show, died of heart failure at age forty-nine. It was such a shock. Harris was a real favorite of all the skaters. He had a wonderful sense of humor and was sort of like a big brother to everyone on the tour. He was always full of energy, always cracking jokes, and always running around making sure everyone was doing okay. I missed him terribly and couldn't believe that yet one more person in my life who I cared about was gone.

The tour ended with two performances in San Jose in mid-July. As you can imagine, I was welcomed back by the hometown crowd like a returning hero. And after so many months on the road, I was very happy to be home. I knew that it wasn't going to be easy adjusting to the relative quiet of home after all the excitement of the tour, but I was looking forward to unpacking and not having to go anywhere.

But before I could settle down, I had to pack one more time.

Laura and Andy invited me to come live with them at their two-bedroom condo until I found a place of my own. Mom encouraged me to go. She'd managed pretty well without me while I was away, and she knew how much I'd like being with Laura and Andy. So one more time I packed my things and moved.

On the tenth of August, a few weeks after I got home, I had the honor of giving Laura away at her wedding. Originally, Laura and Andy were planning to get married on August 10, 1997, but Andy's dad was diagnosed with a rare form of leukemia and wasn't expected to make it another year. Andy's father was a judge, so they were planning to have him perform the wedding. When it became clear how sick he was, they scrapped their plans for a big wedding and quickly arranged an intimate family wedding in the backyard of Andy's parents' house in Aptos, which is right next to Santa Cruz.

The day of the wedding, you would never have known that Andy's dad was sick. It was such a happy day for all of us, and for him as well. But it was also bittersweet. We knew Andy's dad wouldn't live much longer, and as Laura's escort, I was standing in for my dad and for George. I know Laura and I were thinking about both of them as I gave her away, so it was hard holding back the tears.

Three weeks after the wedding, Andy's father died.

One of the things I really looked forward to when I came home was going out with my mom and shopping for a new house for her. I quickly discovered that that wasn't what she wanted to do. She told me that she was happy where she was and that after living in the trailer park for so many years, with all of the memories, and knowing all of her neighbors, she didn't want to move. So, instead, Laura, Andy, and I took Mom shopping for new furniture, and we also had her yard relandscaped. I also took Mom shopping at the nice department stores for new clothes. I think all the shopping was a lot more fun for Laura and me than it was for my mother. She seemed pretty overwhelmed by the whole thing and keeps most of the new clothes in her closet with the tags still on.

Since I didn't buy Mom a new house, I decided to buy a vacation house up in the mountains that the whole family could enjoy. The four of us drove up for the closing in August, then camped out in the house on the floor of the living room with blankets and pillows.

In the middle of the night I was awakened by Mom, who I heard saying, "I can't breathe! My chest hurts! Help me!" I couldn't believe it. Without thinking I said, "Mom, don't do this. You can't be having a heart attack!" I thought this couldn't be happening again, not now that everything was going so well.

Laura and Andy were awakened by my yelling at Mom, and all the commotion woke up Mom, who had apparently been having a dream and was talking in her sleep. With her eyes wide open, she looked at us and said, "What's going on? Why are you staring at me?" I started laughing, then Laura started laughing, then we all just laughed and laughed. Thank God it was just a dream. The last thing my family needed was another tragedy.

What happened next was a real nightmare, but it could have been a lot worse. I thank God that I didn't kill anyone or get killed myself, and in a funny way, I thank God I was arrested.

Just a couple of weeks after Laura got married, I was out at a club with a friend, and I had way too much to drink. While I was on the skating tour, if I drank too much, there was never any danger of getting into trouble on the road because I was either at the hotel bar or I took a cab back to the hotel.

That night in San Jose, I was too drunk to know how drunk I was, and I got into my new car and tried to drive home. I was barely out of the parking lot when I was stopped by the police and arrested for drunk driving. Before I knew it I was in jail waiting for Reuben and Wayne to come get me. I called them because Laura was in Las Vegas at a competition, which turned out to be a good thing. Laura told me later that if she'd been the one I called, she would have left me in jail for a few days as punishment for being so stupid.

Besides being mad at me for doing something so dangerous, Laura was mad at me for not taking my new position in life seriously. I was national champion. There were kids who looked up to me. And here I was out partying, getting drunk, and driving! What was I thinking?

The humiliation of being arrested shocked me into realizing what I'd done and that I had a problem with drinking. Since that day I have not touched a single drop of alcohol.

During the time I've been completely sober I've been able to recognize that I was drinking in large part to keep my bad moods and my anger under control. And since I haven't been drinking, I've had to deal with all of those feelings head-on, and it hasn't been easy.

Despite how I'd dismissed Laura and Andy's earlier effort to get me to see a counselor, they were right. I've had problems with mood swings all my life, and now that I'm able to acknowledge I have a problem, it's time to get some help. But I must admit, even though I've decided to go, I'm still afraid. I guess being afraid is normal. Fortunately, I have Laura and Andy's support, and that makes all the difference.

In the middle of all this turmoil, I had to make a final decision about the future of my career. Since my return home, Laura and I had been talking about whether I'd continue as an amateur and set my sights two years ahead to the Olympics or end my amateur career and turn professional. In practical terms, turning pro would mean I could no longer compete in nationals or worlds, and I wouldn't be eligible to compete for a spot on the Olympic team.

The pros and cons were pretty clear. As an amateur I was always under the do-or-die pressure of competing in the USFSA championships. One bad performance and it was over for the season. As a professional, I could compete in professional events throughout the year, and one bad performance was simply one bad performance. I'd still get to compete in the next event. Also, as a professional I'd have the freedom to explore new creative possibilities without having to look over my shoulder and worry about what the USFSA judges would think. I could simply be myself, skate as I wished, and—not incidentally—provide the kind of financial security for my family that they deserve. The financial rewards of skating as a professional are potentially far greater than as an amateur. My family supported me my entire life, and now I felt it was my turn to provide for them, and I knew I could do that better as a professional.

It was a surprisingly easy decision. Having won nationals, the goal of getting to the Olympics no longer had the same appeal. I'd been competing for most of my life, from one season to the next, and I was tired of the fight. I had my gold medal from nationals and a bronze from the worlds. I was about to turn twenty-seven; it felt like the right time to make a change.

Shortly after I made the decision to turn professional, the USFSA announced who it was sending to compete in Skate America, the premier international competition that the USFSA had chosen not to send me to in the past. And once again, despite the fact I was now national champion, my name wasn't on the list. That just reconfirmed for me that I'd made the right decision. I'd never been able to understand what motivated the U.S. Figure Skating Association, and as a professional I wouldn't have to think about it anymore.

On September 11, we made the official announcement, and afterward, I couldn't believe what a sense of relief I felt. For the first time since I was a child, I wouldn't have to worry about my whole career riding on amateur competitions.

What next? After surviving the premature deaths of family, coaches, and friends; living through the volatile ups and downs of my skating career; struggling through bouts of alcohol and drug abuse; and overcoming depression and racial and sexual prejudice, I wouldn't be willing to make any bets on an unqualified "happily ever after" story. But through all of it, I've managed to hold on to my enthusiasm for life and my sense of humor, and I've learned a couple of very valuable lessons: live one day at a time, and never, ever give up. And I won't.

See you on the ice!

Appendix

The Record

Singles Figure Skating

1996	Hershey's Kisses Challenge	2nd
1996	World Championships	3rd
1996	U.S. National Championships	1st
1996	Pacific Coast Senior	1st
1995	U.S. National Championships	8th
1995	Pacific Coast Senior	1st
1994	Vienna Cup	1st
1994	U.S. National Championships	7th
1994	Pacific Coast Senior	1st
1993	Nations Cup	4th
1993	U.S. Olympic Festival	2nd
1993	U.S. National Championships	5th
1993	Pacific Coast Senior	1st
1992	Prague Skate	2nd
1992	U.S. National Championships	8th
1992	Pacific Coast Senior	1st
1991	U.S. Olympic Festival	5th
1991	U.S. National Championships	11th
1991	Pacific Coast Senior	3rd

1988	U.S. National Championships	10th
1987	Asko Cup	1st
1987	U.S. Olympic Festival	2nd
1987	U.S. National Championships	8th
1987	World Junior Championships	1st
1987	Central Pacific Senior	1st
1986	National Juniors	3rd
1986	World Junior Championships	2nd
1985	Pokal der Blauen Schwerter	2nd
1985	National Juniors	3rd
1985	World Junior Championships	3rd
1984	Pacific Coast Juniors	3rd
1984	National Juniors	5th
1984	Grand Prize SNP	1st
1983	Pacific Coast Juniors	6th
1982	National Novice	1st

Pairs with Kristi Yamaguchi

1990	World Championships	5th
1990	U.S. National Championships	1st
1989	NHK Trophy	4th
1989	Skate America	2nd
1989	World Championships	5th
1989	U.S. National Championships	1st
1988	NHK Trophy	3rd
1988	Skate Electric	1st
1988	U.S. National Championships	5th
1988	World Junior Championships	1st
1987	U.S. National Championships	5th
1987	World Junior Championships	3rd
1986	Skate America	5th
1986	Olympic Festival	3rd
1986	U.S. National Championships, Junior Pairs	1st
1986	World Junior Championships	5th
1985	U.S. National Championships, Junior Pairs	5th
1985	Central Pacific, Junior Pairs	1st

JUMPS AND SPINS

Trying to describe the major figure skating jumps and spins in plain English is no easy task, and for that reason I relied on journalist (and skating enthusiast) Lorrie Kim for the descriptions in this section. Before I get to the actual jumps and spins, there are a few things you need to know about the skate blade and one thing you need to know about the way I skate. First the blade.

The bottom of the quarter-inch-wide blade has a shallow rounded groove down the middle, which gives the single blade two edges: the inside edge and the outside edge. The blade is also divided (figuratively speaking) into forward and back parts. For example, if the skater's weight is on the ball of his foot, he's skating on the forward part of the blade. If his weight is on the heel, he's skating on the back part.

With this blade geography in mind, there are eight skating edges: left foot, forward inside; left forward outside; left back inside; left back outside; right foot, forward inside; right forward outside; right back inside; and right back outside.

Figure skating blades also have toe picks, which are the sharp teeth underneath the toe area of the skating boot. Skaters use the teeth to jab into the ice and launch themselves into a jump.

What you need to know about *me* is that I'm left-handed and like most skaters who are left-handed, I rotate in a clockwise direction when I do my jumps and spins. So all the jumps and spins are described from my perspective. For example, when I do a salchow jump, I take off on my right foot and land on my left. A skater who jumps in a counterclockwise direction takes off on his left foot and lands on his right.

With all of that in mind, it's time for the definitions.

Jumps

Most people have trouble distinguishing between the different jumps. The reason for this is simple: Once a skater is in the air, all the jumps look basically the same, except for the number of revolutions executed by the skater. (In competition, jumps are typically done as doubles or triples—in other words, with two or three revolutions.) What distinguishes one jump from another is the takeoff and landing.

There are six major jumps in championship figure skating. In ascending order of difficulty, they are the toe loop, salchow, loop, flip, lutz, and axel. Except for the axel, each jump is approached while skating backwards. The seventh and last jump on this list is the waltz jump, which is not a major jump, but I mention it several times in the text of the book as a warm-up jump, so I've included it here.

Toe Loop

The skater approaches on the left back outside edge, jabs the right toe pick into the ice, rotates once, and lands on the left back outside edge. The toe loop is the only jump to use the right toe pick. (When skaters do two jumps, one right after the other—which is called a jump combination—the toe loop is often the second jump in the combination.)

Salchow

The skater takes off from the right back inside edge, rotates once, and lands on the left back outside edge. Because the left leg comes behind the right leg during takeoff, the salchow has a distinctive "crossing-over" appearance.

Loop

The skater springs off the left back outside edge, rotates once, and lands on the left back outside edge. The jump is approached in a crouch, with the right leg slightly crossed over the left, as though sitting in an imaginary chair.

Flip

The skater approaches on the right back inside edge, jabs the left toe pick into the ice, rotates once, and lands on the left back outside edge. Often, while preparing to use the toe pick for takeoff, a skater will slightly scrape the ice with the left foot.

Lutz

The skater approaches on the right back outside edge, jabs the left toe pick into the ice, rotates once, and lands on the left back outside edge. This is the only major jump that the skater approaches while skating on a counterclockwise curve. Often the skater is looking over his shoulder during the approach and performs the jump in a corner of the rink.

Axel

Skating forward, the skater takes off from the right forward outside edge, rotates one-and-a-half times, and lands skating backward on the left back outside edge. The skater kicks the left leg forward and swings with both arms during the takeoff. Because the skater takes off from the forward position and lands backward, there is an extra half-rotation. So a triple axel is in fact a triple-and-a-half, which is one of the reasons it's so difficult to execute.

Waltz

Skating forward, the skater takes off from the right forward outside edge, does a half-rotation, and lands backward on the left back outside edge. It is the first one-third of a single axel.

Skaters routinely perform waltz jumps and other half- and single-rotation jumps in their programs, but they are not counted for technical merit; they are done either for choreographic impact, or as connecting elements.

Spins

Again, I spin clockwise, and all of the descriptions that follow are for someone who spins as I do. For skaters who spin counterclockwise, the feet are reversed.

One other thing you need to know about spins in general is that any spin executed with the right foot on the ice is called a "forward" spin and any spin executed with the left foot on the ice is called a "back" spin. For example, you might hear a commentator describe a series of moves in the following way: "In the change-foot spin that the skater just executed, he started out with a forward camel and foot into a back camel, then down into a back sit spin." All of that will make a little more sense once you've read the descriptions that follow.

Combination Spin
The combination spin includes several changes of position.

Flying Spin
The skater jumps forward, similar to an axel takeoff, and goes immediately into a spin upon landing. Two examples are the flying sit spin and the flying camel. (See below for sit spin and camel spin.)

Scratch Spin
This is a very fast spin in an upright position in which the toe pick of the free foot scratches the surface of the ice. The spin is so fast that the skater appears blurry to the audience and the audience appears blurry to the skater.

Layback Spin
The skater bends the head and torso back at the waist while turning out the free leg from the hip; the lower part of the free leg is parallel to the ice. (I'm one of the few male skaters flexible enough to do a good layback.)

Cross-Foot Spin
This spin is done with both feet on the ice, with one crossed behind the other.

Appendix

Sit Spin
The skater spins in a sitting position on the skating leg, with the free leg extended in front of him.

Camel Spin
The skater's torso and free leg are in a horizontal position, parallel to the ice. In ballet, this position is called an "arabesque."

Death Drop
From a right forward outside edge, the skater jumps high into the air with the free leg out and the face and stomach parallel to the ice. As soon as he lands, the skater goes directly into a back sit spin.